T0072561

SKETCHES OF LIFE IN CHILE

LIBRARY OF LATIN AMERICA

General Editor
Jean Franco

Series Editor for Brazil
Richard Graham, with the assistance of Alfredo Bosi

Editorial Board
Tulio Halperín Donghi
Iván Jaksić
Naomi Lindstrom
Eduardo Lozano
Francine Masiello

OXFORD

SKETCHES OF
LIFE IN CHILE
1841–1851

JOSÉ JOAQUÍN VALLEJO
"JOTABECHE"

Translated from the Spanish by
FREDERICK H. FORNOFF

EDITED WITH AN INTRODUCTION AND CHRONOLOGY
BY SIMON COLLIER

OXFORD
UNIVERSITY PRESS

2002

OXFORD
UNIVERSITY PRESS

Oxford New York
Auckland Bangkok Buenos Aires Cape Town Chennai
Dar es Salaam Delhi Hong Kong Istanbul Karachi Kolkata
Kuala Lumpur Madrid Melbourne Mexico City Mumbai Nairobi
São Paulo Shanghai Singapore Taipei Tokyo Toronto

and an associated company in Berlin

Copyright © 2002 by Oxford University Press

Published by Oxford University Press, Inc.
198 Madison Avenue, New York, New York 10016

www.oup.com

Oxford is a registered trademark of Oxford University Press

All rights reserved. No part of this publication may be reproduced,
stored in a retrieval system, or transmitted, in any form or by any means,
electronic, mechanical, photocopying, recording, or otherwise,
without the prior permission of Oxford University Press.

Library of Congress Cataloging-in-Publication Data

Vallejo, José Joaquín, 1811–1858
[Selections. 1911. English]
Sketches of life in Chile, 1841–1851 /
by José Joaquín Vallejo "Jotabeche";
translated from the Spanish by Frederick H. Fornoff;
edited with an introduction and chronology by Simon Collier.
p.   cm. — (Library of Latin America)
Includes bibliographical references
ISBN 0-19-512867-2 (pb)— ISBN 0-19-512866-4
1. Chile—Social life and customs—19th century.
2. Vallejo, José Joaquín, 1811–1858.
I. Fornoff, Frederick H.
II. Collier, Simon.
III. Title.   IV. Series.
F3095 .V2513 2002   983'.04—dc21   2002025118

1 3 5 7 9 8 6 4 2

Printed in the United States of America
on acid-free paper

Contents

Series Editors'
General Introduction

The Library of Latin America series makes available in translation major nineteenth-century authors whose work has been neglected in the English-speaking world. The titles for the translations from the Spanish and Portuguese were suggested by an editorial committee that included Jean Franco (general editor responsible for works in Spanish), Richard Graham (series editor responsible for works in Portuguese), Tulio Halperín Donghi (at the University of California, Berkeley), Iván Jaksić (at the University of Notre Dame), Naomi Lindstrom (at the University of Texas at Austin), Eduardo Lozano of the Library at the University of Pittsburgh, and Francine Masiello (at the University of California, Berkeley). The late Antonio Cornejo Polar of the University of California, Berkeley, was also one of the founding members of the committee. The translations have been funded thanks to the generosity of the Lampadia Foundation and the Andrew W. Mellon Foundation.

During the period of national formation between 1810 and into the early years of the twentieth century, the new nations of Latin America fashioned their identities, drew up constitutions, engaged in bitter struggles over territory, and debated questions of education, government, ethnicity, and culture. This was a unique period unlike the process of nation formation in Europe and one that should be more familiar than it is to students of comparative politics, history, and literature.

The image of the nation was envisioned by the lettered classes—a minority in countries in which indigenous, mestizo, black, or mulatto peasants and slaves predominated—although there were also alternative nationalisms at the grassroots level. The cultural elite were well educated in European thought and letters, but as statesmen, journalists, poets, and academics, they confronted the problem of the racial and linguistic heterogeneity of the continent and the difficulties of integrating the population into a modern nation-state. Some of the writers whose works will be translated in the Library of Latin America series played leading roles in politics. Fray Servando Teresa de Mier, a friar who translated Rousseau's *The Social Contract* and was one of the most colorful characters of the independence period, was faced with imprisonment and expulsion from Mexico for his heterodox beliefs; on his return, after independence, he was elected to the congress. Domingo Faustino Sarmiento, exiled from his native Argentina under the presidency of Rosas, wrote *Facundo: Civilización y barbarie,* a stinging denunciation of that government. He returned after Rosas' overthrow and was elected president in 1868. Andrés Bello was born in Venezuela, lived in London where he published poetry during the independence period, settled in Chile where he founded the University, wrote his grammar of the Spanish language, and drew up the country's legal code.

These post-independence intelligentsia were not simply dreaming castles in the air, but vitally contributed to the founding of nations and the shaping of culture. The advantage of hindsight may make us aware of problems they themselves did not foresee, but this should not affect our assessment of their truly astonishing energies and achievements. It is still surprising that the writing of Andrés Bello, who contributed fundamental works to so many different fields, has never been translated into English. Although there is a recent translation of Sarmiento's celebrated *Facundo,* there is no translation of his memoirs, *Recuerdos de provincia (Provincial Recollections).* The predominance of memoirs in the Library of Latin America series is no accident—many of these offer entertaining insights into a vast and complex continent.

Nor have we neglected the novel. The series includes new translations of the outstanding Brazilian writer Joaquim Maria Machado de Assis' work, including *Dom Casmurro* and *The Posthumous Memoirs of Brás Cubas.* There is no reason why other novels and writers who are not so well known outside Latin America—the Peruvian novelist Clorinda Matto de Turner's *Aves sin nido,* Nataniel Aguirre's *Juan de la Rosa,* José de Alencar's *Iracema,* Juana Manuela Gorriti's short stories—should not be read with as much interest as the political novels of Anthony Trollope.

A series on nineteenth-century Latin America cannot, however, be limited to literary genres such as the novel, the poem, and the short story. The literature of independent Latin America was eclectic and strongly influenced by the periodical press newly liberated from scrutiny by colonial authorities and the Inquisition. Newspapers were miscellanies of fiction, essays, poems, and translations from all manner of European writing. The novels written on the eve of Mexican Independence by José Joaquín Fernández de Lizardi included disquisitions on secular education and law, and denunciations of the evils of gaming and idleness. Other works, such as a well-known poem by Andrés Bello, "Ode to Tropical Agriculture," and novels such as *Amalia* by José Mármol and the Bolivian Nataniel Aguirre's *Juan de la Rosa*, were openly partisan. By the end of the century, sophisticated scholars were beginning to address the history of their countries, as did João Capistrano de Abreu in his *Capítulos de história colonial.*

It is often in memoirs such as those by Fray Servando Teresa de Mier or Sarmiento that we find the descriptions of everyday life that in Europe were incorporated into the realist novel. Latin American literature at this time was seen largely as a pedagogical tool, a "light" alternative to speeches, sermons, and philosophical tracts—though, in fact, especially in the early part of the century, even the readership for novels was quite small because of the high rate of illiteracy. Nevertheless, the vigorous orally transmitted culture of the gaucho and the urban underclasses became the linguistic repertoire of some of the most interesting nineteenth-century writers—most notably José Hernández, author of the "gauchesque" poem "Martín Fierro," which enjoyed an unparalleled popularity. But for many writers the task was not to appropriate popular language but to civilize, and their literary works were strongly influenced by the high style of political oratory.

The editorial committee has not attempted to limit its selection to the better-known writers such as Machado de Assis; it has also selected many works that have never appeared in translation or writers whose work has not been translated recently. The series now makes these works available to the English-speaking public.

Because of the preferences of funding organizations, the series initially focuses on writing from Brazil, the Southern Cone, the Andean region, and Mexico. Each of our editions will have an introduction that places the work in its appropriate context and includes explanatory notes.

We owe special thanks to the late Robert Glynn of the Lampadia Foundation, whose initiative gave the project a jump start, and to Richard Ekman of the Andrew W. Mellon Foundation, which also generously supported the project. We also thank the Rockefeller Foundation for funding the 1996 symposium "Culture and Nation in Iberoamerica," organized by the editorial board of the Library of Latin America. We received substantial institutional support and personal encouragement from the Institute of Latin American Studies of the University of Texas at Austin. The support of Edward Barry of Oxford University Press has been crucial, as has the advice and help of Ellen Chodosh of Oxford University Press. The first volumes of the series were published after the untimely death, on July 3, 1997, of Maria C. Bulle, who, as an associate of the Lampadia Foundation, supported the idea from its beginning.

—*Jean Franco*
—*Richard Graham*

Chronology of José Joaquín Vallejo

1811 (29 August)	José Joaquín Vallejo born at Copiapó (Coquimbo Province, Chile).
1819 (April)	Copiapó destroyed by earthquake: Vallejo moves to La Serena, and is educated at the local *liceo* (high school).
1829	Vallejo moves to Santiago to complete his education at the Liceo de Chile, a private school, closed down in 1831.
1835	Appointed secretary of the Intendancy of Maule Province.
1840	Imprisoned by Intendant Domingo Urrutia of Maule Province. Escapes from prison, moves to Santiago, and takes part in political agitation before the 1841 presidential election.
1841 (September)	Moves back to Copiapó to practice law and speculate in mining.
1841–42	Adopts the pseudonym Jotabeche and publishes his first "jotabeches" in the Valparaíso newspaper *El Mercurio*.
1843 (October)	Copiapó becomes capital of the new Province of Atacama.
1845 (April)	Founds *El Copiapino* newspaper.
1847	Main sequence of "jotabeches" published in book form.
1849 (March)	Elected to the Chamber of Deputies.

1850 (April)	Marries Zoila, daughter of his brother Ramón.
1851 (October)	Represses mineworkers' revolt at Chañarcillo.
1851 (December)	Inauguration of Copiapó-Caldera railroad.
1852 (March)	Reelected to the Chamber of Deputies.
1853 (January–May)	Leads an unsuccessful diplomatic mission to Bolivia.
1854	Onset of tuberculosis.
1858 (27 September)	Dies near Copiapó.

Introduction

JOTABECHE AND HIS WORLD

According to early twentieth-century Chilean writer Alberto Edwards, José Joaquín Vallejo—"Jotabeche"—was the effective founder of his country's "genuinely national literature" and "the first of the truly Chilean writers."[1] This is a perfectly reasonable claim. Vallejo was undoubtedly the first creative writer of any kind of stature to emerge in Chile after the country's wars of independence, and easily the best before the appearance of the novelist Alberto Blest Gana (1830–1920), whose primacy among nineteenth-century Chilean writers is not likely to be disputed. He is perhaps the only Chilean writer from the 1840s who can still be read with unforced pleasure. Most of the essays and sketches he wrote during that decade have worn rather well.

The standard explanation of his pseudonym—"Jota-Be-Che," the Spanish names for the letters J, B, and Ch—is that he borrowed the initials of Juan Bautista Chenau (or Chaigneau), a popular Argentine resident of Copiapó, the northern mining town where Vallejo was born and where he lived most of his later life. This explanation was certainly accepted at the time,[2] and, according to Alberto Edwards, it was still remembered in Copiapó at the start of the twentieth century that Vallejo had been amused when people insisted on attributing his articles to Chenau.[3] Vallejo himself never offered reasons for his choice, but he often referred to his essays as his "jotabeches," so he obviously liked the sound of the name he had invented.

His first appearances in print (1840–41) were as a polemical political writer, turning out caustic and sarcastic articles in which his language sometimes bordered on the gross. These pieces are no longer of much interest, except possibly to students of the background to the Chilean presidential election of 1841. After this short apprenticeship, however, Vallejo suddenly struck his true vein. Over the next six years he published a remarkable series of articles on aspects of Chilean life and society, somewhat in the manner of the recently dead Spanish *costumbrista* writer Mariano José de Larra, whose writings were then being avidly read throughout the Spanish-speaking world. Vallejo was very familiar with his work from the Spanish newspapers that regularly reached Chile, and a collection of Larra's sketches was published in Valparaíso in 1842. According to José Victorino Lastarria, this became Vallejo's "only favorite book."[4] Lastarria's remark was no doubt intended as a putdown, but could well have had a grain of truth. "I adore Larra," Vallejo wrote in 1843, "and rarely go to sleep without reading one of his beautiful pieces."[5]

The Making of Jotabeche

On his father's side, José Joaquín Vallejo Borkoski was the grandson of Gabriel Alejo Vallejo, a Spaniard who moved from Mexico to the north of Chile in the mid-eighteenth century and held a minor official post in Copiapó. His mother was the granddaughter of Juan Cristóbal Borkoski, a Polish migrant from Danzig who had arrived in the north sometime before 1750 and became a successful miner. Vallejo's parents were thus of respectable lineage by Spanish colonial standards, but were by no means well-to-do. They held neither the mines nor the lands possessed by the richer families in the mineral-rich Chilean north—the desert and semi-desert area nowadays called the Norte Chico ("Lesser North"), to distinguish it from the still more northerly provinces (the Norte Grande or "Greater North") conquered from Bolivia and Peru in the War of the Pacific (1879–83). Vallejo's father, Ramón, worked much of his life as a silversmith, which did not give him much of an income in Copiapó, an undeveloped, peripheral settlement whose population was no more than 2,500 in the 1810s.

José Joaquín was born there on 19 August 1811, less than a year after the Spanish colony known as the Captaincy-General of Chile had started its move toward independence, which was formally declared in February 1818. In April 1819 Copiapó was devastated by an earthquake, and the seven-year-old boy was taken south, to La Serena, the capital of Coquimbo Province, where a sympathetic uncle saw to it that he attended the local *liceo* or high school, one of only three in Chile at the time. Its educational standards were not very high: Vallejo's earliest writings reveal rather defective spelling. He was nonetheless, in due course, appointed as one of the schoolteachers there, and was thus able to contribute to the family income. When the La Serena *liceo* was closed down, basically for lack of funds, he moved to Santiago to continue his education at the Liceo de Chile, a private school founded by the distinguished Spanish Liberal José Joaquín de Mora, then briefly residing in Chile, where he had been the chief inspiration for the new Constitution of 1828. The congressional deputy for Coquimbo arranged for the young Vallejo to be given one of the forty-two scholarships instituted for the school by the Liberal government of President Francisco Antonio Pinto (1827–29). Vallejo, whose attendance at classes began in March 1829, made some good friends during his time there, including two future Conservative politicians of note, Manuel Antonio Tocornal and Antonio García Reyes.

Mora's school, unfortunately, soon fell victim to the political crisis that engulfed Chile in 1829–30. The 1820s had been a mildly agitated decade. After 1823, with the overthrow of the country's liberator-dictator, Bernardo O'Higgins, a series of Liberal governments had aroused the bitter hostility of their Conservative adversaries, who in September 1829 enlisted the help of the army and mounted a successful rebellion. Following their triumph, and under the inflexible leadership of Diego Portales, the "omnipotent minister" of the new regime, the Conservatives took a very tight grip on the country, a grip that was not to be broken during Vallejo's lifetime. Under Portales, persecution of Liberals became the order of the day, and in February 1831 Mora was expelled from Chile. With the Liceo de Chile shut down, Vallejo took a class in law at the Instituto Nacional, the country's premier educational institution, but abandoned it in 1832 because of his impoverished circumstances. For the next two or three years he worked as a shop assistant or clerk in Santiago. One of the few escape routes for somebody in this position was a government job. In 1835 Joaquín Tocornal, father of his former classmate Manuel Antonio, and incumbent Minister of the Interior, offered Vallejo the post of Secretary to the Intendancy (governorship) of Maule Province. In the direct way that was always characteristic of him, Vallejo informed the Conservative president, General Joaquín Prieto, that he was an opponent of the government. The president told him that this really did not matter; what the government needed was honest officials.[6]

Vallejo's new superior, Colonel Domingo Urrutia, Intendant of Maule Province, quickly took a liking to him. Later, when Vallejo had resigned the secretaryship after eight months, the two men went into business together in Cauquenes, the provincial capital. Here Vallejo established himself as a respectable citizen, becoming a captain in the local militia battalion. In 1840, however, he and Intendant Urrutia had a serious falling-out, for reasons (probably business related) that neither of them ever divulged. In Conservative Chile it was never wise to antagonize an Intendant, the powerful satrap of the still more powerful president. Trumping up a spurious charge, Colonel Urrutia had Captain Vallejo court-martialed, twice slamming him in jail, on the first occasion for five days (in irons), on the second for twenty-three. On the night of 31 August 1840, with the help of friends, Vallejo escaped from prison. In his fury, Urrutia arrested some of Vallejo's militiamen and a few of his friends, one of them a blustering Englishman who was working mines in the province, for whose benefit Urrutia coarsely insulted Queen Victoria.[7]

Vallejo, meanwhile, made his way to Santiago, where news of his acquittal by the court-martial followed him soon afterward. He found the capital in a state of mild political excitement. President Prieto's second consecutive five-year term was nearing its end, and under the new, Conservative-dictated Constitution of 1833 he could not stand for an immediate third term. Who would be his successor? The opposition Liberals were pinning their hopes on former president Francisco Antonio Pinto. Given his liberal leanings, Vallejo could well have been tempted to join them, but probably for personal reasons decided to throw in his lot with his former benefactor, Joaquín Tocornal, the candidate of the more traditional faction of the Conservative party. Despite Tocornal's faithful record as a cabinet minister, the government was passing him over for the succession in favor of President Prieto's nephew, General Manuel Bulnes, the victorious army commander in the highly successful war Chile had recently fought against the Peru-Bolivian Confederation (1836–39). Bulnes's standing as a war hero, the government sensed, could be used to reinforce the legitimacy of the Conservative regime. To oppose him, Tocornal's supporters created a news-sheet, *Guerra a la tiranía*, to which Vallejo contributed a number of articles, pouring crude invective on Bulnes, whom he nicknamed Bulke Borrachei ("Bulky Drunky"), in an allusion to the well-built general's gargantuan appetite for food (this was true enough) and for drink (somewhat less true).

Chilean governments of the period (and until nearly the end of the century) systematically "fixed" all elections and made no secret of it.

Opposition parties could sometimes elect a small number of candidates to the Chamber of Deputies, but stood no chance of capturing Senate seats, elected (until the 1870s) on a single national "list," still less the presidency, which was decided by an easily manipulable electoral college. The hopes of Tocornal and the Liberal candidate Pinto were doomed from the outset. General Bulnes's victory was a foregone conclusion. The voting in the electoral college was: Bulnes 154, Pinto 9, Tocornal 0. Vallejo's first political "campaign" was thus a complete failure. From the point of view of literature, this was a definite blessing. It sent him back to Copiapó (on a northward-bound steamship a few days after President Bulnes's inauguration in September 1841) following an absence of more than twenty-two years. More important, it allowed him to discover his true vocation as a writer. It turned José Joaquín Vallejo into Jotabeche.

He would return to politics later. In the meantime, there was no lack of opportunity for him in Chile's far north—Atacama Province, as it became in October 1843, when the government redrew the political map of the Norte Chico. Copiapó, now rapidly growing (with a population of around 12,000 by 1850), became the provincial capital. Vallejo was invited to become Secretary of its Intendancy, but, remembering his experiences in Maule Province, was not even tempted. In any case, he no longer needed a government job. Boosted by the dramatic silver strikes at Chañarcillo (to the southeast of Copiapó) in 1832, Atacama was living through its classic nineteenth-century mining boom, exporting large quantities of silver and copper to the international market. The mines of Atacama and Coquimbo Provinces were the motor of nineteenth-century Chile's flourishing export economy and the source of all the largest Chilean fortunes of the time. Vallejo opened a law office (even though not fully qualified) in Copiapó, and speculated successfully in mining, the goose that laid the golden eggs for him and for so many others in the north. Unlike the others, who merely made money, he was able to fix the moment on the printed page, and so to bring it to life again for us. Between May 1841 and September 1847 he wrote the forty-one sketches that established his literary reputation. Many were printed in the Valparaíso newspaper *El Mercurio*, founded in 1827 and today the oldest Spanish-language newspaper in the world. Others appeared in the Santiago magazine *El Semanario*, and a few in the provincial newspaper *El Copiapino*, which Vallejo himself would start in 1845. He was probably the highest-paid writer of the time, receiving a fee of two ounces of gold per article from *El Mercurio*. In October 1847 thirty-eight of the essays were published in book form, with a eulogistic preface by

Vallejo's old classmate Antonio García Reyes. By then the name of Jotabeche was familiar to every Chilean who could read. In the 1840s, that meant around one in ten.

The "Movement of 1842"

Literary life in Chile ran at a very low ebb in the first two decades after independence. The new nation's heroic military role in the liberation of Peru from Spain, the political ups and downs of the 1820s, the harsh Conservative stabilization of politics after 1830—the times did not allow much in the way of serious cultivation of the arts. Nothing that could be called good-quality literature appeared in the 1820s. Nor were the 1830s very propitious for literary activity, although they brought to light the first poet of the "national" period to rise (just about) above the pedestrian, Mercedes Marín del Solar (1804–66). Her single most celebrated poem was occasioned by the brutal murder by mutinous soldiers (June 1837) of the awesome minister Diego Portales, whose far from tender leadership had been the chief factor in the Conservative consolidation of stable political institutions. Gradually, however, the repressive atmosphere of Portales's time was dispelled, or at any rate diminished. With more settled conditions prevailing, victory in the war with the Peru-Bolivian Confederation, and the gradual expansion of overseas trade (spurred by the silver pouring from the Chañarcillo mines), a softer climate quickly developed. General Manuel Bulnes's two terms in the presidency (1841–51) were marked for the most part by genuine governmental tolerance, with the harsh emergency powers so often used in Portales's day now mostly in abeyance, though still very much on the statute book. They would be used again (extensively) by Bulnes's successor in the 1850s.

Political relaxation and growing prosperity brought the first serious stirrings of cultural life. A number of educated Chileans of the younger generation became strongly interested in creating a "national" literature. They emerged on the scene in the "movement of 1842," as it is usually called, perhaps a little too grandly, for it was hardly a "boom" and still less a "renaissance." It did, however, represent the end of the previous cultural inertia. The two cardinal influences on the handful of writers (more accurately, would-be writers) who came to the fore at this point (most of them now long forgotten) were the Liberal publicist José Victorino Lastarria (1817–88) and the great Venezuelan polymath Andrés

Bello (1781–1865), who had settled in Chile in 1829 and was now widely recognized as the most remarkable Latin American intellectual of his time. Lastarria was a tireless literary entrepreneur and (something rather too transparently emphasized in his own retrospective accounts) the principal stimulus to the "movement" insofar as it achieved organized form. To some extent it did, at least for a while, in the shape of a Literary Society (*Sociedad Literaria*), which held eighty-six meetings in 1842–43 before lapsing into inertia. Andrés Bello (whose sons Francisco, Carlos, and Juan were prominent members of the Society) was an altogether more formidable figure. Vallejo greatly admired him. Bello was already established as the supreme educator of his adoptive homeland, where he had become a citizen and was both a senior civil servant and a senator, adding to these roles in July 1843 when he was appointed first rector of the newly created University of Chile. His patiently exercised influence on the next two or three generations of educated upper-class Chileans was incalculable. In the long run, it easily outweighed any influence Lastarria (or anyone else) could bring to bear.

Although they respected each other, Bello and Lastarria never really saw eye to eye. Lastarria's doctrinaire liberalism did not square well with the more measured approach favored by Bello, both in literature and politics. Open battle between them, however, was rare. Their most important public polemic in the 1840s concerned the writing of history, of which there had been virtually none since independence. Lastarria proposed what he termed "philosophy of history," history of a general, reflective nature designed, in effect, to further his own reformist liberal political agenda. Bello, by contrast, advocated scholarly research and a strict adherence to the narrative method. In this debate Bello was the clear winner,[8] and his ideas were to help mold the brilliant tradition of Chilean historiography that flowered over the next few decades and prolonged his intellectual influence into the twentieth century.

The Bello-Lastarria debate over history is of no great relevance to Vallejo's story, but it at least reminds us that the "movement of 1842" was born in a definitely polemical atmosphere. A contributory factor here was the arrival in Chile in the early 1840s of numerous Argentines, refugees from the long-running and at times bloody "federalist" dictatorship of Juan Manuel de Rosas. Many sought their fortune in the northern mining zone, where Vallejo rubbed shoulders with them and overheard (as some of his sketches show) their interminable conversations on Argentine politics. Others were intellectuals, the two most prominent of whom were Domingo Faustino Sarmiento and Vicente

Fidel López. Sarmiento, the future president of his country, made an immediate impression in Chile with his pugnacious journalism. He was not a hesitant man, and his tangles with his Chilean hosts landed him in trouble more than once, the trouble including a brief stay in prison and a fistfight with a rival journalist.[9]

In some of his early articles Sarmiento castigated the Chileans for what he saw as their literary inertia and backwardness, coupling this with a passionate advocacy of French Romanticism and corresponding denunciations of "grammarians" and "classicists." The chief grammarian and classicist in Chile, Andrés Bello, was stung into a reply, in which he chided Sarmiento for his affection for everything French, quoting the eighteenth-century Spaniard, Padre José Francisco de Isla:

> *Yo conocí en Madrid una condesa*
> *que aprendió a estornudar a la francesa.*
> I once met a countess in Madrid:
> she learned to *sneeze* in French, she did.[10]

The strictures of Sarmiento and other Argentines were not well received by Chilean writers in general, and quickly attracted fierce responses, many of them little more than howls of aggrieved patriotism. At a more popular level the Argentines were nicknamed *loros* ("parrots"), for their animated conversational style. "Their habitual frankness," as Lastarria was to put it, "contrasted with our national seriousness."[11]

It would be misleading to claim, as nearly everybody does, that the "movement of 1842" was simply a reflex action, something goaded into life by the Argentine exiles, though the irritant of their presence doubtless added to such vitality as it possessed. Lastarria's ideas were already moving independently in the same direction as Sarmiento's. He took up Sarmiento's support for French Romanticism and made it a principal theme of his opening address as the newly elected (in effect, self-appointed) first director of the Literary Society (May 1842). Much of Spanish literature, he said on that occasion, was "retrograde, without philosophy." Quoting Victor Hugo's opinion that English and German Romanticism were dead and that French literature was the only one still alive, he exhorted his followers to "read the most noted French writers of the day, not to copy them . . . but to learn to think, to steep yourselves in that philosophical coloring that characterizes their literature, so that you can follow the new path and vividly portray nature."[12] Lastarria obviously hoped that Romanticism, the "new path," would become a kind of literary orthodoxy for emerging Chilean writers, writers preferably directed by himself.

Although he is often placed there in Chilean textbooks, and while it provided the context for his appearance as a creative writer, Vallejo cannot be said to have been completely a part of the movement of 1842. His first pieces appeared before the movement got fully under way. He was several years older than Lastarria (and had very little time for him) and considerably older than most of Lastarria's bright-eyed troupe of followers, though he was on friendly terms with many of them. Moreover, despite occasional stays in Santiago, he lived and worked much of the time in the north, and was therefore on the sidelines of the diminutive literary world of the capital. This does not mean that he was out of touch, or that he was unaware of the polemics of the moment. On the contrary, he joined in with gusto, taking particular pleasure in mocking both Romanticism and the Argentines. A minor war of words broke out between him and Sarmiento, whom he once described privately as "that literary anti-Christ,"[13] a phrase that seems to have enjoyed a wide circulation. For his part, Sarmiento later paid tribute to Vallejo as his "most formidable" Chilean adversary. He liked him as a man, and also as a writer—"a model of incisive and witty terseness," as he put it a few years afterward.[14] Vallejo also willingly collaborated in the creation of the short-lived literary magazine that emerged from the movement of 1842, *El Semanario* (1842–43), which, partly at Andrés Bello's behest, contained a certain amount of anti-Romantic (and indeed, anti-Argentine) material. Its successor, the equally short-lived *El Crepúsculo* (1843–44), more faithfully reflected Lastarria's new orthodoxy of Romanticism, with heretics like Vallejo firmly excluded.

Orthodoxy, in modern times at least, has not usually been a good seedbed for literature. If Lastarria seriously hoped to foster a generation of distinguished authors through his energetic cultural entrepreneurship, he was to be badly disappointed, though it was not something he could ever bring himself to admit. Vallejo's literary achievement was far stronger than that of any of the writers who strove to emerge from the ferment of 1842. We should not be too dismissive about all of them. Lastarria himself wrote one short story, "El mendigo" (1843), which still receives respectful attention from literary scholars, though his novella *Don Guillermo* (1860) does not read well today. The poetry of Salvador Sanfuentes (1817–60), in particular, deserves a closer look than it commonly receives. Alongside the essays of Jotabeche, it is surely the most valuable Chilean writing of the 1840s. Yet none of the writers of that decade (not even, perhaps, Sanfuentes) came quite as close as Vallejo to finding a distinctive individual voice, and a voice that was both regional and national as well as individual. It is also worth mentioning that the novelist Alberto Blest Gana, who made his reputation in the 1860s, owed little or nothing to Lastarria's literary circus. He owed more than a little to the example of Jotabeche.

Jotabeche's "jotabeches"

What is usually termed *costumbrista* writing — sketches and vignettes of society and local customs — enjoyed an enormous vogue in the Spanish-speaking world in the nineteenth century. Because of its sheer variety, the genre eludes easy definition.[15] There is probably a case, however, for seeing the kind of short essay cultivated by Jotabeche as its purest form. Spanish Americans of his generation were especially impressed by the models provided by three Spanish *costumbrista* essayists in particular: Mariano José de Larra (1809–37) and his longer-lived contemporaries Ramón Mesonero Romanos (1803–82) and Serafín Estebáñez Calderón (1799–1867). Larra's importance to Vallejo has already been noted. The parallel between them, though often made during Vallejo's life, should not be pressed too far: Vallejo's temperament was altogether sunnier, more positive than that of his Spanish mentor, and he saw life from a provincial perspective, unlike Larra, whose focus was the metropolitan society of Madrid. What else Vallejo may have read, apart from Larra, we simply do not know, though it can be assumed that he was reasonably conversant with the Spanish classics. He seems to have known his *Don Quixote*; there is probably a conscious echo of its opening line in the sketch "A Practical Joke." Francisco Montero, the protagonist of the second of Jotabeche's two "historical" narratives, dies clutching his sword Tizona, the name of one of the two famous swords of El Cid, as recounted in Spain's national epic.

When reading Jotabeche, we need to bear in mind that his themes, not surprisingly, are closely related to the world that was most familiar to him, and it is important to remember that his vision of Chile is essentially that of a *northerner*. The Norte Chico, the mining zone, was always a rather distinctive part of the republic. Politically it tended to be more liberal than the rest of the nation. Only a few years after Vallejo's death it became the birthplace and stronghold of Chile's great Radical Party, whose contribution to the democratic advance of Chile is indisputable.

Its society was always more fluid (and distinctly more cosmopolitan) than that of the Central Valley, the classic region of the great haciendas and their patriarchal, hierarchical way of life. The inert, slow-moving world of the haciendas, of the *patrón* and the *inquilino*, of master and man, is not one depicted by Vallejo's pen, though he obviously takes it for granted. Some brief throwaway remarks (in the essay "Items of Interest") on the arrogance of the landowners of Colchagua Province and the stupidity of their tenant-peasants can hardly be taken as a serious criticism of the country's highly unequal agrarian system. The distinctive world of the Chilean south, the world of the "Frontier" (beyond which the Mapuche, the Araucanian Indians, still stubbornly maintained their independence in the 1840s), is also absent from his picture, except as the setting for the two "historical" narratives he wrote at the end of his main sequence of jotabeches. And while he devotes somewhat more attention to Santiago and Valparaíso, Chile's two most important cities, his picture of them, though lively, is by no means comprehensive. Whenever he describes them, it is always from the standpoint of the kind of provincial visitor depicted, classically, in "The Provincial in Santiago." His true focus remains the north, his *patria chica*.

Not everybody liked or understood the north as he did. The Polish scientist Ignacio Domeyko, starting a notable residence in Chile in the early 1840s, paid an early visit to Copiapó. "For the first time in my life," he would remember, "I saw what is meant by a . . . society without agriculture, without neighbors, without traditions or inherited ideas, whose principal and exclusive aim is to get rich . . . . Wherever one pauses, whether in the street, a café or an inn, the only talk one hears is of money, of mines, of lawsuits."[16] The prosperity that followed the Chañarcillo silver strikes soon left its mark on Copiapó. The German miner Paul Treutler, seeing it ten years after Domeyko, noted that it by then had gas lighting, and that its main streets were paved, some with sidewalks—evidence, for him, of a "high level of civilization."[17] Most foreign visitors, however, thought it a fairly unremarkable small town. An American who passed through in 1851 observed that

> With one exception the houses are of a single story, and constructed much lower than those to the southward, because of the greater frequency of violent earthquakes. Like the dwellings at Santiago, they have two or three patios, and the arrangement of rooms is commodious, if not in accordance with European ideas of elegance. . . . As there is very little mud at any time, and few suitable pebble-stones

nearer than a mile and a half, only a street or two has been paved, nor has the municipal council given much thought to the necessity of sidewalks.[18]

Vallejo himself, though intensely loyal to his hometown, is always aware that it scarcely bears comparison with Santiago, and the first of his essays on "Afternoon Walks" draws attention to, for instance, the modesty of its cemetery and the litter that *copiapinos* have left lying in its vicinity. A careless attitude to the disposal of litter, alas, is still far from unknown in the Norte Chico.

Whatever their limitations, the Copiapó oasis and its surrounding mineral-rich wastelands are nonetheless Jotabeche's fundamental reference points. His sketches of the mining zone bear out Ignacio Domeyko's observations. This *was* a world in which the making of quick fortunes was the driving obsession. Discoveries and deals were the conversational staples of virtually all northerners. The great silver strikes at Chañarcillo, and other, less legendary copper or silver finds, were inextricably a part of the local folklore. Speculators and prospectors very frequently set out on the kind of wild-goose chase depicted in "The Map to the Lode of the Three Mountain Passes." Although Jotabeche scarcely undertakes a sociological study of the mineworkers, his description of them contains a good deal of covert admiration for their strength and endurance, qualities they certainly needed, for, apart from primitive ore-crushers and smelters, there was little in the way of labor-saving machinery in the Norte Chico; it was only just starting to arrive in Jotabeche's time. Jotabeche is moderately indulgent toward the mineworkers' universal practice of *cangalla*, the theft and smuggling of ore from the mines they worked—a practice that drove most of the mineowners to fits of furious indignation, though it was not something that they could easily control. Jotabeche sees it as an understandable or at least inevitable perquisite for the less privileged.

Although Atacama Province was the most open, least traditional region of nineteenth-century Chile, the festivals, social rituals, and amusements to be found in Copiapó itself were much the same as in any Spanish-American city of the period, large or small: religious holidays, with their processions and masked figures, the pre-Lenten Carnival with its rough horseplay, the regular evening *tertulias*, the chief social gatherings of the time—all these are vividly and precisely brought to life by Jotabeche. The social (as distinct from the entrepreneurial) world described here is still in many respects a very traditional, Hispanic one, very reminiscent of the not-so-distant colonial era. But Jotabeche is also keenly aware of the ways in which modernity (in its nineteenth-century form) is beginning to make an impression. Some of the most attractive passages in his writing reflect the excitement felt at Caldera (the "Port of Copiapó" described in the essay with that title) when the steamship calls there, and his own obvious relish at taking trips on board these novel artifacts of high technology, so new to Chile and the world in general. (It is a shame that he was no longer writing his jotabeches when the railroad made its appearance, only a few years later.) Modernity is also present, less directly, in the way he captures the general climate of ideas—liberalism, progress—that was taking hold of educated Chileans in the 1840s. Without rejecting the fundamentally Catholic framework of Chilean life, Jotabeche is clearly on the side of progress, though quite capable of mocking the pretensions of its more vocal advocates. He is also fully conscious of the general atmosphere of liberalism beginning to pervade the country, especially its political class. His classic essay "The Liberal" may poke gentle fun at partisan Liberals, very much the party of the "outs" in the 1840s, but also grasps the fundamental point that the nominally Conservative government of the period, which he mostly supports, also uses the language of liberalism, and appeals to liberal values, in its quest for legitimacy. This was an accurate understanding of his own time and place.

Underlying much of Jotabeche's work, we feel as we read it, is a secure sense of social and political stability, something educated Chileans were beginning to feel proud of as they contrasted their fledgling republic's record with the turbulence so often reported from the surrounding countries, especially Argentina. Jotabeche is never, to be sure, flamboyantly nationalist. He does not view Chile's recent past as by any means impeccable. Yet his basically very positive disposition enables him to take a quietly optimistic view of his country's prospects, and his affection for the Chilean scenes and human types he portrays is palpable. His approach is not, however, one of sentimental or romantic evocation. On this score it is hard to disagree with Raúl Silva Castro, who could not find "a single drop of romanticism in Vallejo's soul."[19] Jotabeche is capable of "lofty and noble thoughts" on his excursion into the Maipó canyon (who could avoid similar feelings in that awesome spot?), but his sketches are essentially down-to-earth and realistic, and he can be tongue-in-cheekishly self-deprecating (as in "The Port of Copiapó") about his inability to express the proper romantic emotions. His clear-sighted realism, however, is always tinged with his own unsentimental "take" on what he observes and describes. Above all, we sense, he is *amused* by the sights and sounds of his native land, and his amusement is persistently reflected in his general tone of light irony, of gentle mockery that somehow never quite turns savage. Content with his lot, content with (though never complacent about) a country that seems to be on a steady path of improvement, his chief concern is to pinpoint the quirks and foibles of his fellow countrymen, their standard conversational commonplaces, some of the nuances of their society. Perhaps his deepest impulse is simply to make Chileans laugh at themselves.

Costumbrista writers in general took a strong interest in history, and elsewhere in Spanish America often drew on the colonial past and its chroniclers for the subjects of their essays and sketches. Jotabeche's chief concern is with contemporary society, but the last articles he published in his main sequence were two "historical" narratives: "The Last Spanish *Caudillo* in Araucania," and "Francisco Montero. Memories of the Year 1820." Both recount episodes from the wars of independence, but not, interestingly, from the epic main campaigns of the liberators José de San Martín and Bernardo O'Higgins, already prominent in the new republic's mythology and themes that would soon be taken up by a notable generation of Chilean historians, some of whom Vallejo knew as young men. Jotabeche's chosen episodes both come from the much less well-known *guerra a muerte*, the peculiarly savage "war to the death" between patriot soldiers and royalist guerrillas on the Araucanian Frontier in the south, which went on intermittently from 1817 to 1827. Whatever his reasons for choosing these particular episodes (he gives at least one in "Francisco Montero"), there is no denying the verve and skill, the sure sense of pace, with which he handles them. Had Jotabeche persisted in his literary work, he might well have become one of Chile's great storytellers—possibly even its first novelist, beating Alberto Blest Gana into second place for that prize. Be that as it may, his achievement was striking enough. He effectively created the Chilean version of an international genre, and one that did not die with him.

Situated in his own time, at the opening moments of a national literary tradition, and with no serious competitors, Jotabeche was almost certain to exercise some kind of influence on those who came after him. His example was important for several generations of Chilean *costumbrista* essayists, some of whom expanded the range of themes treated and got closer to colloquial Chilean Spanish than he did. Names that might be mentioned here include Pedro Ruiz Aldea (1830–70), Román Vial (1833–96), Daniel Barros Grez (1834–1904), Arturo Givovich

(1855–1905), Daniel Riquelme (1857–1912), Manuel Ortiz (1870–1946) and Joaquín Díaz Garcés (1878–1921). Writers like these lacked (for the most part) Jotabeche's literary flair, but successfully prolonged the *costumbrista* tradition in Chile for the better part of a hundred years. Their work can, in fact, legitimately be seen as one of the currents that fed into the mainstream of *criollismo*, "creolism," the main literary trend of the early twentieth century. In their concern to explore and depict the local, the distinctively national, the "creolist" novelists and short story writers could be said to be advancing an agenda originally set by Jotabeche, whose underlying aim, as Enrique Pupo-Walker sees it, was to create literature that would "define the cultural profile of his new nation, and in a larger sense, of Spanish America."[20] Probably Vallejo himself would never have consciously conceptualized his work in quite such grand terms. If it *was* an unconscious aim, he can be said to have succeeded in ways he himself would scarcely have been able to foresee.

Businessman and Politician: Vallejo's Later Years

Vallejo's main sequence of articles came to an end in 1847. Indeed, his production of jotabeches slackened noticeably after 1842, his *annus mirabilis*, when he wrote nearly half the entire sequence. The year 1845, with eight sketches, was his last serious period of writing in this vein. Asked by a friend in 1846 why he was no longer writing his jotabeches with his former frequency, he blamed pressure of work and the lack of stimulus he encountered in his provincial seclusion, where the only conversation at *tertulias* was about mines, and the only pieces of music played by young ladies were Strauss waltzes—all this, he said, was "enough to dry out the brains of a horse."[21] He was concentrating more than ever on his business interests, and found the stimulation he lacked in politics. The businessman and politician, it might be alleged, killed the writer. We cannot be absolutely sure of this, as he apparently went on writing, though without publishing his efforts. His failure to do so may just possibly have been one of the tragedies of Chilean literary history. It seems more likely, on balance, that Jotabeche never quite recovered the inspiration that had seized him so memorably in the six years after 1841.

His interest in politics did not remain dormant for very long. In 1843 he was elected to the municipal council of Copiapó. Two years later, in April 1845, he founded *El Copiapino*, a notable provincial newspaper that lasted until 1876. He himself made very little money from it, soon tired of the tasks of editorship, and sold it after its first seventy-one issues. Vallejo used his newspaper to boost the campaign of a favored candidate in the 1846 congressional elections. The candidacy was not "official" (i.e., supported by the government), and was easily defeated in ways described by Vallejo in his indignant article "Elections in Copiapó." Three years later, he himself ran for the Chamber of Deputies as an "independent" candidate in the Vallenar-Freirina district in the Huasco valley, announcing himself as a staunch defender of provincial interests and throwing himself with great vigor into the campaign. The government did not regard him as an ally, but despite the best interventionist efforts of the Intendant of Atacama Province, Manuel José de Cerda, he was elected. Once again, the best description of the election was provided by Vallejo himself.

At the time Vallejo entered the Chilean Congress, the "era of good feelings" that had marked Manuel Bulnes's presidency was giving way to a new phase of political conflict. The logjam of Conservative hegemony was about to be broken—largely by fissures within the ruling party itself. By 1849 a number of dissident Conservatives had become strongly disaffected from the incumbent Minister of the Interior, Manuel Camilo Vial, President Bulnes's cousin, largely because of his flagrant nepotism. In the congressional elections of that year they strove, against the minister's wishes, to elect candidates of their own. Vial naturally had no difficulty in frustrating their efforts and packing Congress with an overwhelming contingent of his own followers. Only four of the Conservative "rebels" were elected to the new Chamber of Deputies. Shortly after the election, however, Vial had a falling-out with President Bulnes, who almost certainly regarded him as developing excessively liberal schemes, and he was fired as Minister of the Interior. The president appointed a new cabinet (June 1849) that included two of the newly elected Conservative dissidents, Vallejo's old schoolmates Manuel Antonio Tocornal and Antonio García Reyes. Vallejo aligned himself with them in the Chamber against the *vialista* deputies who were the majority in the 1849 sessions, and who now suddenly constituted the opposition to the new cabinet—an opposition from whose ranks would emerge, in due course, the great Liberal party of the later nineteenth century.

Vallejo's debut as a congressman was disconcerting. In one of the opening sessions, in a not altogether parliamentary manner, he impugned the credentials of his newly elected fellow-deputies Juan and Carlos Bello, on the grounds that they had been born in England (where Andrés Bello had lived from 1810 to 1829) and hence lacked proper Chilean citizenship. Why he did it remains a mystery. It may simply have been a clumsy political maneuver (Juan Bello was among the *vialistas* he despised), but many found it a bewildering move, given his well-known friendship for the Bellos. He had been particularly anguished by the early death (at the age of twenty-eight) of their brother Francisco in June 1845, and he sincerely admired Carlos Bello's efforts as a dramatist, which enjoyed much local success in the 1840s. During the debate that followed Vallejo's initiative, he mocked the pretensions to talent of Lastarria, who had sprung to the Bellos' defense. "*Es verdad, lo tengo y lo luzco*" ("It's true: I have it and I show it to good effect"),[22] retorted the vain Lastarria—one of the more famous parliamentary ripostes in Chilean history. Vallejo was providing political commentaries on the 1849 sessions for *El Mercurio* at the time, and frequently used Lastarria as a target for his sarcasm. "Señor Lastarria is a man of convictions," he wrote, in one of these pieces, "and there is nothing easier than to have some convictions one day and others the next."[23]

Vallejo was too independent, too much the maverick, to be a very good party man. His instincts were similar to those of moderate Conservatives like his friends Tocornal and García Reyes. He loathed the increasingly high-flown rhetoric of the opposition. Nevertheless, Lastarria's later description of him as "a violent partisan of the omnipotence of authority"[24] is monstrously wide of the mark. His own election had been fought (very spiritedly) against "authority." The historian Diego Barros Arana, whose own credentials on this score were unimpeachable, remembered him as a "truly liberal spirit."[25] He was quite happy, in fact, to support a major proposal to reform the 1833 Constitution presented (unsuccessfully) by the opposition in July 1850. The suspicious Lastarria interpreted this as a maneuver to embarrass the opposition,[26] but it is clear from Vallejo's letters that his support was genuine. "This reform," he wrote, "is a vital necessity for the country, and above all to improve the administration and condition of the provinces." He himself favored an amendment to allow religious freedom, something that was still absolute anathema to virtually all Conservatives, who firmly upheld the exclusive status of Catholicism. Although he declared himself satisfied with the "foundations" of the 1833 Constitution, the changes he envisioned in 1850 (the abolition of the "single list" for the Senate, the elimination of two-term presidencies, the popular election of Intendants)[27] closely resembled some of the main points of the Liberal agenda of twenty years later, although the popular election of provincial (since 1974, regional) Intendants has never found favor in Chile; they are still appointed by the government, just as department *préfets* in France were from Napoleon's time to the 1980s.

It cannot be said that Vallejo became one of the legends of the Chilean Congress. He was better at interrupting than speaking. Benjamín Vicuña Mackenna was to remember him, in these congressional sessions, as having "an ardent face, lively and a bit sour, a military bearing, a hollow and brusque voice, impatient gestures, an incisive and cutting tongue . . . a high forelock over a large brow, a twisted moustache above a narrow and audacious mouth—in a word, a retired colonel with thirty years' service, discontented, grumbling."[28] Yet despite his limitations as a speaker, he can be credited with several important legislative initiatives, notably the abolition of internal passports, and the relaxation of restrictions on the coasting trade, hitherto reserved to Chilean ships, most of which in 1848–49 had vanished north of the equator, laden with wheat and flour to help feed the California Gold Rush.

Vallejo had always led an active social life. Although we know little or nothing of his earlier romances, he had certainly had several. In April 1850, and (judging from his letters) more or less on impulse, he married one of his nieces, Zoila, by whom he had four children, the first of whom died in infancy. He devoted as much time as possible to family life and his business interests in Copiapó, which were prospering as never before. Vallejo was now a rich man, much of his wealth coming from the Candelaria silver mine at Chañarcillo. He was particularly excited by the building of the railroad from Copiapó to its port, Caldera. This was the first substantial track (fifty-one miles) in South America, and was opened in December 1851. He was one of its promoters, invested 50,000 pesos ($45,000), served on its board of directors, and later wrote some of its annual reports. He did much, apparently, to put it on a sound business footing. At the time of his death, shares in the railroad company were at 60 percent above their original price.

But, whatever his newfound domestic happiness and entrepreneurial successes, Vallejo could not remain indifferent to the deepening political crisis now overtaking Chile. Faced with a tidal surge of Liberal agitation, the Bulnes government turned to the notoriously intransigent Manuel Montt (formerly both a cabinet minister with a reputation for authoritarian attitudes, and a strict principal of the Instituto Nacional) as its choice for the presidential succession in 1851. Vallejo had often expressed admiration for Montt, but, like his friends Tocornal and García

Reyes, was persuaded that his election would bring violent political conflict, as it did, not once but twice. He would have much preferred a compromise candidate such as the prominent trader Jerónimo Urmeneta (Finance Minister, 1850–51), who seems to have been his favorite. "Montt for me," he wrote to a friend, "is like one of those healthy and delicious dishes which have given me indigestion, so that I cannot eat them again."[29] He was still hoping for a compromise candidate as late as October 1850, by which time Montt's succession was a done deal. Whatever his doubts about Montt, he gave him strong support in the election of 1851, as did most of the mining magnates and businessmen of Atacama Province, who believed that their province was the most advanced, most enterprising section of the republic. Montt's much-trumpeted emphasis on material progress, in their view, was just what Chile needed, a standpoint also adopted by Montt's great friend Sarmiento, who vigorously publicized his cause in just such terms.

The political agitation of 1849–51, however, had developed its own momentum. Armed rebellion by the Liberal opposition (and the not exactly Liberal but highly ambitious General José María de la Cruz, the defeated presidential candidate) broke out even as Montt moved into the presidential palace in September 1851. Vallejo sprang immediately to the government's defense. Had it not been for the fact that his wife was pregnant at the time, he would have joined the soldiers sent south from Copiapó to attack La Serena, one of the main centers of the rebellion. In October, when the mineworkers at Chañarcillo revolted and sacked their mining camp, ostensibly in support of General Cruz, the Intendant of Atacama, with whom he had previously been on very bad terms, gave him the task of repressing the uprising. He did so with severity. His hastily mustered force of one hundred soldiers and militiamen killed one of the rioters and took ninety prisoners. All but sixteen were subsequently exonerated by a Copiapó magistrate, an action that did nothing to enhance Vallejo's popularity among Montt's enemies. In December 1851, at the tail end of the civil war, largely defenseless Copiapó was briefly captured by local rebels. Vallejo, who was high on their hit list, was forced to beat a hasty retreat. Happily for him, he was at Caldera at the time. A friendly fisherman took him out to sea, where he intercepted a northward-bound steamship, and next day, while the ship was in port, he hid among the stokers, with the rebels searching for him in vain. By the time he returned from his involuntary trip to Peru, the steamship's destination, order had been restored in Atacama Province. He rewarded the friendly fisherman with new tackle and a new boat.

Vallejo was reelected to Congress in 1852, but did not take his seat, mainly because the Montt administration named him (in November 1852) Chilean chargé d'affaires in Bolivia. There had been almost nothing in the way of diplomatic contact between the two young republics prior to Vallejo's mission (January–May 1853), and there was not to be much for some years afterward; not until 1866 did Chile send another envoy to Bolivia. Vallejo's single diplomatic experience was a chapter of accidents, misunderstandings, and frustrations. The Bolivian government, then in the hands of the rough dictator General Manuel Belzú, refused to receive him formally until he gave satisfactory explanations for the presence in Chile of some of Belzú's political adversaries. Vallejo knew nothing about this and improvised a reply that was sufficient to win him a reception by the dictator. The reply, however, did not meet with the approval of the Chilean government, and Vallejo was instructed to leave La Paz, the Bolivian capital, immediately. Arriving in the Peruvian city of Tacna, on his way home, he rejoiced that he was once again "in the civilized world."[30]

Although Vallejo was happy to serve the government in this way, his earlier doubts about Montt seem to have become more serious as his presidency proceeded. Even though he never lost his respect for the president, he at least once described him as trying to run the country in the way he had earlier run the Instituto Nacional, surrounded by "schoolboys, inspectors and beadles."[31] He stood aside from politics, devoting himself to his commercial interests and his happy domestic life. His old friends Tocornal and García Reyes had given active personal support to Montt in the crisis of 1851, but their moderate, tolerant brand of Conservatism did not appeal to the autocratic president, who preferred compliant yes-men, and they were gradually marginalized. García Reyes died in 1855. Tocornal and his father, the veteran politician Joaquín, now took a major hand in organizing a great Conservative defection. In 1857–58 the bulk of the party deserted President Montt and formed an alliance with the opposition Liberals, a notable political realignment that paved the way for the comprehensive liberalization of political life in the 1860s and 1870s. It is likely that Vallejo, had he lived, would have supported the new "Liberal-Conservative Fusion." It is rather less probable that he would have approved of Atacama Province's dramatic but unsuccessful armed rebellion against President Montt in 1859, though it was led by *copiapinos* he knew and liked.

Such speculation is pointless. While Vallejo must have been aware of the first phase of the political realignment, he was by then past caring about such things. He was falling victim to advancing tuberculosis, the first symptoms of which had become apparent in 1854. In April 1857 he set out on a journey to Europe, hoping to find relief in Italy or the south of France, but got no further than Argentina. In 1858 he and his wife Zoila, also succumbing to the disease, went to Peru in further quest of a favorable climate. On 24 June, while they were at Jauja in the Central Highlands, Zoila died, a blow that undoubtedly hastened Vallejo's own final collapse. The end came soon after his return from Peru, on 27 September 1858, at his hacienda near Copiapó. He was forty-seven. In his will, notarized two days earlier, he instructed the tutors of his children to pay proper attention to their religious education and to place them, "as soon as possible, in commercial offices with strict discipline."[32] An obituary in one of the Santiago newspapers predictably described him as "The South American Larra."[33] He would probably have been pleased. He apparently left a large number of unpublished writings, including poetry. All his manuscripts were burned by his executors, who feared that they were infected.

In more recent times in Chile Vallejo, while never failing to be recognized as an important early figure in the country's cultural panorama, has been distantly venerated rather than widely read or studied. This is not very surprising. The real "giants" of Chilean literature, all twentieth-century figures, and including the two Nobel prizewinners Gabriela Mistral and Pablo Neruda, have understandably attracted a much wider readership and more critical attention than any of the authors of the nineteenth century. Yet the "first of the truly Chilean writers" is not likely to be forgotten.[34] We do not need to make exaggerated claims for him. His achievement was in some ways that of the *petit maître*, but it was an achievement that has strangely retained its value. Jotabeche's jotabeches give us a vivid portrait of the early Chilean republic, especially its all-important mining zone in the northern deserts. Those who want to get a sense of what Chile (or some of Chile) looked like and felt like, in those important, formative years will always be able to go back to his sketches. And this anthology now makes them available to English-language readers unfamiliar with Spanish. Fred Fornoff's sparkling translations very precisely capture Jotabeche's tone, his crystal-clear, straightforward, supple prose with its built-in ironies and gentle sarcasms, and its delightful colloquial interpolations. Those who know the essays in their original tongue (and those who do not) will *hear* Jotabeche's distinctive voice. It is a voice that brings, or should bring, smiles to our faces.

Notes

1. *Obras de don José Joaquín Vallejo (Jotabeche)*, ed. Alberto Edwards (Santiago, 1911), pp. xxii–xxiii. Hereafter cited as *OJJV*.

2. See, for instance, Domingo F. Sarmiento's article "Zamora de Adalid a Jotabeche," *El Progreso*, Santiago, 4 January 1843.

3. *OJJV*, pp. xxi–xxii*n*.

4. José Victorino Lastarria, *Recuerdos literarios* (Santiago, 1878), p. 176.

5. *OJJV*, p. xxiv.

6. Raúl Silva Castro, *José Joaquín Vallejo* (Santiago, 1969), p. 27.

7. Robert Erskine Newland to President Joaquín Prieto, 10 September 1840, printed in *El Buzón*, Santiago, 23 September 1840: *OJJV*, pp. 322–34.

8. See Iván Jaksić, *Andrés Bello. Scholarship and Nation-Building in Nineteenth-Century Latin America* (Cambridge, 2001), pp. 133–42, and Allen Woll, *A Functional Past. The Uses of History in Nineteenth-Century Chile* (Baton Rouge, 1982), pp. 29–48.

9. See Iván Jaksić, "Sarmiento and the Chilean Press," in Tulio Halperín Donghi et al., eds., *Sarmiento. Author of a Nation* (Berkeley-Los Angeles, 1994), pp. 46–47.

10. *El Mercurio*, Valparaíso, 12 May 1842.

11. *Recuerdos literarios*, p. 167.

12. *Recuerdos literarios*, pp. 113–35.

13. Vallejo to Manuel Talavera, 14 December 1843: *OJJV*, p. 496.

14. Domingo F. Sarmiento, *Recuerdos de provincia* [1850], 9th ed. (Buenos Aires, 1961), p. 137.

15. See Enrique Pupo-Walker, "The Brief Narrative in Spanish America: 1835–1915," in Roberto González Echeverría and Enrique Pupo-Walker, eds., *The Cambridge History of Latin American Literature*, 3 vols. (Cambridge, 1996), I, 490–92.

16. *Mis viajes. Memorias de un exilado*, 2 vols. (Santiago, 1978), I, 403.

17. *Andanzas de un alemán en Chile, 1851–1863* (Santiago, 1958), p. 77.

18. Lieutenant J. M. Gilliss, *The U.S. Naval Astronomical Expedition to the Southern Hemisphere during the Years 1849–'50–'51–'52*, 2 vols. (Washington, D.C., 1854), I, 251–52.

19. *José Joaquín Vallejo*, p. 139.

20. *Cambridge History of Latin American Literature*, I, 495.

21. Vallejo to Manuel Talavera, 19 December 1846: *OJJV*, p. 502.

22. Chamber of Deputies, 8 June 1849.

23. *El Mercurio*, Valparaíso, 6 July 1849.

24. *Recuerdos literarios*, p. 177.

25. *Un decenio de la historia de Chile, 1841–1851*, 2 vols. (Santiago, 1905–06), II, 308.

26. Lastarria, *Diario político* (Santiago, 1968), p. 88.

27. Vallejo to Nicolás Munizaga, 13 and 29 July 1850: *OJJV*, pp. 516–18.

28. "La niñez de Jotabeche," *El Mercurio*, Valparaíso, 28 September 1880.

29. Vallejo to Nicolás Munizaga, 29 July 1850: *OJJV*, p. 517.

30. Vallejo to Antonio Varas, 16 May 1853: *OJJV*, p. 542.

31. *OJJV*, p. xli.

32. "Testamento," 25 September 1858, reprinted in Raúl Silva Castro, *José Joaquín Vallejo*, pp. 219–22.

33. *La Actualidad*, no. 210, 7 October 1858.

34. In terms of Chilean topography, he cannot easily be forgotten: a 19,300-foot mountain in the Andes, on roughly the same latitude as Chañarcillo, now bears the name Nevado Jotabeche.

Note on the Text and Translation

The texts translated for the present collection have been taken from those printed in *Obras de don José Joaquín Vallejo (Jotabeche)*, edited by Alberto Edwards (Santiago, 1911), in the Biblioteca de Escritores de Chile. This is by far the best edition of Jotabeche's essays, and also includes a selection of his correspondence and articles from before and after the principal series of jotabeches between 1841 and 1847. The texts here are of thirty-three articles from the main 1841–47 sequence, together with three (indicated by asterisks) from outside the sequence. Original titles (in order of appearance in this collection) are:

I

"Copiapó," "¡Quién te vió y quien te ve!," "Mineral de Chañarcillo," "Los descubridores del mineral de Chañarcillo," "El teatro, los vapores y el hospicio de Chañarcillo," "La mina de los Candeleros," "El derrotero de la veta de los Tres Portezuelos," "Los cangalleros," "Vallenar y Copiapó," "El puerto de Copiapó."

II

"El Carnaval," "Corpus Christi," "La Cuaresma," "Copiapó: las tertulias de esta fecha," "Paseos por la tarde, Primer artículo," "Paseos por la tarde, Segundo artículo," "Las salidas a paseos," "Carta de Jotabeche a un amigo en Santiago," "Carta de Jotabeche," "Una enfermedad," "Algo sobre los tontos," "El provinciano en Santiago," "El provinciano renegado," "Los chismosos," "El Liberal de Jotabeche."

III

"Cosas notables," "Carta," "Un viajecito por mar," "Extractos de mi diario," "Suplemento a los extractos de mi diario," "Un chasco," *"Las elecciones en Copiapó," *"Elecciones de Huasco," *"El levantamiento de Chañarcillo," "El último jefe español en Arauco," "Francisco Montero. Recuerdos de 1820."

I

COPIAPÓ AND
THE MINING ZONE

Copiapó

In the past, there was another period in which this island in the desert flourished. There followed a long series of years in which poverty, hunger and thirst, pestilence, and earthquakes imprinted the seal of misery on it one after another, forcing its inhabitants to emigrate or die, razing the town limits, and wearing down the verdure of the valley in which it was situated until it looked just like the wasteland surrounding it.

In my youth I visited Copiapó. A terrible earthquake had just laid it waste. The people had abandoned it almost completely and were wandering among the arid boulders scattered around the town weeping over their lost homes and trying to placate the wrath of God by doing penance. Its streets, marked at that time by parallel lines in the rubble, provoked an overwhelming sadness, a suffering as mute as the silence of its ruins. Nothing is more melancholy than the sight of an empty yard in a town where no one lives any longer. A cemetery has more signs of life: the crosses, the epitaphs, and even the sepulchres that vanity has adorned with decorations—these reveal to us a new existence, the existence of eternity; but an abandoned city is the image of chaos, the general destruction of the universe.

3

On May 10, 1819, I left here in the company of several families who were emigrating to Huasco and La Serena. All of them overcome by bitterness, they said their goodbyes to the land of their childhood, almost as if they were taking leave of a friend, leaving him abandoned in a state of irreparable misery. They were fleeing from a place in which they feared they would find their graves, but they were weeping, because even a happy refuge in a foreign land makes us remember with double bitterness the misfortunes of our homeland.

Twenty-two years later I have walked once again on this ground that back then depicted the image of a malediction. What a difference! What a contrast between what I see now and my memories of what it was then! Luck, or Fortune, or whatever invisible entity it is that rules the destinies of men and towns!—everything I see, everything present in this place is a manifestation of your power, an astonishing sign of the incomprehensible rules of your will!

Commerce, agriculture, arts, and luxuries have now erased with their riches the very memory of those times. The sound of a great gathering, always busy and active, ever occupied in speculations and business deals or given over to the happiness of nocturnal amusements, echoes today through those places where previously nothing could be heard but the cry of a bird of night, or the barking of the dog who, patrolling the ruins, still felt the urge to keep watch over the destroyed fortune of its fugitive masters.

From whichever direction you travel to Copiapó, you have to cross deserts of sand, arid crags, and vast plains stripped of all sign of vegetation. Heat and thirst, perhaps, don't mortify the traveler as much as the horrible aspect of lifeless, graceless nature, garnished only by boulders as black as the complexion of an African native, and by hills whose tangled strata and harsh ruggedness resemble the wrinkled brow of the old miser trying to defend his buried treasures against the world's greed.

On drawing near to Copiapó, therefore, and catching sight of its groves of trees, its tall willows whose cheerful verdure stands out against the pallor of the heights that complete the landscape, the soul thinks it's awakened from a hateful nightmare, and involuntarily our excitement surfaces as if after a long voyage we discerned the shore of our country and the air were carrying the fragrance of its forests to us. Cheers, lovely valley, enchanted oasis of the desert! The weary traveler approaches you as happily as he would the home of his parents; he catches sight of you like a friend after a long absence and blesses you as a pilgrim blesses the room that lodges him for the night.

The town of Copiapó, because of its layout, is different from many others. Its narrow streets, irregular and twisted, are far more adapted to variety, the only fixed base that until now we've seen prevail over the usual taste of the human species: two straight lines, endless and parallel, of white houses are a constant monotony, a life given over to idleness. In Copiapó it's not like that. At every turn we come upon different looking houses, different kinds of fig trees, different locust trees. Farther along, a long, narrow cart of which, only a few yards back, we could only make out the horns of an ox; then there's a small plaza; right in front of us, then, a foundry oven that, two minutes later, has vanished from sight, and then we're entering a sandy lot where we encounter a church half-buried. Another half-turn, a new scene! An ancient carob-tree with its trunk transformed into a cross, then a smelter, and then a tiled house, ground down, crumbled, its tiles broken off by earthquakes; and so it goes as we walk forward always surprised by something you can't see unless you follow the humps and twists of the streets.

There's something unpleasant about the buildings, whose roofs are low and covered with mud, but for that very reason we are surprised when we see the comfort, ease, and luxury with which the interiors are adorned.

The inhabitants are for the most part foreigners, and of these a large number are Argentines, yet we can't be sure that tomorrow or the next day we might not have a different mix in Copiapó, because every day entire squadrons show up to surrender their weapons to these authorities, though they wouldn't be of much use to the Republic (the weapons, I mean) since they're as knicked and abused as, apparently, the United Provinces of the River Plate[1] must be. Their conduct in this town earns them credit as men of orderly habits; if they have been as brave in battle as they are here in matters of love, there's no way to explain their defeats except as some ill turn of fate, some caprice of fortune.

The fair sex in Copiapó is like the fair sex everywhere, and I mean this as homage. Where is it that women aren't pleasant, lovely, gracious, and endowed with goodness and talent? Who is the wretched fellow who, in whatever clime, hasn't found them to be charming in habit and custom, attractive at play, and conducive of warmth in the head, attributes without which it is impossible to live among them? When I was young and traveled, as I now travel being old, I had the good fortune, which many men must have had, to find in each town six or eight houses with two girls each, all of whom I liked simultaneously. The one who didn't have green eyes had blue ones or black ones; if they were brown, a color regarded as insignificant in eyes, I found them to be irresistible for the curly lashes around them, and I even recall that I almost fell for two that were crossed and seemed enchanting, because I discovered in them a certain *je ne sais quoi* that was impossible to define. It was the same with all their features; I found them all delightful; and the same thing would happen to me today in Copiapó if my faith in baptism didn't weigh so heavily on me. What a collection of eyes of different sorts! Even now, when my blood circulates just so as not to lose the habit, a kind of leftover from the impulse I'd ascribe to youthful ardor in past years, I feel knocked for a loop by sleepy eyes whose intriguing sadness fills my soul with joy; by some dimples, or a mole . . . and by a thousand other small treasures that in those days I coveted by day and fanned my fantasies with in nightly visions.

There's a neighborhood here too that's called Chimba, where every stroll ends up, and from which no one ever returns without a pretty cluster of carnations and jazmins. It's in this part of the town where the orchards and flower and vegetable gardens are most carefully cultivated, because of which the residents of Chimba are visited assiduously by all who know how to appreciate the simplicity of their hospitality and the coolness of their grape arbors and groves. The way back from these strolls on moonlit nights is delightful. A soft breeze from the west sprinkles the balmy air with the fragrance of the magnolia, not to mention the spectacle of a bright, pure, crystalline sky that any enamored poet would be compelled to compare to the gaze of his beloved's eyes.

Man's labors end at six in the evening, and shortly thereafter begin the labors of the guitar strings. Any young man or woman who goes to bed without dancing a country dance can exclaim like that emperor when he retired to bed without having performed an act of largesse: "I've wasted the day."

"Hey, how's it going, man?"

"Great. I just got a letter from Chañarcillo. Two deals almost settled."

"Great news! We'll have to celebrate this. Where will I see you tonight?"

"At N.'s house. We've arranged to meet his pretty cousins there."

"Perfect! I'll show up with the girls next door, and I'll get so-and-so and his pal and you-know-who to pay us a visit with what's-her-name and a couple of her friends."

"Sounds good. Hey, I've got to get to the smelter."

"And I've got to buy me some hammers."

And so they meet, chat it up, and say goodbye, only to meet again where they said they would, where they continue to make further arrangements. The house hosting the visits provides the tea; the men, usually, only ask for water. But this water from Copiapó, perhaps because of the metallic particles floating in it, is so crude and indigestible that, as a precaution, they have to spice it with sugar and cognac, which makes it perfectly drinkable.

"Let's do it! Square dance . . . French quadrilles . . . waltz . . . a minuet for the ladies who can't keep up with the waltz . . . slippery stuff. . . another square dance: have them sing the *Trovador*,[2] the *Sajuriana*, and another and another . . . try the American quadrilles . . . the National Anthem . . . *Sambacueca* . . .[3] and now a square dance to rest a bit."

"Hey, the girls are leaving! Grab the ladies!"

"Jesus, it's late! . . . I've got a sick brother at home. . . . We live so far away!"

"No, for God's sake, love. Look, it's only eleven-thirty. Just another little square dance, and then, no more. . . . Hey, the girls have agreed to dance!"

"Let's do the *moza*, the *moza!*," everyone shouts.

The women take their places again, because although they would have preferred to ignore so much badgering, they can't find a way to just leave. So they dance the *moza;* and since the girls can't go out into the cool air while they're sweaty from dancing, while they cool off, someone hands one of them a *vihuela* so they can all sing . . . "her voice is hoarse, she's forgetting the words, she only knows old clunkers, she's sung too much"; she tunes up the instrument, the first chords ring out, and she begins:

"Oh, how bitter absence is . . . !"

When the first chorus is done, another sweet chord sounds out from the grape arbor in the inner patio . . . the birds are singing! It's dawn!

A general "Jesus!" rings out on the dance floor. A thousand "carambas" of disappointment from the men. They were just beginning to enjoy themselves! They say goodbye to the owners of the house, who are sad as they can be that everyone is leaving so early; but, on the other hand, everyone assures them they've had a great time, and that the next evening they'll take more time.

(*El Mercurio*, February 1, 1842)

If They Could See You Now!

F ew towns have had an infancy so prolonged and so similar to decrepitude as the village of San Francisco de la Selva, now the city of Copiapó, capital of the Province of Atacama. But it's also true that very few will have experienced more rapid or more ostentatious progress than that which has suddenly seen fit to descend on this beloved corner of ours in the last few years. You can say of it what they say about the child who suddenly suffers a huge growth spurt: *he's growing right before our eyes!*

All those countrymen of mine who aren't trying to pretend they were born yesterday will remember what it was like here thirty, forty, or fifty years ago: a mining district with five or six machines for processing gold or silver, and this gold or silver was the only inducement, on the occasion of the death of a bishop, arousing the interest of some speculator, who was as brave as the one who in our times carries his indigo and glass beads deep into the interior of Araucanian territory.

Trees like the carob, *chañar* bushes, or *dadín* plants not only divided one property from the next, but they provided shade for buildings and spread to the patios and sidewalks of the city. In the main plaza, we're told, these native plants grew in the same peace and freedom they enjoyed before Diego de Almagro[1] came from Peru to bring turmoil to this previously quiet valley.

A subaltern official of the Catholic monarchs governed the entirety of the jurisdiction of Copiapó, just as the subdelegates[2] of the Republic govern today in Chañarcillo and San Antonio. I'll explain what I mean: they were charged with overseeing the welfare of the region, but at the same time they had the power, authority, and the money raised from fines to do ill, if they so chose. So in reality it was always a special favor and an act of mercy if they decided not to hang you when you least expected it. The town back then was like a huge monastery of both sexes, and it lived, ate, and slept to the chiming of bells. Early in the morning the priest summoned them to mass; at twelve noon, the sacristan rang *the agony of lunchtime;* at the oration, he rang the bell again so everyone could go yawn through the reading and the distribution; and later, at around ten, curfew sounded, the hour when the subaltern official ordered his people to go to bed and turn out the lights, under penalty of a week of hard labor in the jail or a fine of a certain number of pesos. Back then, everyone knew that the pesos were for the subaltern official: today no one can swear for sure exactly which abyss they're going to end up in.

In those days, there were only a few rich men and an anthill of the poor, as poor as Adam. The former made up the royal court of the subaltern official; they were all military officers with commissions from the king, the only title still conserved today with all its privileges and perquisites; the latter have returned to what they were, have turned to smoke.

The only matter classified then as *public interest*, and which was capable of moving the community to a state of excitement, seems to have been water rights. One authority was stoned by the people for having distributed them favoring the rich; and there was another who, having failed to distribute them favoring them, had to join the people in attacking them, going so far as to burn their crops in order to institute reforms.

The only law was the inquisitorial power exercised by the parish priest, whose authority was not limited to marrying you against your will, but also included locking you in jail or casting you from the fold by permanent excommunication, a stigma that was passed on to your descendants.

The Commanders of the Order of Mercy and the Guardians of San Francisco constituted another terrible power. Consequently, it was regarded as a great honor in those days to have them act as godfather to your children, and a veritable blessing from God to receive visits from them; on the contrary, to fall from their favor was the heaviest stone that could fall on top of an individual.

Family gatherings were seldom held at night, and nocturnal celebrations were only organized on the occasion of a wedding, an anointing, or some other occasion for rejoicing. The minuet performed by the most distinguished female, usually not the prettiest girl, opened the session, after which all the ladies were permitted to come out, one by one, to reenact that elegant pass, that exhibition of grace and beauty to which this magnificent custom from the past has been reduced. The protocol of allowing the young woman who was considered queen of the ball to open the dance with a minuet was for a long time the cause of quarrels and charges of favoritism. But later on it was arranged that that prerogative should go to the oldest young woman, so there came a time when no one wanted to accept such an honor. Women have always been impossible to understand.

The furniture in the main room of a house consisted of a long platform with a rug over it and a mouse-family underneath; on the platform and along one wall, there was a row of semi-Moorish pillows with chintz backs or finely woven cotton cloths used as wall hangings. This was exclusive seating for the ladies, and no man, unless he were the friar who rang the church bell, could profane that sanctuary. Nestled like a cabbage against one of these backed cushions you'd find the mistress of the house seated on a small rug, by her side a small coffer inlaid with silver mosaics and conch shells. In front of this raised contraption you'd find a bench and several stools made of wood so unvarnished it looked like it might take root and send out new shoots; this was where the men sat. Beneath the bench and stools the house-doves slept, spiders wove their webs, the little girls kept their dolls and the older girls their favorite shoes; and since no broom ever passed under them, it wasn't surprising to see a *chañar* seedling or two sprouting. The only other furniture was an enormous table, usually made of willow, on which the family's miracle-working saints, the *mate* and silver teapot, a small box with mirror inside, a freshly watered flowerpot, several bottles of *chicha*, and the mistress's pet cat lived in perfect harmony.

That, more or less, is what Copiapó was like in those days of its prolonged infancy. That's how it vegetated for nearly a century, without the lives of its inhabitants suffering any crises other than those caused by an occasional silver strike or by the strong earthquakes felt there from time to time.

The revolution of independence managed to shake up these customs and this mode of existence of our town, despite its isolation from the theater of events and reforms. It introduced a certain fermentation in the life of inertia lived here, and, as elsewhere throughout the territory, people discovered it was possible to think and act, and they thought and acted in a circle wider than the one they had known existed until then.

But it's undoubtedly true that Copiapó has only really begun to move ahead in the past ten years. The exploitation of Chañarcillo, San Antonio, and the other rich mines; the frequent communication we've established with other towns and other people; the immigration of the Argentines; and a number of other important circumstances have given great impulse to our population, business, industry, and cultural customs, improvements that would be much weaker if they had been brought about only through the effect of our civilizing revolution.

Six establishments servicing the silver mines with noisy machinery and abundant capital now threaten to pulverize and dissolve every hill in the district. The opening of these important companies is like an obsession now: some are just starting up, several more are planned. It's truly amazing and somewhat heartening to see that the more machines there are to devour metals, the greater number of cash registers are brought in to the companies. The combination has provided an admirable boost to this industry.

They've assigned an Intendant now to run the public business of the district, and it may well be that throughout the province there are no problems worse than those caused by the imprudence and idealism of these officials.

A large population is now at work in industries of all sorts, in this city and throughout the valley. The advances in agriculture are truly unbelievable, if you consider that five or six years ago it was in a state of utter abandonment.

Theft and lying are very rare, because work provides the poor classes with an adequate living. Property is distributed, there are countless small businesses in full operation, and commercial speculators keep the market abundantly supplied. Everything is expensive, but everything is available.

The priests and clergy have stopped putting on airs that can't be maintained except by mystifying the people and keeping them in a perpetual state of ignorance. Now they're no longer feared, but loved, because they love everyone, and because they favor the poor, persuading the rich to give to charity, open schools, build temples, and undertake projects whose primary goal is to benefit humanity. I don't want to leave anyone out, but I feel obliged to mention here the names of the excellent canon D. Joaquín Vera and Fray Francisco Bustamente: both of them, because of their work, their selflessness, and their noble and evangelical virtues, have won the gratitude and love of our people.

There are no longer any platforms, benches, or stools. Elegant furnishings have replaced this collection of respectable grotesqueries. Woolen shag rugs, sofas, and horsehair chairs, marble, mahogany, mirrors, and pianos now fill the reception rooms, whose walls are no longer covered by cotton hangings but by pretty wallpaper.

Our social life, when it chooses to, can offer all the pleasures and attractions of the best provincial towns. All that's needed is for people to seek to have a social life, for them to prefer the tea served by a young woman to that prepared by servants in the houses of bachelors, and that after the store is closed, where we've been cheating half the world, for us to seek out places where everyone can cheat us. Remember those beautiful times that sometimes shine in this excessively masculine life we lead, like a beautiful day in snow-covered winter; remember those September nights, and think of all the elegance, all the kindness that's been left behind there in unworthy oblivion, in pitiful inaction.

Considering the contrast between the Copiapó that used to be and the one we now see, there's every good reason to exclaim, with our hands beside our head, *if they could see you now!*

(*El Copiapino*, April 10, 1845)

The Mines of Chañarcillo

I have seen this settlement, not of houses but of caves. I've seen a hill covered with round holes, like a piece of wood drilled by moths.

Twenty leagues south of Copiapó and at the end of a chain of mountains that extends over a long distance in different directions, its surface the color of maize or different metallic shades, a man hunting guanacos in May of 1832 discovered that deposit of silver, its value incalculable even today. There people have found their great fortune or added to the one they already had; others, driven by greed, have lost the fortunes they previously possessed, and a good many, after becoming astonishingly rich extracting from Chañarcillo its treasures, have fallen back into misery through prodigality, imprudence, and mad dissipations. In fewer than ten years this region has produced more than twelve million pesos, and if one could calculate in cash even a quarter of the hopes currently riding on it, long strings of ciphers would be needed to express it. There are more than a hundred mines in operation; some of them are rich; others are run on speculation; but all of the calculations and probabilities seem to guarantee in almost all of them the desired yield, to secure which their owners plod with the same dogged tenacity, wiles, patience, and strategems one uses to conquer the heart of a haughty and beautiful woman. The veins of Chañarcillo that have been mined to the appropriate depth yield a rich ore. The general efforts of the miners, then, is to reach that depth, which they call strata, a line where no hope has failed to be satisfied, and where fickle fortune, weary of resisting her tenacious conquerors, rewards their constancy.

A mine is a rare testimony of the power and audacity of man, though perhaps the undaunted plowing of the stormy ocean is a better measure of his destiny than running through the dark caverns he himself has constructed and shored up beneath the enormous weight of mountains ever ready to buckle and shift. A thousand hopes gird the mariner in his peril; a boat, a plank, can carry him safe to shore. Only darkness surrounds the miner; once his foot slips from the hard path guiding him, nothing can save him from foundering; he doesn't even get to look death in the face, for it surprises him in the act of performing the most vigorous exertion of his existence.

The horrible blast of dynamite that scorches the miner as he swings his pick, the commotion produced in the enormous mass whose center he's cutting into, and the roar repeated a thousand times by the echoes from other concavities and crevices in the mine, no experience could be more imposing than this sublime expression of the omnipotence of industry, or, as the miners say, this moaning of the mountain as it feels its entrails cut to pieces. No matter how prepared he might be to hear that tremendous din, he is nonetheless overcome by a violent terror without being able to shake it off even after the phenomenon has passed, doubting whether he'll emerge in one piece without being buried on the spot, and, for all his effort, breaking off only a few pieces of stone in order to lay bare the metal of the vein he's pursuing.

The operations in the Descubridora [Discoverer], Chañarcillo's chief mine not only because it was the first but also because it's the richest, have cut their way to a greater depth than all the other mines. To see a half-naked man appear in the mouth of this mine, carrying on his back two or even three hundred pounds of rocks after having climbed with such an enormous weight through that long succession of galleries, pits, and chambers, and then to hear the painful howl he makes when he finally gets a breath of fresh air, we conclude that the miner belongs to a more accursed race than man, that he's like a creature emerging from another world less fortunate than ours, and that the deep sigh he emits when he finds himself among us is a bitter reproach directed at heaven for having excluded him from the human species. Between the mouth of the mine and the open space where he dumps the metals you can see sweat pouring copiously from all his pores; each plodding step he takes is marked by a violent grunt; his stooped body, his staggering walk, and finally his violent panting, show how much he's suffering. But scarcely does he throw his burden to the ground than he stretches his beautiful torso, gives a happy whistle, anxiously drinks a glass of water, and then disappears back down the arched labyrinth of those dark precincts, chanting an obscene song.

The mines that are currently in a fairly presentable condition are the Descubridora, the Guías, the Carlota, the Santa Rita, the Rosario de Picón, the Colorada, the Guía de Carballo, the Reventón Colorado, the Santo Domingo, the Esperanza, the Bolaco, and the San José. A good number of others, despite being barricaded by day, wouldn't be sold by their owners except for prodigious sums, which proves how deeply rooted their hopes are; to which we should add that a mine could scarcely be called abandoned just because it's been denounced[1] by one or more who continue to work it until they find in it their fortune or their ruin. Chañarcillo, then, is a place where people work amazingly hard, with a constancy worthy of better rewards. For many years it will go on being one of the most solid bases of the wealth of this Republic, on which heaven spreads its blessings for the happiness of its children, and in which so many noble Americans end up drying their tears in their misfortunes.

In the center of the mining region a village called Placilla has sprung up. It is there where the miners go to seek solace at night. Gambling, love, liquor, and all the vices lead them to consume in an hour the entire product of their labor as well as the value of the precious stones that in good conscience they feel obliged to steal from the owner so he won't make so much profit, working so much less than they. Placilla is a Babel, its confusion not of languages but of all the fortunes of Chañarcillo. Finding themselves within its purview, where notions of mine and thine are abolished, the miners sell the metals that have come into their possession in the vicissitudes of the day with the same frankness with which the owner of the mine feeds into the machine at Fragueiro and Codecido[2] the ore he's been able to save from their pilfering.

(*El Mercurio*, February 2, 1842)

The Discoverers of the Chañarcillo Mines

Excellent topic for a Lenten sermon in which the orator proposed to describe the fleetingness of earthly treasures and conjure up not just one but many prodigal sons without resorting to parable. I, who am no orator, and who have not been burdened on this earth with the arduous task of herding restive sheep from one place to another, though I'm proud to own some and frequently find myself trailing after one who's gone astray, have chosen this matter to write an article.

It's hard to say whether fortune meant to favor or mock those who discovered the first veins and strata of these famous mines. Waking up one morning possessed of fabulous wealth, by nightfall they found themselves in a state of poverty more dire than any they'd lived in before the blind goddess led them in the direction of Chañarcillo. They had rich stores of cash, unrivaled credit, and made many others rich; they had their haciendas, their servants, and could count on the respect and servility of everyone around them. Before long they didn't even have a place to live; they were ruthlessly evicted; no one would lend them a spare closet; finally they even removed the title of *don* from their names, since it only covered them with humiliation, as if the continued use of that wretched title obliged them to maintain certain relations they could no longer afford or profit from. What a race, these humans! How are you any different from a prostitute, except that you will never grow old enough to change your ways.

The ass-keeper Juan Godoy was out hunting a guanaco on May 18, 1832, and exhausted by the tenacious chase he'd given him, only to be mocked by that agile denizen of the desert, he sat down to rest on a rock, waiting for his dogs to return with bloody mouths to announce they'd caught the prey and would lead him to the site of their triumph. It didn't take him long to notice that he had for a seat an outcropping of rich silver ore, and this was the instant when Chañarcillo was born into the world, the instant when heaven bestowed such a magnificent boon on this happy Republic. Godoy, overcome with surprise, forgot all about the guanaco, and would have forgotten his donkeys too, who were wandering nearby, had he not conceived the plan to load them up with rich rocks instead of firewood, and go straight to Copiapó where he intended to get advice on what he should do, as if some great calamity had befallen him.

The first person he confided his secret to, so as to get some sort of guide for conduct, was Juan José Callejas, an old miner and professional snoop or warrant server who despite having known about all the veins and deposits in that district for over forty years, had managed to accumulate only a wealth of experience, but no wealth. So just like that, Godoy gave this guy a third of the treasure he'd discovered, which the old man signed over to a former boss of his, from Copiapó, out of gratitude for the many favors he owed him.

Our discoverer, after having deflowered his treasure, sold the other two-thirds he had left and, liberated now from the cares of working the mine, settled down to enjoy the pleasure of being rich. Don Juan Godoy, as he was now called, turned out to have a lot of relatives, lots of very close ones he had never related to before, except when he'd sold them firewood. However, it was now unavoidable that he acknowledge and recompense all those extremely courteous demonstrations of affection, showing himself to be properly sensitive to the overwhelming anxiety they displayed in ingratiating themselves to him. A meal would be followed by a dance, the dance by some girls they'd introduce him to, the girls by lunch, lunch by a visit to some gambling den, until when all was said and done he had no oil for his lamp, and I'm not talking about that marvelous lamp of the thousand and one nights. The crowd then started thinning out, taking French leave, so to say, each one by a different door, and one day Juan Godoy, as he was now called, woke up as he had just a few months ago feeling that all the lovely things he'd dreamed weren't real. Poor wretch! He didn't even have any burros left . . . ! The generous boss of his pal Callejas, learning about the misery in which the guy was once again immersed, gave him a part share in the Descubridora mine, which earned him 14,000 pesos. With that sum his famous benefactor got him to buy himself a cornfield in Coquimbo where, no longer pestered by his friends, he went to die in peace, leaving his family a truly mediocre inheritance.

Old Callejas had found the perfect way to escape this catastrophe. Happy to have made his benevolent boss rich, he enjoys amid the most exemplary sobriety, the gifts with which he in turn has been blessed. His favorite place on earth is the Descubridora mine, which he loves like the child of his own eyes; his favorite places to take a stroll are in the mineworkings called Pique del Agua, Frontón de Castillo, El Fenómeno, La Paloma, and all that muddle of abysses the fruitful invention of which he has been principal director. The Descubridora is for him a beloved daughter, beautiful and diligent in the arms of a friend he idolizes; and with every new discovery they make there ten more of his white hairs fall out from sheer joy, as if it were a brand new grandson for him to hold in his arms. Happy old man, who taught you your philosophy?*

Not far from this mine stands what was formerly called the Manto de los Bolados. This powerful deposit of silver balls can only be seen by day; it's a huge round hole, which to those who know its history and the history of those who discovered it calls to mind nothing if not a bone depositary, the contrast between what a man was and what he ends up being. Four miners discovered this charmed spot. Without putting a price on the silver dust and ore that each one of them gave to the infinite comrades constituting the fickle retinue of fickle fortune, it's been verified that it produced for its owners more than 80,000 eight-ounce silver coins, at least 700,000 pesos. What became of this capital? Its appear-

---

*   I had finished writing this article when I learned of the death of don Miguel Gallo, Callejas's boss, the benefactor of Godoy and many other poor men. He died suddenly in Chañarcillo on the eighth day of this month (March), after spending three hours walking through his Descubridora mine. He left his children a large fortune and a spotless memory, the example of the most excellent social virtues.

    If I can leave my children a legacy like that, how happy my eternal rest will be!

ance on the scene happened so fast that no one can answer this question to anyone's satisfaction, not even those who, to all appearances, merely played the role of capitalists.

One of them has simply disappeared. His large family is probably the poorest in the whole province.

Another is currently involved in a lawsuit with the village priest over a plot of land his now deceased wife left him. If the priest wins the lawsuit, the guy's on the street.

The third lost not only everything he got from the mine, but also the best part of what he owned previously.

The fourth has nothing left except the many children born or still to be born to him and his wife.

These same four men also discovered the rich mine called El Bolaco, which today belongs to other owners.

The Colorada, famous for its abundant yield of silver marks for its owners, for the river of nuggets stolen by the miners, and for lawsuits initiated by half the people in town, was discovered by Manuel Peralta, who no longer exists. Generosity ruled this miner like a passion, and he ended up giving to different individuals more than twelve-fourths of his find; and he would have gone on giving it away like that if its total petering out hadn't brought an end to the requests. Those who now own this mine got it through a formal denunciation:[1] they worked at it, they got it, and here's where the fun began. Each one of the stockholders filed at least one lawsuit; each lawsuit was for a fourth share; each share had twelve litigants, and each litigant estimated the value of his stocks and challenged all counterclaims before his royal highness as having greatest claim by law, each swearing that he wasn't proceeding with malicious intent. One asked for an embargo, another for arbitration; this one for a summons, that one for total restitution, damages, practical judgment, settlement, or legal acknowledgment of his rights; and they all asked for costs, damages, and reimbursement; and beyond that, exemption from further litigation. What a mess!

I mentioned that Manuel Peralta died, the wisest course of action for the poor guy, because they probably carried him out the way they brought him in, without knowing what he'd done nor even what people expected him to do. The poor wretch died really tired of hearing himself called "stupid ass" by the very ones he'd given everything away to.

The mine called La Guía, or Prospect, that opulent collection of veins, strata, and promising geological formations that even now is thought to be loaded with virgin silver, because the working of it continues to proffer new rewards day after day, was discovered by the pick-man

Juancho, who hurried and sold it before all that dazzling treasure played out. With the money the deal brought him, he too decided to have himself a good time; he started throwing sumptuous feasts; in one of these, a friend stuck a knife into him, as a result of which they had to amputate his arm. His last nickel went to the apothecary, and in no time the sacristan and the grave-digger were fighting over who should be attending to him. The discoverers of Red Lode have extracted from this mine nothing but a few drawersful of legal complications impossible to resolve, more like cold lead, whose profits up to now are undetectable. Keep up the good fight! And they aren't even unitarians or federal agents . . . ! [2]

This little piece would get longer and longer if I chose to add all the little anecdotes I've left out, which anyway are identical in the way they turn out: desperate poverty or lawsuits, just like those uprisings and battles that ensue when Peruvians think they've found a way to agree on something.

Whenever I write something, unless it's a letter, I'm faced with the problem of not knowing what to say when I see it's time to end it; but for now I have to fulfill the idea I had when I started to sketch these sad episodes in the history of Chañarcillo. I want to remind those who've gotten rich from these mines to pay some attention to the families of those who discovered them. No one has more legitimate claim than they do, all those naked little kids swarming about in anticipation of the generous protection of the rich miners of this town. To support and educate some of their children would only require some minimal endowment, approximately, for example, a single day's yield of the ore discovered by their parents.

When you're strolling out from Copiapó to visit your mines, say about two hundred yards before you get to the chapel of Tierra Amarilla, stop off at the poor shack off there to the left, beside the main road. You'll find a mother and seven small children, I won't say "living," rather, "huddling" there. This is the family of one of the discoverers. I only ask that you go inside that hut, which is one of life's totally painful learning experiences, and I'm sure you won't come out without agreeing that it's a place where you can purchase peace of heart for almost nothing.*

(*El Mercurio*, April 4, 1842)

---

* The current owners of the Descubridora mine in Chañarcillo are millionaires. They live in great opulence in Santiago: they distribute generous sums of money to churches and hospitals. Meanwhile, the children of the discoverers from whom they purchased, for forty dollars, this immense treasure, are living in indigence. How much more virtuous their vanity and conscience would feel if those wealthy men would spend their alms educating the children of their benefactors! *Jotabeche* (May 1847)

The Theater, Steamships, and the Chañarcillo Hospice

Have no doubt, all of this exists on that famous hill. The law of compensation is as true in the life of man and society as gravity in physical nature: good and evil are almost always balanced as if they shared this property of fluids. To anyone we hear complaining that there's a subdelegate[1] in Chañarcillo, we can say: *but there are also some good things there, as should be the case, because everything can't be to our liking.* And, in fact, even this can be an excuse for giving up.

The theater of the mines is, as they say, one of those things, though still in its infancy, and the players in the company don't put on airs. People of experience, they know very well that the members of the audience are quite creative in expressing their impressions, that their applause is like hooting, and their hooting like grapeshot; hence, the primary goal of the company, after collecting the price of entry, is to prevent a tragedy from being staged there, in which some actor plays the role of St. Stephen. Before starting the production, they provide music to soften the hearts of those seated in the orchestra, preparing them for reconciliation with what they're about to hear and the costumes and characters they're about to see. The bravest of these steps forward first and by way of prologue says to the spectators: *Respectable public, there are many of you here who understand theater, and many more who do not, but who will understand it shortly. As for the first group, there's no problem; as for the second group, I beg you to maintain order and not applaud until the farce is presented following the play: thank you.*

The curtain goes up, and two hundred seat-pads that had been pressed between the floor and the buttocks of that many ticket-holders are waved in the air immediately. The dust and the smell of burnt gunpowder make those who understand theater step back; these, ready to leave at a moment's notice, stand in the rear to keep their dress-jackets and frock-coats from taking on the hue of the miners' ponchos and cotton smocks, which are always the color of ochre, ash, or mold-green of the ore in the mine where they work.

During the performance you don't in fact hear any noise that's too alarming. Yawns of boredom, raucous laughter during the more sentimental or pathetic scenes, the thudding sounds of those falling from their perches on the walls, the crying of the mineworker's small child, whose mother never leaves him home, and now and then a shout "my four *reals* . . . !" protesting the cost of the spectacle, these are the only, though oft-repeated interruptions heard in the theater. Beyond this, the sound of the swords of the grenadiers, which always announces the imposition of a fine or a trip to jail, keeps everyone in a state of moderation, which the Ministry would desperately like to introduce into the Democrat Clubs.[2]

Just as it's true that in Chile and elsewhere the public worship of any but the Catholic religion is prohibited, though anyone can worship God as he sees fit, so in Chañarcillo there's a prohibition of the public sale of any drink other than *horchata*, which doesn't stop anyone from getting drunk however he chooses. In the theater, then, the only refreshment is this almond liqueur made with water from the Molle and then fermented, which is delicious, especially if it's been chilled in snow.

Because of the effects of this drink, the farce is brutally hooted, booed, and interrupted. The procession of San Tristeza excites those who are already excited sitting down, so you would think that this could be nothing but two rival political clubs demanding simultaneously that the national anthem be sung and that it not be sung, that the hymn of freedom be played and that it not be played.

The bell that sounds curfew, or rather, that threatens everyone with fines, puts an end, at ten o'clock, to the riot. Everybody departs, on their own or someone else's feet, for their homes or else they head for the powder-shack, which the miners' insatiable need for a *tertulia* has turned into a secret café, where they can drink long and gamble hard without anyone being inconsiderate or courageous enough to go and interrupt them.

The steamships. Could anyone who hasn't lived for a while in Copiapó imagine what they call steamships in Chañarcillo? A fine invention that does honor to those who created it! Two poor entrepreneurs came up with the idea of filling, for their own profit and as a public service, a need that the administration neither acknowledged nor had any intention of satisfying; I'm referring to the frequent and regular communication between this town and its rich mines.

About three years ago two men, each of whom owned three or four horses, started making the trip from here to Chañarcillo once a week, establishing their scheduled days and hours of departure and arrival at both places. At first they transported fruits and vegetables, but once they became known, once people knew that on a certain day they would be leaving from a particular point, and on a certain day they would arrive at another point, and that on a certain day they would return, people started paying them to deliver their private correspondence and as many small and large packages as they needed to have sent, carried, and brought back between two places whose communication with each other was expanding rapidly. The people gave these travelers the very significant name of steamships, and since each one arrived at the mines on different days of the week, they distinguished between them by calling them the steamship *Peru* and the steamship *Chile*, after those that travel along our coastline. Today the two travel in convoy, apparently having teamed up to conduct the business as a company.

Their departure from this city is scheduled for each Saturday at dawn, and they accept mail up to that hour, packages up to midnight the night before. They also regularly transport families or women who are traveling to visit their parents or husbands who work in the mines.

They arrive at their destination on Sunday at sunset, a time when all the inhabitants of Chañarcillo are gathered in the plaza, which is the port where they drop anchor. Everyone comes here to receive what he or she is expecting, because in addition to the predictability of the arrival of these men, as soon as they come into view they are announced with repeated cries of *the steamship! the steamship!*, which is echoed across the hills.

Each package is carefully labeled or attached to the letter that goes with it. The exact freight or postage is paid in Chañarcillo, which, in conjunction with the orderliness and reliability observed, augments their earnings substantially. General opinion assures us that they've never accepted for delivery any smuggled ore or any liquor except that carried for personal consumption, nor have they given passage to persons who don't have a passport from the authorities.

On Monday afternoon both coaches set out from Chañarcillo, carrying as return cargo all the dirty clothing and correspondence handed them; there's no charge for this, no freight to pay. The letters and packages whose recipients did not show up are deposited in the respective agency until they come to pick them up.

On Tuesday they're back. The laundresses receive the clothing, and quite a few poor mothers a memento, made of silver, from their sons.

The hospice. Mining, like the profession of war, also has its dead and wounded, unfortunately more than just a few. Accidents, risk-taking, carelessness, overconfidence, gunpowder, and iron take their daily toll on the miner through one of the many dangers that threaten his existence. And it's not just in the mines that this industry seems to take its quota of victims, because it isn't uncommon for workers to lose their lives or an arm or a leg in the smelters, machines, and metal-processing operations. In this connection, we might legitimately mention the conduct of some of the owners of these companies, who, when an employee or worker has been killed or mutilated on the job, have continued paying the same salary to the widow of the one who died or to the individual incapacitated for work.

The miner with a pick or drill is exposed, more than others who work in the mines, to this kind of misfortune. The formation of an auger-hole in the stone where the work is being done is one of those operations that cannot be completed without fatigue and suffering: consequently, the miner can't accept the possibility that a job that has cost him so much effort should yield no profit. This is the cause of his injury.

Once the augur-hole has been prepared, loaded with powder, and the shot tamped, the worker lights the fuse and runs to a hiding place until the explosion and rock-fall is over. It frequently happens that the powder doesn't ignite and *the shot remains unexploded.* In such a case, the safest thing would be to drill a new hole, but who wants to waste all that time and work? *What will people say* if he delays longer than his companions in getting to the ore? The poor miner doesn't think any more about it, and driven by a foolhardy anger he goes about unloading hell, not with a scoop that would protect him from any danger if he's patient, but with the steel tip of his pick, which is the same as holding a burning coal against the powder. This operation almost always has a happy ending, but there are times when while he's doing this the powder ignites, the shot explodes, and our man pays with his life for his boldness: if he comes out alive, usually, it's without eyes. A week ago the best pick-man in the Colorada mine died on the job in one of these accidents: the pick with which he was unloading the shot ended up buried in his skull.

Therefore, there are many blind drillers, totally incapacitated in the robust fullness of youth for earning a living in their chosen profession. But these young braves of the industry, who with more justification than others could live on public charity, continue earning their living with the sweat of their brow. In Chañarcillo, eight of them live together in a humble shack, which is impossible to visit without your heart experiencing one of those emotions that are pleasant if you happen to be generous, sad if you aren't. Do you know what those blind men do to earn their daily bread? They pound and soften the leather that the mineworkers use to make their sandals. The calloused hands and strong teeth of these invalids are better than any tool for tanning the stiff material distributed to them. The great need for this leather guarantees their survival, and the social environment in which they live and work, the nonstop chatter they keep up, give this poor hospice the lively air of a workshop full of happy young workers.

Unfortunately, there's someone moving in on this industry of the blind men of Chañarcillo. A man who's sound and healthy, who in his profession not only earns his living but puts away substantial savings, wants to compete with them and has established a shop to sell this material prepared in his own house by peons who work for him. The blind men brought him up before the subdelegate, but they lost the case.

It's a pity that the subdelegate did not add to his long list of totally arbitrary decisions a decree declaring the industry of softening leather for sandals to be the exclusive province of the blind.

(*El Copiapino*, December 6, 1845)

Candlestick Mine

Every treasure buried in the bowels of the earth has its owner; and this owner, usually, is a spirit who defends it, hides it, and watches over it, sometimes in the form of a guanaco, at other times that of an enormous fox, and not all that rarely in the form of a vulture, lord of the air. Infinite miners, no matter how little time they've spent nosing around in the solitary mountains of Chanchoquin, Punta del Diablo, Checo, etc., bear irrefutable witness to this truth. And I say truth because I do not wish to scorn such an ancient tradition, and because it would be discourteous to say that thousands of men are lying.

It happens from time to time that one of these spirits decides to contribute to the happiness of a man gathering firewood, and when the man is uprooting from the desert floor a few tree trunks for his donkeys to carry home, he discovers a vein that is not so much metal as it is pure gold or silver. It's true that the good intentions of the spirit are never brought to fruition, since most of the time the one who made the discovery stands there loading wood so someone else can smelt the silver that the vulture, fox, or guanaco had intended to give him. But this does not in any way invalidate the first proposition, and merely proves the axiom: *he who was born to be poor will never get rich.*

On other occasions, a shepherd, who has gone out looking for a lost goat, will be running over the crags, breaks, and ravines in the early morning, and while he's running he gets a thorn in his foot, and the pain makes him sit down to pull it out. He'll be sitting there cursing that instrument of his wretched luck, when he sees strolling right past him a reddish fox with its tail held straight up and its back bristly. It's the very one that murdered his goat! He stands up, runs after the voracious beast, whistles for his dog Corbata, who's nowhere to be seen, and in his frustration he picks up a stone with the reasonable intention of crushing the ribs of that butchering fox. . . . Surprise stays his wrath . . . the stone he's holding in his hand is very heavy. . . . He examines it and discovers that it's a nugget! Pure silver! After examining the hill he discovers the outcropping from which the nugget broke loose. A hundred donkeys couldn't carry the rich metal that's just lying there in the sun! But the shepherd is walking and can only take with him two small chunks whose value is at least thirty marks. He has no doubt that the reddish fox is the owner of that astonishing wealth; he's afraid, of course, that by some whim, which he knows to be very common among spirits or witches, as he calls them, the treasure will disappear, so to mark the place where it's located in a perfectly foolproof manner, he stacks up a huge pile of stones, hangs his cloak on a nearby carob tree, records many signs and calculated measurements, and at last the dog who had just run up to him ends up also tied to the trunk of a small carob tree, eating a thick chunk of bread that his master leaves him until he returns to untie him. As he moves away, he continues to mark signs here and there and tries to step where his footsteps will stand out so they can guide him back later.

He doesn't take long getting back to the sheep-fold, known by the name Green Water, or black, or yellow, it doesn't matter; he calls to his father secretly, then to his two older brothers, and finally to his mother. He begins his story, starting with him setting out before dawn and recounting point by point and step by step the trail he followed, what he did, what he saw, and what happened to him; they all stand hushed, dominated by a stupid terror, as if they were listening to the story of the murder of a well-known miner and were afraid to hide his murderer. After these inexplicable moments have passed, things are different. The father makes his calculations, has four donkeys saddled, and telling the rest of the family that he's going out for firewood, he leaves with his three sons, each one riding his respective donkey. The shepherd spurs his donkey to take the lead, the old man follows, and then come the other two boys, and the parade is rounded off by a squadron of bone-thin dogs of all sizes and colors. The guide starts recognizing the places he'd marked: there are his signs, the white stone there in front has done its job; now they can see the blue cloak tangled in the carob tree, and the squadron of dogs take off when they hear Corbata barking. They're only a short distance away . . . now they're there.

But, what has become of the outcropping . . . ? There's something. . . ! The shepherd picks up the stone he'd used to break off the two chunks . . . ! They look everywhere, then look again and again; all in vain. The treasure isn't to be seen . . . they've hidden it . . . ! A flock of vultures, black as ebony, circles over their heads, and this apparition obliges men, dogs, and donkeys to abandon that spot. Is there anyone living who hasn't seen some time later the stones marking Fox Outcropping? Is there a wood-gatherer anywhere who doesn't know about Vulture Ravine?

A hundred stories like this are told on winter nights around the fire. There's hardly a mineralogical collection that doesn't contain a nugget or a rich stone whose original mine has never been found, or has disappeared after having been found, due to the influence of confusing causes, anytime reason sets out to investigate them. How to respond to so many facts, how to refute so many and such respectable witnesses with nothing more than the word "concerns"!

Happy romanticism! For the imagination that you have created, that word isn't worth a fig. For the imagination anything that astonishes and amazes is true, without the insipid need to understand it. Your children have spread out the world and existence to infinity, and do not feel confined by any limits other than those of the marvelous and immense concepts of the spirit. To them I dedicate the following story that has the further advantage of not being very long.

In the middle of the last century, in a village situated two miles southeast of Copiapó, called Village of the Indians, because in fact those who live there are Indians, there was a family of Indians that was quite poor; suddenly, though, it began to prosper, without anyone knowing how, it being a mystery to everyone. Good clothing, good horses, rich harnesses, constant drunken sprees and feasts, attended by the whole neighborhood, had replaced the plain cotton cloth that formerly covered them and the barley flour that had been their normal fare and pleasure. There were four men in the family, and the name of one of them was Campillai. This man, finding himself one night visiting Copiapó, in the house of a friend of his, after sharing with him countless glasses of liquor and inspired by the generosity and openness strong liquor produces, told him he was going to make him rich by telling him a secret.

Pushing his confidence a bit further he told him that he and his three brothers were secretly working a mine a league and a half from Copiapó, from which they were taking ore so rich that in the Huasco,[1] where they sold it, they were paid little less than they would get for smelted silver.

But he said that the four Indians, to keep from arousing the greed of the rich men from Copiapó, had taken an oath to keep the secret of such good fortune, and that anyone who revealed the secret would lose his life, so he should be very careful to keep it. He also told him that they owed this discovery to an old woman who had died a long time ago in the Village of the Indians with a reputation as a sorceress, and that they had sworn to her they would never share that immense wealth with any white person. Immediately he invited him to climb on the back of his horse and ride with him to see it, and to take all the ore he could carry in two saddlebags they took with them for that purpose.

They left in the cover of darkness and after a long gallop they came to the foot of a hill that is today called De Los Candeleros. Leaving the horse tied there, Campillai and his friend climbed up a narrow path to the summit. Campillai told his friend they were there and that since his brothers were in the Huasco there was no danger of their being caught, and that he shouldn't be frightened by what he would see. Then he took him by the hand and led him into an excavation, but the friend almost fell dead when he saw that that hole was the cave in which an enormous bird was sleeping and which, its sleep interrupted, unfolded its wings and flew out making horrible screeches. Campillai, not at all intimidated, put two large rich stones in the saddlebags and, encouraging his friend, they climbed out of the cave and went down until they found the horse, which took them back to the place from where they had started.

Tradition is not very clear about the circumstances and events that followed this, but from what I've been able to gather, after much investigation, the generous Campillai was shortly thereafter murdered by his brothers and the law got after them and they were never seen again; also the mine was undoubtedly transported to another place by the bird that was guarding it, since neither the friend of the Indian nor any of the infinite persons who looked for it during that period were able to find it, and this is the origin of the name "Mina de los Candeleros." About a year after the murder of the Indian, another Indian unknown to the parish priest of Copiapó showed up, telling him that in the church he would find a basket of silver nuggets that were being given to pay for a mass for the soul of the deceased Campillai, after saying which, he disappeared. On that same night they found the nuggets, and the pious priest sent the silver to Lima to pay for making a pair of enormous candlesticks, which still exist on the main altar of the parish church, where they daily illuminate the celebration of the Divine Mysteries.

(*El Mercurio*, February 5, 1842)

The Map to the Lode of the Three Mountain Passes

Man, before heading anywhere, by some accursed rule of prudence, marks out his path so as to give himself the illusion he's not heading for uncharted territory. He traces his road, calculates anything that might befall him on it, his plucky and foresighted imagination smooths it out and negotiates all obstacles, then he takes his first step, then the second . . . and smash! . . . he's rolling down some steep ravine or sunk up to his eyes in a quagmire. Bitter inconvenience for our faculty of reason! A condition that, regarded philosophically by some, has caused them to live totally without plan, without forming or following any path other than heaven, the only infallible way, the only path, as we see it, on which there's no danger of getting stuck in a bed of eggplants, and which, if we stray from it, as happens at every step so as to allay the monotony of the journey, it's no great matter getting back on it and continuing on our way. Solitary places of refuge, venerable asylums of innocence, and for me, deep fonts of the only science we need to learn in this world; only the many caravans you hold enclosed in your sacred walls lead us down the true path for crossing life's deserts!

I have seen, and unfortunately experienced as well, so many false paths, that I'm utterly resolved in advance never to follow any of them, and to live without plan and without anything resembling a plan. The social world, the world man thinks he created, is not the work of man, but of the pure whims of chance, of that divinity, spirit, or demon, whose permanent amusement is to keep the puppets of the proud human species dancing. I intend to develop this doctrine later on, and to do that I'm just waiting for the arrival of those hours I usually dedicate to boredom, during which I generally bore myself until I grow weary. In such moments I write love letters, seek out people to talk politics or lawsuits with, make some Argentine tell me the story of Rosas[1] or Aldao,[2] and in short I find a way to let my ennui reach its climax, which for me is usually in sleep, while for others it might be the very sane determination to commit suicide. For now, I'm going to find a way to try the path announced above; and I say *I'm going to find a way* because it's likely that I'll do so before many digressions. I've already arranged it. My only plan is not to follow any.

Anyone who doesn't understand about mines and comes to Copiapó, is coming to not understand himself or anyone else. He'll walk up and down the streets, go into a smelter or a foundry, visit the gardens of

Chimba, but after all that he won't know what to say about any of it. Old men like to talk about everything, about such and such a lode of silver that is virgin, another of dubious quality, about the wooden rakes for washing silver ore, about those scoundrels who steal ore, and the work foremen who steal more than anyone. Young men, even when they're talking about love, say rather, "I pulled a good one," or "This thing happened"; they call an old nag "arsenic," a pretty girl "ruby silver"; about a girl who's stuck up they claim she's "cold metal" and is low in calcium, or needs someone to teach her what's what. If she isn't snooty, then she's a silver ingot, an outcropping of pure silver, worth a fortune, solid metal, richest silver dust. And even the young women themselves enjoy describing the rare stones that make up their collection, which is the dossier of girls from Copiapó. In each chunk of ore they have a souvenir of some boyfriend, and in all of them together, the bounty of the spirit or genie inspiring Chañarcillo, San Antonio, Bandurrias, Pampa-Larga, and the infinite poets whose verses are preferable to all the hymns, songs, and dirges of Mount Parnassus. How I love that literature of Copiapó!

Now maybe my story will begin. One night I was in a gathering with several good friends, having a cup of tea, which is fragrant and delicious, so pretty and ruby-red around a glowing table, alternating swallows with the bright, festive things that at times like that make your conversation shine. I don't have to tell you that we were talking about mines and not gossiping, which sometimes spices up the delicious infusion of tiny leaves from China. The owner of the house told us that he had a bona fide map to a really rich vein, but that he hadn't gotten around to following it yet because he was so busy. He didn't wait for us to beg him to show us that precious jewel, which was a piece of paper torn at every fold, and as dirty and worn as hands of the miner who generally doesn't wash them except when he goes in to town for Carnival.

In case you'd like to take advantage of the indications it contains to make your fortune as quick as you can say Jesus, I'm going to reproduce this document, the writing down of which was done by the same priest mentioned in it.

Map that on the occasion of his last rites the ass-keeper Fermín Guerra revealed to his confessor don Nicolás Prieto, unworthy priest of this Parish. You'll walk about two leagues along Paipote ravine and turning off at a canyon that has two very thick carob trees at its entrance, you'll walk as far as a pass that has lots of thistles and then you'll climb up that pass and on the other side after a few ravines you'll find an arroyo that has a lot of gramma grass, and then you'll turn left along a plain that has lots of thorn bushes, and after walking as far as some very large rocks in the middle of that plain, you'll walk to the right following a steep cliff until you get to some sand hills. From these hills you'll discover, by looking toward the sea, a string of hills, and you'll walk until you get to them, walking straight toward three mountain passes you can see from far away. In the one on your left, which you'll climb up, you'll find a vein that you'll follow to the right until you come upon a hole dug with a pick about a yard deep, and a little beyond this there's an outcropping of lead on which there's a cross carved with a knife. When you find this treasure you should have a special mass sung every Friday of the year for the soul of Fermín Guerra, the one who discovered it, paying the priest Prieto twenty pesos for each mass, and he'll provide the alms to pay for a final response. And I warn you that if you fail to do this things will go bad for you. It should be noted that Guerra discovered the vein because he got lost coming back from the Chañaral and Pueblo Hundido mines, but later he went back there and brought back some stones that in his last rites he showed to said priest, and they will pay for his burial. At the foot of the pass in the middle there's a good stream, an easy place to hunt huanacos and wild asses. Copiapó, July 4, 1792.

Written for Fermín Guerra, who doesn't know how to write.

— Nicolás Prieto.

From reading this document, and from various other circumstances referred to in it, it turned out that three of us who were present determined to follow the map just to see, we said, how it turned out; although for my part I set out with hopes the size of a tower. We agreed on our departure time, and when the time came we headed out. We took pack-mules, two bags of food and water, and two servants who were somewhat familiar with the wasteland we'd be traveling through. We thought that a compass would be very useful, so we took one along. All that day we trotted along Paipote ravine, and almost at nightfall we discovered the canyon of the carob trees. It's impossible to say how happy we were to find this first indication of the fidelity of the map. "We're on the right track!" we exclaimed in our excitement.

We slept under one of those solitary trees that perhaps over many centuries have dropped their few leaves onto the desert floor, and at dawn we started walking again up the canyon described in the map. At midday it seemed to us that we'd gone about far enough, and sure enough, at two in the afternoon we started up the Mountain Pass of the string of hills. At five we arrived, almost dead with hunger and thirst, at the arroyo of the gramma grass, where our mules came back to life, since they were dying of hunger and thirst.

On the third day we decided to continue on our way with just one servant and a light load, mostly water, leaving the rest at that spot with the other mules. Shortly after sunup we entered the plain on the left, where we noted with pleasure the thorn bushes indicated on the paper; and after walking along it in the same direction until two in the afternoon, we saw the large rocks and dismounted at the foot of them. Very close by we saw the steep cliff we were to follow to the right; we rested until four; the animals drank a few swallows of water, and we continued our journey. Night fell without our having even glimpsed the shadow of the sand hills; it was very easy to get lost; a terrible fatigue hit us, the animals could scarcely stand up, and it was necessary, finally, to suspend our trek, although the moon provided plenty of light. That was a very sad night. In fact, the map, up to that point, had not misled us; but it's not possible to stay calm in the middle of a frightening wasteland, without shelter, without refuge, and without hope of returning to the company of human beings, lacking the fragile support one sees disappearing without cease on all sides. A thousand times I cursed the map and my madness. I imagined my companions were doing the same, because like me, they chewed in silence the poor dinner prepared by the servant. Before going to bed we agreed to keep moving ahead until noon the next day, at which time we would turn back if we didn't find the sand hills.

The fourth day dawned and we continued. At ten the cliff we were following had vanished, but very far ahead, we saw in profile some heights that could only be the sand hills we were looking for. How could we stop! Perhaps the string of hills would be nearby, and the mountain passes, the vein, and the water! In two hours we were sure to cover that distance; but five passed before we crossed it. On foot and with great difficulty we managed to climb those hills, because the shifting sand of which they were formed moved with us at every step. Holding hands we reached the top; immediately our eyes looked in the direction of the sea, and simultaneously also we heard each other cry out in frustration and despair. The only thing in sight was a sea of sand forming a horizon on every side! However, after standing there staring for a long time, we thought we could see, at an incalculable distance, a kind of shadow or discoloration on the earth that seemed darker than the sky, which, if it wasn't the string of hills of the three mountain passes, must be the one of the boundaries of hell. Because, what would be strange about discovering hell in these regions?

"Let's turn back. I'm not taking another step. That Guerra, the devil, and the priest Prieto created that damned paper to mock us."

"It's your fault."

"The hell you say."

"There's no reason to start quarreling yet. We're in grave danger, because neither the animals nor the water will last the two days we need to get back to the arroyo with the gramma grass where José stayed with the mules. From there to here we've followed an angle. I'm of the opinion that if we cut straight across here we can save distance. South is the way we should go."

We got down. Of the water that remained we made four small rations, and what was left over we split among the mules, who couldn't even wet the reins with their dry tongues. I led the way, no longer consulting the accursed paper that we would have liked to bury in the sand of the hills, but the compass like a sailor keeping watch at the helm.

At nine o'clock at night the servant's mule gave out, and he climbed on the one that had carried the food. Shortly after that we took a rest until dawn, which when it came magnified our discomfort. An immense sand plain surrounds us on all sides, and there's no hill in sight. At noon one of my companions was left on foot and he climbed on the back of my mule. The servant's mule lived until two in the afternoon; by nightfall, an hour when we had no reason to believe there was any likelihood of our being saved, the whole caravan was made up of infantrymen. We took shelter, and at midnight, by the light of the moon, we started walking. We exchanged not a word; any word that crossed our lips would have been a prayer to heaven or a curse. The descending mist that always comes at night to these wastelands came to refresh us, and the atmosphere and the desert were overcast until ten in the morning of the sixth day. Then we discovered very close by some hills that the mist had hid from us. The servant recognized in them the ones called the *ravine of the souls*, which comes down from Paipote ravine, which meant that we had escaped from Inferno and were now in Purgatory. Even so, we were very happy in spite of how little strength we had to make it over the craggy heights looming ahead of us, and in spite of not knowing when we would find water, which we badly needed then.

Finally, after unspeakable fatigue and anxiety, we climbed and descended the hill. At nightfall we found a waterhole that was salty and full of insects that seemed delicious to us. On the seventh day some wood-gatherers rented us their burros to get back to Copiapó, where we arrived afflicted by a thousand aches and gripped with fever on the morning of the eighth day. Happily this expedition had been a secret for everyone, except the owner of the map that he entrusted to us, after we had signed a document guaranteeing him a sixth of whatever we found;

had our friends known about it, the customary mockery would have embittered even more the cruel joke we suffered.

Six days behind us José arrived, who had left the gramma grass arroyo, believing us already dead in the desert.

(*El Mercurio*, February 22, 1842)

The Cangalleros

Speaking frankly, there aren't just *cangalleros* in the rich mines; the treasury has them too, and very talented ones: everyone takes pride in embezzling its funds, and the treasury itself takes pride in embezzling the income of every citizen. The biography of an ore smuggler will make you die laughing, and the only risk the smuggler runs, assuming he isn't caught, is the risk of being taken, for the rest of his life, for a clever, talented fellow, a quality that, it should be mentioned in passing, isn't always a recommendation in the considered opinion of many fools.

With regard, then, to *cangalla* and *cangalleros*,[1] I'm of the opinion that before we draw back in consternation and stare in horror at Chañarcillo, before we visit the silver smelters to witness this shocking phenomenon, we should first look for them in other places, which are sure to offer them up for our inspection.

Who doesn't celebrate the cleverness of the passenger who carries or transports a trunk full of correspondence without paying shippage to the gringos running the steamship? Are there any among us who haven't forced a friend to help us smuggle that pittance, with the honest excuse of preventing the letters from getting lost?

Proportionally speaking, how many *cangalleros* are there for each one of our merchants? In the first place, the rats on the ship transporting his merchandise eat his tastiest loaves of bread and his finest silk cloths; next in line, the rats in the shops of this port, these accursed animals devour whole packages of merchandise, including lumber and strongboxes; finally, the oxen pulling the carts and the pack-mules, what do they do?

They deliver to him here, on clean, dry sand, a shipment as heavy or heavier than what they were given in the port in wheat, flour, and beans. When you get right down to it, all this is *cangalla*.

And water—show me a dunce who doesn't divert some from his neighbor's field. In Copiapó, don't they play *your turn to irrigate* the way kids play *grab what's yours?* Don't I steal some from you because my neighbor above me steals it from me?

Let's go to a dance, a dance paid for communally by subscription, and not counting all the love-*cangalleros* swarming over the dance floor, how many do you suppose there are guzzling down all the wine and dancing nonstop without having contributed to the cost of the party, just like someone enjoying the benefits of a mine without contributing to the working of it? That's the way the world goes, each of us stealing as decently as possible whether it looks that way or not.

But the famous *cangalleros*, those currently parading by in open carriages, are the ore-smugglers. He's a pure Atacama specimen, a man whose industrial ingenuity, if today it's merely tolerated by the subdelegate of Chañarcillo, in ancient Sparta they would have raised statues to his prowess, and he would have won everyone's admiration if he had stepped forth, in those days, to exhibit his remarkable prestidigitation.

Considering that the world never was any better or worse than it is right now, it should be acknowledged that there were smugglers from the first moment mines popped up to the surface, and most likely, as long as God lets us have them, the devil will see to it that there's someone to rob from them: we'll be doing well if we can keep them from walking off with the whole thing.

The yield from a mine is marked, to some extent, by the happenstance of its discovery; the respect conferred by law and tradition on the notion of *mine* and *thine* is not applicable here: ordinary folk instinctively believe that because the man didn't have to sweat buckets to get it, because he won that fortune playing mines, which up to a point is the same as playing the shell game, it's fair to charge him and skim off some of the profit. This may be the origin of the lack of scruples and the audacity with which the miner is challenged over the exclusive right to his discovery. The most incorrigible *cangallero* may find the theft of a sack of coins repugnant, while he won't think he's committed even a venial sin when he carts off three times that amount in smuggled ore.

Several local circumstances, among them the fact that until a few years ago a number of respectable men encouraged this system of thievery and the fact that over a long period of time these rich stolen nuggets have been circulating in the market as just another negotiable currency, have caused the authorities and ordinary citizens to look upon this corrupt business with a certain indulgence. There are men who would consider two hundred lashes a fair punishment for stealing a horse, but would call any judge a hangman who brought even the leader of a gang of *cangalleros* to trial. This may be because, when a judge is unavoidably obliged to rule on a case of ore-smuggling, he looks on the case with even more levity than the thief, and postpones the trial. It would be barbarous to convict a man who stole nothing but ore.

The race of *cangalleros* is divided into three castes. The *ratero* or common-thief smuggler; the *marchante* or wholesale smuggler; and the *habilitador* or middleman smuggler.

The first type is numerous, and there reigns among its individuals the same spirit of family and fraternity you find among gypsies. They have, as gypsies do, a language all their own, a system of telegraphed signals by which they recognize each other, deal with each other, and inform each other, instantaneously, of any dangers confronting them, the negotiations to make, or what to do next. They wear long cotton smocks, a belt and wide cotton trousers, and a sash the size of the large skirt or swallowtail like those on our modern dress-jackets. They used to wear a cap in the shape of a half moon, with their hair drawn into a long tuft on top wrapped in large leaves, but these items, being no help to them in this line of work, have fallen into disuse. They still wear the other garments because they are the indispensable tools of their craft. Take away the belt and sash, the pockets of the trousers and smock, and they'll steal about as much ore as if their hands were tied. Anyone who, at this point in time, tried to introduce reforms in this uniform would be excommunicated from the guild as a reprobate; he'd be persecuted as a violator of the laws and guarantees of the community, and only by running away would he be able to shield his worthless person from the derision, provocations, and serious threats to which he'd be exposed daily.

The *ratero* smuggler makes no mystery of his trade, except when the law tries to prove something against him. Neither does he try to hide it from anyone: his boss or his foreman can subject him to the same insulting scrutiny as a warden in a prison, confident he won't be offended. The more obstacles set in place to stop his inevitable rapacity, the easier his conscience is when he prevails, because then the appropriation seems more legitimate to him. The foreman says, in his heart, to the *cangallero*: "I'll do whatever I have to to keep you from stealing from me," and the latter, observing the other's zeal, responds, smiling: "You long-legged bird, you'd better not blink!"

If by some coincidence rarer than a strike in an intersecting vein of ore, the *ratero* happens to be caught in the act of flipping a rich nugget into one of his bottomless pockets, then he lowers his head in shame and berates himself pitifully, but his anguish has nothing to do with being caught stealing; it's because he knows his clumsiness will bring down on him the derision of the whole guild. If as a consequence of his blunder he's beaten by the foreman, all his guild-brothers applaud the flogging, shouting "he's clumsy; that's what he deserves," just as others would say "he's a thief and a rogue; that's what he deserves."

Much time will have to pass, and the *cangallero* disgraced in this way will have to do some fancy stealing, if he's ever going to win back the respect of the others. A man who's incompetent is a disaster and compromises the progress of the industry in general, exposing one of the tricks and infallible maneuvers of his mysterious profession, and enabling the watchers to prevent the theft by countering the maneuver. The first dunce who let somebody see him wrap a nugget in his cotton sleeve as he pretended to roll it up has caused more harm to the interests of this guild than all the measures taken by the security forces of Chañarcillo against it.

They hold public meetings in the kitchens of the work crews, but these amount to little more than acquainting each other mutually with the maneuvers most recommended for their results and undetectability, informing each other which *marchantes* will be arriving, which mines have hidden reserves, and which others would be worth exploring as a group; all of this is discussed and talked about in slang and seasoned with jokes that tend to be crude and provoke boisterous laughter. These meetings are the schools where neophytes are initiated into the language and, shortly thereafter, into the total immorality of the ore-smuggler.

The entire caste is irrevocably dedicated to drunkenness and even more so to gambling: they'd give up smuggling before they'd stop practicing these vices, especially in Chañarcillo, where the police have provided the added incentive of making them gamble and drink clandestinely, which in itself adds to the charm and fun of it. First pleasure: get drunk; second pleasure: break a rule; third pleasure: laugh at the judge who's as stupid as the rule.

The *ratero* smuggler has his own moral principles. Only deception is acknowledged by him as the legitimate means of appropriating someone else's silver ore; any other recourse is degrading, and used only by the plebians of this caste.

He'd let them pull his teeth before he'd reveal the secret of his societies and accomplices: informing is an infamous crime, punishable by death.

If he goes to jail as a gambler or a drunk (nobody goes to jail as a smuggler, of course), and has no money to pay the fine, no problem: some brother will advance him the money until the next ore strike in the *Descubridora* or the *Valenciana*.

In another article we'll discuss the other two castes.[2]

(*El Copiapino*, June 7, 1845)

Vallenar and Copiapó

They are two neighboring towns, two sister towns, and this is more than enough to cause them to live in eternal discord.

There are times when I too start thinking about the origins of our civilizations, because I like to think that prior to *illo tempore* we were more animal-like than we are now. Did men get together, I ask myself, so they could love each other more easily? No. They got together because when one was wandering over here and another over there, it was harder to bite each other and tear each other to shreds. In this sense it's true that, when they gathered into tribes, they did so for the sake of convenience. The first time man felt the need to have a friend, was when he saw that he could not dismember another person all by himself. It probably didn't cost him much to get what he needed by promising to do the same for his ally; that must have been the occasion of the first reciprocal services our ancestors performed for each other, and of those their children far more commonly do for each other. Such too was the origin of the word Friendship, sign of a virtue poets think is the daughter of heaven, and with good reason, because it's quite true that there was a God-man; but a Friendship-man?, a Friendship-woman?, no way, not even those who believe in the communion of saints could conceive of such a mystery.

Back to the topic. To get from Copiapó to Vallenar[1] you have to cross fifty leagues[2] of sand plains, sand cliffs, and sand ravines; you have to ride, almost always, on trans-Andean mules, whose least bothersome habits are biting, kicking, and bucking; you have to drink water from the horns you have to carry it in and pretend to like it, and spend the hour of the midday sun, which is hotter than the fires of purgatory, beneath a sun-blasted carob tree whose shade is scarcely wide enough to cover the hundred snakes and lizards who live among its roots. Even the names of the places you pass by or get a glimpse of contribute to suffocate the soul. "There's Devil's Point." "That one's Devil's Hill." "The one behind it is Devil's Gap." "Tonight we'll sleep in Little Hell." "Before the sun gets too hot we'll reach Demon's Water-hole." To put it more succinctly, almost all those places are consecrated to the same gentleman, because it seems all too true that they were all territorial sections of his dominion. If while you're following this road you hear someone say good water, sweet water, willow grove, iron-wood grove, for God's sake, don't go thinking you're going to find any delightful shade trees or crystalline brooks, because all you'll find is fire, or at best, in place of water a frothy liquid that not even the most wicked apothecary could cook up. Names like those are a cruel irony, the bitterest jest anyone could play on the traveler.

Just a few days ago, I passed through those regions for the first time. (Anyone who thinks it's inaccurate to call them regions, please be so kind as to go have a look at them.) On the afternoon of the second day of my journey, at the time of day when the sun is still slamming you with its oblique rays though it's no longer managing to suck all the coolness from the breeze, one of my companions who was riding beside me asked:

"How long do you think it will be before we sight Vallenar?"

"Who knows! I wish it were right now, because this mule, with its trotting, hasn't left a single one of my bones in place."

"I think it's not too far. Do you see that road twisting along that hill in front of us?"

"Yes."

"Well, we'll be going up that hill, and from the top we'll be able to see the town."

"I tell you, it doesn't look all that short to me . . . ! Damn you, mule, and damn the guy from Cuyo who tamed you!"

"You'll be free of him in less than four hours."

"Four hours! . . . four hours of torture . . . ! But what's that? Hey, the river, those trees!"

And my companion broke out laughing at my surprise. We were on the brow of a steep, almost perpendicular cliff . . . . Vallenar was right below us, at the bottom of a narrow ravine, deep, which was why it can't be seen except all of a sudden, and not gradually the way most towns reveal themselves to travelers. What a pleasant surprise! It's like suddenly coming face-to-face with a tender gaze our eyes hadn't dared hope to see!

We made a stop right there to contemplate the most beautiful view nature could offer us, even without having spent two whole days moving through nothing but inhospitable expanses of sand. A narrow valley, but stretching out toward the setting sun until it was lost in the shadows of the distance; small, pretty pastures separated by groves of willows that looked as though the wind had combed them; a town symmetrically laid out among infinite green stands of trees and wooded areas, with a rushing stream passing through that scenery, marking its course with frothy white bubbles everywhere; all of this, beheld from the height we stood on, was like a precious miniature landscape.

I greet you, too, lovely Eden, planted among the arid expanses of the north, like a rose among thistles and brambles! You're the compatriot we embrace far from our beloved country where they rocked us in our cradle! You're nestled among the barren wastes around you, one of those bolts of joy shining through the storm clouds of existence!

In fact, Vallenar is a precious town. Of course it's true that after such a difficult crossing, one is disposed to wax enthusiastic over anything at all that might offer a more beguiling vista, but even without that circumstance you can rest assured that the Huasco valley is among the most picturesque and beautifully cultivated spots in our territory and that its main settlement is one of the prettiest cities in the Republic. I'll never forget the pleasant sensations intoxicating me as I strolled down its streets at sunset, breathed in the air perfumed by its gardens, roses, passionflowers, and other fragrant vines climbing up the walls between the houses; or when I was visiting a family and they took me out to see the orchard. A charming disorder reigns in orchards that are really gardens. At the foot of a cypress tree grow a small chirimoya tree and a jasmine, then there's an orange tree with a rosebush or carnation plant beneath it; next there's an arbor with golden clusters of grapes; then you come across a bed of cabbages, a lily, and a Brussels apricot tree, several rows of onions, a peach tree, a pomegranate and a myrtle; in short, a labyrinth where happily there are no pear or fig trees, nor any squares or triangles or circles or figures laid out in so-called good taste.

It's a pity that the buildings aren't designed in a similar relaxed confusion. Any swindler who wants to brag about his conscience, let him say he's straighter than a Vallenar street, and rest assured he'll never have to tell any lie bigger than that. What for me is a defect, I'm well aware that for many it's quite the contrary. Its public promenade, although it's quite new, can rival the best in Chile, as long as it maintains its gramma grass and its rosebushes. Neither would I want them to erect any temple other than the one now standing in the center, looking out over the whole town from its tower. I don't know why this seems so religious to me, so poetic. Countless houses around this house of God form an expressive scene full of simplicity, piety, and enlightenment.

The inhabitants live here in a state of peace that's utterly boring. Not a lawsuit or a rowdy marriage, no gatherings where men can argue politics, no dances, not even any malicious gossip. They get up early, skip lunch, eat in the old style, take their siestas, their *mate* tea, go out to the orchard, come back in to do their rosaries, give their kids a snack and put them to bed; the ladies play card games like Pandorga or Burro, the girls read or sew, eat supper and . . . good night. I like the trees a lot more than the men! When I say men I'm not talking about the women, about whom there's no need to talk. That's a seedbed that's bewitching everywhere!*

There's only one exception to this impassiveness on the part of the men, which I never failed to toss out in order to liven up a gathering that since time immemorial has met every day in the back room of one of the shops. The stimulant I'm referring to is the word Copiapó mentioned casually as if it had no special meaning. No one stays calm on hearing it; its sound produces a commotion in the nervous system; anyone dozing off comes full awake, and everyone is ready for a fight.

"What did you say about Copiapó?"

"I was telling the man how progressive that town is. . . . As you know, those Chañarcillo mines are an inexhaustible well of silver ingots . . . !"

"Chañarcillo . . .! That was nothing but a metallic glint in the sun. I've said that from the beginning, and Copiapó, when that hill plays out, will return to its former misery."

"Well, I think you could say the same about Vallenar, it too would lose a lot if the silver mines closed."

"Vallenar? No, sir! Its copper, its black bronze, and its agriculture would sustain it in the same flourishing condition it's in right now! We don't have mines in Chañarcillo, and we don't want any, because those men with their greed would kill us with lawsuits and intricate litigations, as sure as if they were cudgels. No, sir, let them keep their treasure, and we'll see what happens in due time. . . ."

* Anyone who has visited Vallenar for any length of time will know that in these few lines I've judged them most frivolously. Its inhabitants aren't the way I've described them. I've had a thousand opportunities to convince myself that I was wrong to write about them in this way. *Jotabeche* (May 1847).

"And do you really think Vallenar wouldn't lose anything if those mines played out through some misfortune?"

"No, sir, not a dime."

"Come on, man, admit it. I know that many products that are sold in Chañarcillo for their weight in gold and at exorbitant profits, they'd rather buy them from you or from someone else in this valley, at a very good price . . . ."

"And what's that got to do with us? You'll discover that even to buy a good piece of fruit, the Copiapinos need us. They're lazy, and then, there's no water on that damned hill . . . ! Let them be, eventually they'll go back to stealing and eating dry eels."

"My dear sir, if the principal mine in Copiapó plays out, you won't get even three thousand marks here in the Huasco tax office. Those monies come from Chañarcillo, through the back door . . . ."

"What are you trying to say? That we're stealing those three thousand marks? That we're buying ore smuggled out of the mines by the *cangalleros?* Is that the kind of crap those fools are saying about us? If they're too stupid to keep their miners from stealing ore from them, does that mean we're supposed to be too stupid to buy the nuggets they come to sell us? Aren't the merchants from Copiapó engaged in the same business, haven't they always been? Hey, for God's sake, this burns me up . . . !"

"Look, you all know that this stealing of ore is almost inevitable; not even the Copiapinos care if there are merchants who buy it, because ultimately it's necessary for someone to buy it, but the real reason they complain about you is that here you engage in the immoral practice of letting them profit out in the open in the smelters, which they think encourages robbery, hides it, and up to a certain point, even offers it protection."

"What protection, sir, and what pumpkins! You go tell them to watch over their mines personally, and not to laze around town; tell them to pay their foremen better so they'll serve them like honorable men; tell them to set up a security system in the mines, that this will be more rational than all the measures the authorities take against the *cangalleros* and against us. Tell them nothing would please me more than to see them. . . ."

"But sir, I'm not going to tell them anything. Calm down."

"Friend, I can't. I've never wanted to see us involved in a war, but if that misfortune comes about, I can assure you Copiapinos that with just twenty of our citizens we'll demand satisfaction for a million insults we've received . . . ."

"Christ, man, how can that be! I've never heard any Copiapino speak about you with disrespect."

"Let's cut this short! My whole being is in a turmoil."

He squeezed my hand and left to my regret. When I returned to Copiapó it was quite a different matter.

"How were things in Vallenar?"

"Fine, just fine."

"And what are those poor folks up to?"

"They're just living there . . . working their mines . . . ."

"What mines? Why, their mines produce about as much as the pilferings from Chañarcillo. They've got no shame at all!"

"Hey, slow down. Look, they're fine people, and after all they're our close neighbors."

"I wish they weren't so close! We can't even live here with that plague of devils who live in that miserable settlement just so they can come here . . . ."

"In the city of Vallenar, you mean, because it's legally a city."

"A city! Because of some law! There's another law that says anyone who knowingly buys stolen property should go to prison, and, if that law were enforced, where do you suppose all those so-called citizens would end up?"

"What do you mean?"

"What I mean is we shouldn't allow anyone from the Huasco valley in Chañarcillo."

"That's impossible. Not everyone who comes into the mines has to be a thief."

"Every single one; yes, sir, they're all *cangalleros*. I wish that city were so far away we didn't even have to hear its name!"

With anyone else standing in his place the dialogue would be the same. Hatred plays the same role in the moral life of man as certain poisonous effluents from the operation of his machines; without them, their functioning is suspended and finally, the whole thing dissolves. A person who doesn't love anybody, who abhors everything he looks at, we baptize with the respectful titles of lunatic or misanthrope; but start acting humanely and compassionately, love your neighbors, and right away they'll suspect you're an imbecile, they'll swear you've lost your mind and appoint an executor to watch over you, or lock you up forever in some house of charity.

(*El Mercurio*, April 5, 1842)

The Port of Copiapó

"What are you doing, good man? Always pen in hand . . . !"

"I'm going to write a letter."

"For don *Mercurio*, eh?"

"No. Everyone knows who that guy's correspondent is."

"You're probably right, but the only reason I'm here is to give you an invitation. The steamship is scheduled to arrive at the port day after tomorrow, if they aren't playing games with us as usual. Shall we go down there this afternoon? They've got fast horses, games of chance, a bottle of port for everyone . . . ."

"Did you say port wine? Enough said. All our problems are solved. We'll leave at four."

"Agreed. See you at four."

It was four o'clock in the barracks, in the jail, in the municipal building, in the criminal and civil courts, in the office of the notary public, and even in San Andrés when we left. I don't need to tell you that the dust in the narrow streets of La Bodega blinded us, or that dust kept blinding us over and over again at several points along the way . . . I still rub my eyes every time I think of it. The most interesting thing I saw on the way was one of those horrible trophies that don't so much conjure up feelings of justice served as they denounce in our societies clear tendencies toward cannibalism: I'm talking about two human arms nailed to a gibbet, and arranged so that if you just stuck a nightcap up on top, you'd have the living image of the coat of arms of the Argentine Republic.

At ten o'clock at night we arrived at the port. How pleasant it is to check into a room after a long gallop! We checked in at an inn whose owner is an old Italian of such good will that he makes his guests feel welcome and cheerful with it alone when he has nothing else to offer them, which is frequently the case. This time he served us fried fish, and the promise of a good lunch for the following morning; with this, and a bottle of red wine that was as sour and insipid as the face of a tax collector, we went to sleep happy as hens.

When one arrives by night at an unfamiliar place, he wants the light of day to discover what's all around him, and it was this more than the pesky fleas that caused me to get up early and go down to the port. At dawn I was already walking along the cliffs overlooking the bay and the town. Standing on a cliff into which the ocean waves were crashing one after another, I caught myself gazing into the immensity of the water without a thought or idea of any kind in my mind. I must be really dumb, I told myself, to be standing in this place without thousands of brilliant poetic or philosophical reflections occurring to me. It occurred to me that the posture I had adopted was preventing me from being inspired, so I immediately sat down with my legs crossed, resting my cheek on my right hand, of course, and pulling my cap tight down on my head; and because I was lacking the book that I should have had unfailingly closed in my left hand resting casually on my thigh, I took out my notebook and sat waiting in that enticing position for my muse to come calling. But despite all this, it didn't show up, so after a bit, feeling that I might well fall asleep, I abandoned that spot, for fear a bad dream might cause me to fall body and soul into the abyss yawning at my feet.

At ten that morning the announcement *Ship in sight!* went out, and at three in the afternoon the Chilean ship *Esperanza* docked. The deck was crowded with people, who by the varied colors of their garments left no question about their gender. The port captain is back for a visit.

"Captain, I see lots of ladies on board. Are they families coming from Valparaíso?"

"No, sir. The *Esperanza* always brings in young girls. This time there are twenty-four."

"What do you mean, young girls?"

"Well, young girls, sir, young girls . . . from Valparaíso. Eh? Don't you get it? Young girls of certain consequences . . . ."

"Ah, now I understand. And don't they put the boat, the cargo, the crew, and the young girls in quarantine? May God protect the recipients of such merchandise! One of these days the *Esperanza* is going to bring us cholera."

The ship's launch is beginning to unload the cargo, and the first are the young girls. Each one is carrying, in addition to the hat with feathers or the flowered coif, an elegant parasol. (Virginal Saint Barbara, it's not parasols we need, please send us lightning rods against this storm!) Now they're ashore. Now we can see those faces whose freshly applied makeup gives them the fleeting sheen of recently scoured earthenware; those elegant dresses that not long ago perhaps were worn by some honest but now defunct beauty; those lace drawers; those outfits, in short, which if the graces themselves were wearing them would only elicit from the curious bystander observing them a forlorn *How sad!* It wasn't long before the beach was covered with dressing tables, carpets, lavatories, cushions, chairs, trunks, disassembled cots, and all the other ad hoc possessions of these girls who, some of them petting their parrots, others calling to their seamstresses, went off in groups to look for lodging. The coast of the port of Copiapó is very odd because of the capricious forms and dimensions of its rocks and cliffs and because of its grottos and the variety of shells and little stones scattered all over the beach. Because of this, a morning or afternoon stroll is entertaining and pleasant. There aren't, it's true, trees with copious boughs for the wind to sigh through, no winding little streams, no birds chirping, items that are sine qua non for a romantic; but on the other hand the geologist can find there motives for study and for sublime meditations. How many years does this vast quantity of shells and petrified marine plants represent? How long did nature take to work this phenomenon? Those caves, those holes in those large rocks, are they the result of the constant pressure of the waves over centuries and centuries, or was it the finger of the Creator that poked and polished them like that? Those hills turning yellow out there in the sea, are they made of bird shit or not? And, if they are, how many birds and how many centuries did it take to form them? These are questions that, if they forced me to resolve them, I'd feel like they'd condemned me to life in prison. Happily, my school dismissed them as being unpleasant, beneath contempt, and, if that hadn't been the case, thousands, I among them, would have said to hell with it, preferring to learn from the cultists of the prophet than from educators like Dumas and Victor Hugo.

At six in the morning of the second day that I saw dawn in the port, I awakened to cries of *steamship, the steamship is coming, the steamship's in sight*. Half-dressed, I left my room and began to run behind several persons who were heading toward the cliffs mentioned earlier. In fact, the steamship was approaching, vomiting a whirlwind of black smoke, its hull surrounded by crests of foam on all sides. The town was in a state of total confusion. People are climbing up, going back down, running, stopping to look, shouting, asking questions, and explaining what's happening. The empty mercury casques that serve as bells alert the unloading crew and the guards; the sailors are inflating the launches and small boats; our innkeeper sends up a whole array of banners and flags; the passengers arrange their baggage, and their friends get ready to bid them farewell on the same ship. The ladies adjust their hats, scold their boys, call out to their husbands, fix their daughters' hair, give instructions to their servants, and sneak a look in the mirror. Everything is movement, no one stays in one place; it's as if each one had a steamship inside. Meanwhile the steamship *Chile*[1] approaches, its mast sporting no other colors than the British flag, as black and smoke-colored now as one of those hemp cargo nets, which might lead you to think some pirate ship had hoisted it. Five minutes later it slows down, its bright paddle wheels stilled; they start up again for a moment, then stop, then start again, like a man walking with the sounding-lead hanging down from his hand until the floating guest is persuaded this isn't Quintero with its treacherous rocks,[2] then finally letting the anchor drop down from the prow.

The beach is crowded with spectators waiting for the return of the coastguard boat. It's coming now, and so is the launch, two longboats, and a variety of other crafts bringing ashore taciturn Englishmen, haughty Frenchmen, stiff Germans, happy Italians, pale Peruvians, Argentines straight as ramrods, phlegmatic Spaniards, and Chileans dressed up like *huasos*. The first ashore is the amiable Captain Peacock.[3] What a lot of hugs and smiles and furious handshakes!

"How was the voyage?"

"How are you?"

"Everything O.K.?"

"Anything to tell us?"

"Why so late?"

"Couldn't be helped."

"Lots of passengers on board?"

"Quite a few."

"Anything new in Peru?"

"Plenty of new guano!"

"How many new generals?"

"Seven tons heading for England."

"You didn't understand my question. I asked if the Peruvians have taken up arms against General Ballivián[4] yet, or are they still stuck in the swamp."

"Yes, sir. They'll never run out of guano."

"Screw the guano!"

While this is going on here, over there two friends who hadn't expected to see one another recognize each other, congratulating themselves that they'll get to travel together; there, some people are reading letters and newspapers delivered on the steamship; some launches loaded with baggage are heading for the ship, and now some men and women are getting onto longboats that will put them aboard. How happy those girls are, and how nervous they might get seasick on the ship.

"Sit down here, mama."

"Take my hand."

"Careful, child!"

"Don't all get on one side!"

"Oh, no, it's turning the wrong way."

"Don Ramón, don't make such a fuss!"

"Why do you think I came along?"

"Holy Virgin, help us!"

"Everything's O.K."

"Let's go, boys!"

The last to embark are the bars of silver, the sweet fruit of the Chañarcillo mines, and once they're aboard, the bell rings calling the passengers. "The steamship's leaving! The steamship's leaving!" In no time the bridge is covered with men, women, and children, some leaving, others staying behind. A little girl asks to be picked up, another isn't sure how she feels, the color is leaving her cheeks, drying her lips, and her head is leaning on the bosom of a girlfriend.

"Take her to her cabin."

"Man, don't forget my message."

"Take good care of my girls."

"Be sure they feed the parrots."

"Don't stay too long in Santiago."

"You'll have a great time."

"If you get seasick, this will help."

"Don't forget to send me a letter by the return voyage."

"How pretty that girl is!"

"She's a brand-new bride from Lima."

"Happy the man standing beside you sighing!" exclaims a poet, for there's always at least one wherever more than four men get together.[5]

The sailors are lifting anchor, and the bell rings again to say goodbye to the visitors.

"Goodbye!"

"One last hug!"

"Happiness."

"Bon voyage!"

"God be with you!"

"My regards to so-and-so."

"Goodbye, light of my life."

"Goodbye, baby girl!"

And amid jests, hugs, tears, sighs, and upset stomachs, the most affectionate farewell transpires.

Our boat has barely swung free from the ladder when the steamship's paddle wheels start pounding the water and the prow cuts through it as a vulture cuts through the air, unfolding her wings and seeming to plummet down from the cliff where her chicks are nesting. People are still saying their goodbyes, and when these can no longer be heard, they wave their handkerchiefs and hats in the air, as if to say: "I can still see you! Don't forget me!"

When we step ashore, what a sadness! What a silence everywhere! A small dog was howling on the beach, looking for its master who had sailed away. I felt an inexplicable emptiness in my heart. Will there ever be a time when the cup of pleasure leaves no bitter dregs at the bottom . . . !

(*El Mercurio*, April 8, 1842)

II

PICTURES
OF SOCIETY

Carnival

All farewells are sad. Tears, sobs, or a mute, despairing ache are the unfailing companions of goodbyes. And yet, the festival of goodbye we annually bid to the flesh is a rowdy one. With three days of dances, games, parades, madness, and extravagance we say farewell to exquisite roasts, tasty beefsteak, beef jerky in sauce, meatballs, and ordinary stew. It's quite true that nowadays things are set up so that this absence is brief, because of which we are little afflicted. Today's stomachs aren't like those of yesteryear; they're as ill-equipped to digest beans and dried fish as our consciences are for digesting and eliminating the sins of gluttony.

Long before February 6 the preparations for such furious goodbyes were begun, and they had to be drowned, not in tears, but in pastries, roast turkeys, water, husks of bran, wine from Oporto, cognac, waltzes, folk dances, masquerades, horse races, loud shouts, laughs, and all-night sprees. God help us! If our entire lives were spent in this kind of tumultuous confusion, would we call it heaven or hell?

The waterfight may well be an uncivil and detestable custom; let those who judge things with a circumspection I envy not say what they will, the fact is that Carnival games have for me and other lively souls a delightful appeal. I'm crazy about their evanescent intrigues, their pratfalls, their soakings, and all that nonsense. Let a pretty hand brush starch across my poor face everyday, as long as I get to feel it pause briefly on my lips! Pleasant barbarism, find a way to resist the attacks of civilization until I'm no longer capable of getting drunk on your caresses!

Finally Sunday came. A great masquerade ball, which we had prepared for that night, kept us busy all day sprucing up our costumes . . . . Nine o'clock at night! A multitude of Turks, Greeks, Romans, military officers, miners, sailors, harlequins, gauchos, old men, and fops, all imbued with the spirit of madness, arrive one after another to where the retinue was scheduled to meet. Only the leader recognizes each one, distributes among them numbered cards, orders the files, gives the signal, and the parade bursts forth to the sound of a rousing march presaging a thousand triumphs and delights. The street of the parade route is crowded with groups of curious spectators. The multitude accompanying us is huge, and everyone is shouting "Long live Chile!" as if they were rushing into battle. Sublime exclamation we never fail to hear when Chileans have happy hearts!

A beautiful patio with pretty decorations was the dance floor. The grotesque retinue poured into it amid the most charming hubbub.

"Look at the Turk!"

"What a pretty dress!"

"Who's that old guy?"

"Jesus, what an ugly man! Who's going to dance with him?"

"That guy with the long feathers is what's-his-name."

"No, he's the old man with the huge hat."

"What a belly!"

"Look at that queer, he's carrying my fan!"

"Hey, I loaned him that silk coif yesterday!"

"Bring my apron."

"Which one is my uncle so-and-so?"

"The one dressed as a playing card."

"That officer is Eugenio."

"Hey, Eugenio!"

"He turned to look, girl! We nailed him!"

"Look, pretty mask, tell me for God's sake, I'll keep your secret, which one is Captain Yungay?"

"What a drag not to know anyone!"

The masks begin to arouse everyone's curiosity more and more. Guys call the girls by name; they refer to events and circumstance only a friend of theirs would know about; they inquire how a certain matter is going that almost all of them fall for, and they laugh at the embarrassment they put them in with their questions.

The cry, *square dance!*, circulates once again around this immense well of activity and life. Precious moments those in which, hiding behind a mask, you can get doubly intoxicated with the pleasures of the dance without the disadvantage of anyone catching you looking! How pleasant it is to hear yourself addressed by all the titles and formulas of respect by the same girl we were chatting with on a familiar basis earlier, she pretending to know us at the dance by the few words we addressed to her; to ask permission to visit the girl who receives us in her living room every day; discovering the identity of another with a name we know she likes to be called, to confide a secret in her and then watch her happy anger when, through some sign or mysterious expression, she recognizes a few minutes later the same one whose name she had mistaken for the other sly masquer!

At one in the morning everyone knew who everyone was, despite the new combinations and transformations of costume. In vain did the Turk put on a diaper, the sailor breeches, the miner a turban, the Greek a headdress, and the gaucho a helmet or a suit of armor; before he could even step onto the dance floor his name was on every lip. The act of taking off the masks was the last stage and the sign that the dance was going to start up again. For the rest of the night, contredanses alternated with enchanting waltzes, whose swift turns so well imitated the ardor and violence with which the blood circulates in the gossamer bodies of those dancing them; with the *zambacueca*,[1] whose music must have been composed by some lover immersed in a state of voluptuous melancholy, and with all the other dances that grow more and more exciting the closer dawn, which will bring them to an end, approaches. At five in the morning, you could still hear music in the streets. Then they were singing the national anthem. Everyone paid homage to the beloved land where a man can freely give himself up to his vigorous labors and to the embellishment of his existence.

Other no less noisy amusements were available on Monday morning, after restoring your energy with a few hours of sleep. At noon a multitude of champions were already gathered to play water battles.

They're waiting for us at such and such a house. "Let's get over there!"

The attack plan is drawn up; the forces are deployed; in the vanguard go those using certain instruments capable of throwing streams of water over a long distance; these are the launchers, the water-rifles; behind these go other columns armed with bottles, containers filled with starch and packages of flour, and in the rear those who've volunteered to seize the jars, buckets, tubs, and other instruments from the smiling enemy. The latter, on sighting the approaching masculine army, greets them by waving their handkerchiefs in the air, assuring them that they're ready for war if they dare try to cross their entrenchments. The door to the street is wide open, but who will set foot on the patio first? Two double columns are ready to baptize the men right down to their fingernails with materials that, mixed together, make up the stickiest kind of paste.

"Charge, boys!" shout those in the rearguard, who start pushing those in the center and soon everyone is pushing those in front. The opposing army is in a similar state of disorder. The water, the flour, the starch, the bran husks, and other stuff rains down in torrents and cloudbursts; the sun grows dark; the battle is shrouded in darkness, and before a minute has passed it looks as if everyone were bathed in a river of mortar. The accursed amazons, knowing the terrain, after hitting the mark with their first shots, beat a retreat to their rooms, whose doors are locked with keys and deadbolts; robust and hefty servant women persist in this maneuver, so that after so many dangers, sliding falls, and valiant sallies and sacrifices the only captive women, the only prize for valor ends up being the cook, the laundress, and others hiding in the rat-holes of the house. The poor conquerors indulge their need for vengeance on these sad spoils of war, until one or more of them succeed in escaping; she runs to the garden and comes back with formidable reinforcements made up of dogs who, on announcing their arrival by barking, completely rout the men's army, whose soaked clothing won't even let them run as fast as they'd like to. The cries of victory then ring out from all the windows and dormers of the fortress.

However, shortly thereafter they congregate again in a suspension of hostilities stipulated by a thousand assurances of good faith, not always kept by the mischievous beauties who, even in their abuses, charm us. Cups of liquor or other refreshments are served . . . a foot-stomping *sajuriana* . . . a brief song . . . the inevitable national anthem or else the wild "Hear ye, mortals!"[2] . . . and so long. "See you tonight. I claim you as partner for the second contredanse." "Agreed. Now go get those wet clothes off." And the lovely ingrate accompanies this send-off with a sweet look that could all by itself cure the worst kind of cold.

The other social classes engage in amusements no less tumultuous. Great gangs of miners on foot, paired off with arms around each other's necks, a wild troop of horsemen armed with bladders filled with water, not always mixed with aromatic essences, go up and down the streets drenching people left and right; or they attend dances where couples in love hold hands to form a great circle to dance the Vidalai. This ancient native dance is performed to the sorrowful sound of a flute that, heard from afar, inspires a tender sadness rather than excitement. On hearing this music, the miners, who are so fond of quarreling, placate their anger, seek out their enemy, offering him a bouquet of sweet basil as an olive branch and inviting him to take a place in the dance circle.

That's how the second day went, and the second night also ended with dancing. On the third day there was a reenactment of the same attacks, the same defeats, the same truces with their respective infractions, and finally, the same dates for the second contredanse, which is inevitably consecrated to the sweetest of feelings.

"Today's the last day . . . !"

And before morning comes to awaken us to the sad memory of what we are, before that melancholy Wednesday dawns in which they'll tell us that the lovely eyes we adore are nothing more than a bit of crystallized earth, everybody wants to throw a final spree. The poorest insist on having a sumptuous feast in their humble huts. By noon you can already smell the fragrance of pastries cooking in the oven. An excellent hour to attack the fortresses of the water nymphs, because then the truces are signed under the gracious auspices of a golden fountain, replete with everything God created to arouse one's appetite.

The sun of ash[3] surprised many who were coming back from the dance, when others were already on their way to the sacred ceremony of the *memento homo*.

The festivities of Carnival had been paid for by subscription, and there's still some money left. It was necessary to use them up so that on the night from Wednesday to Thursday we could have as pleasant a time as on the three previous nights. Today, Friday, I see almost none of my friendly companions in Copiapó. They've all disappeared. The mines have swallowed them up . . . !

I hope I see them again after a discovery as rich as the one they've been waiting for for so long at any moment.

(*El Mercurio*, February 24, 1842)

Corpus Christi

"The French call this *the day of God*, and in fact the solemnity of its ceremonies make it more divine than any other festival celebrated by the Holy Mother Church. It is perhaps the only one in which Catholicism consecrates itself entirely to its God without mixing in any memory that is not celestial and divine. No saint, none of those heroes who seem to compete with the Creator for the adorations of humankind, has any role in this majestic commemoration. It celebrates, not the victories of a man over the enemies of the soul, nor the wonders that another man wrought amidst martyrs and butchers, but the alliance of the Lord of the Universe with the accursed sons of Adam and Eve, the reconciliation of God with man to restore to him the patrimony of glorious immortality that he had lost.

"This is the mystery of mysteries consecrated by the festival of Corpus Christi.

"But there is a fact bright like sunlight that illumines us, that immortalizes this memory. Today is the day of the man-god, founder of the Gospel, that heavenly republican who, nineteen centuries ago, preached on earth all the social principles that civilization, more triumphant now than ever before, marches forward to attain. In the Corpus Christi it is a precious thing to see the anniversary of the sermon, preached by God himself, on tolerance, liberty, equality, and all the rights of man. The more enlightened nations become, the brighter this solemnity and the less obscure and mysterious the great reasons urging us to celebrate it."

Such were the words spoken to me by a democrat in the plaza of this city on Thursday the eleventh day of this month, one hour before the procession of the Sacrament wended its way through it. And without a doubt his religious-profane enthusiasm was based on solid rational grounds. Because if indeed social progress has cast out countless mystical vulgarities, it has on the other hand added an imposing luster to the ceremonies in which the nation is called on to assume its proper role. Our religion and our civilization owe their existence to the same progenitors: God and Reason.

If a festival of Corpus were to be celebrated today with the morris dances and circus rigamarole of times past, we would judge its purposes entirely unworthy of our epoch. What was previously meant as a tribute, an act of homage presented to the divinity, today would be seen as a scandalous and sacrilegious mockery, or at the very least a frivolous supplement to what was intended to inspire only veneration and respect.

If we compare the Corpus of the eleventh day of this month to any of those we celebrated not that long ago, what convincing proof we'll have of the progress we've made!

To begin with, on the eve of the festival, we would see the governor and the priest come to an agreement concerning the levying and distribution of the public "contributions" needed to cover the costs.

Each muleteer was obliged to place along the route of the procession a wreath made of white-linen foliage decorated with ribbons, liturgical stoles, dolls, maniples, small mirrors, veils, and streamers, which the merchants and the sacristan rented to him for the price of one ounce of gold, his drove of mules or donkeys being held as security for damages, breakage, or loss.

Another contribution, for the construction of four altars, was levied from the merchants, though they were able to recover their costs from the muleteers and other paying customers who on the occasion of the festival came to them from all the mining centers of the district.

The decoration of the plaza was, in truth, something to see with all the trinkets everywhere.

As for the four altars, each one consisted of a skeleton made of limbs of untreated willow sheathed in an old rug and placed against the best-looking bedspread they could get from one of the wealthier couples. This screen served as background for the temporary altar inevitably formed by three or four tables stacked one on top of the other, largest on the bottom, smallest on top, on top of which stood the statue of a saint, a prodigy of miracles perhaps, though certainly not of sculptural refinement. Each of the stacked tables was covered with a frontal and a tablecloth, the visible protrusions or "steps" of each with pots of flowers tied together and held in upright position as tightly as one of our military officers in parade uniform. The altar was topped off with an artificial crown in the shape of those enormous battle sombreros still used by the military in Copiapó, though they've gone out of fashion, the sombreros as well as the . . . altars.

The Corpus of those happy times also featured companies of clowns, Turks, and other turbaned figures, who to the rhythm of flutes, guitars, and tambourine performed their dances and pantomimes in honor of the sacrament, the priest, the governor, and anyone else who was providing or consuming drinks. These dances were the main event, the sacred procession merely an accessory to them.

We also had the whirling confusion of the papier-mâché bull and hobbyhorses and giants and the *tarasca* serpent and the cats and the cripples, who came there to perform a thousand clever mimes and an equal number of vile and obscene gestures. Many still long to see, in this festival, Uncle One-eye and Fat John riding on Uncle Juan Pinto's black burro, who, black burro as well as uncles and Johns, put on a show in the plaza as deliciously wicked and stupendous as anything tradition has handed down to future ages.

The procession would start out along its decorated route, a theater of the lame, a succession of games, and it would start out from the very same cave that still bears the name of parochial Church of our faith, the only grotesque still surviving of all the grotesques of the *Corpus* of those days. From time to time the priest would stop chanting the psalm of David he was addressing to the God he carried in his hands, to scold as beasts those who neglected to kneel because they were watching the cripples; the ecclesiastical prelates would come to blows over who got to carry the brass censer; the mayors and aldermen would also fight over the best seats and the privilege of holding the cross of the brotherhood, whose members would also fight over the poles holding up the pallium and the places closest to Our Lord; each of them won honors and privileges with his fists.

Such was, more or less, the festival of Corpus in times not very remote, in times that vanished only yesterday. Each year, enlightenment and good sense have gone about proscribing a few more of its blemishes and abuses, its silliness. Today, we consider this festivity free of rubbish of this sort and so solemn that it can well be pointed to as the noblest and most brilliant of our religious functions. It should be noted that whenever we've had in our parish a priest as enlightened as Taforó[1] or Father Barinaga, this reform has been maintained by them with such energy and success that they have filled with satisfaction all those capable of appreciating the dignity of the faith and the progress of the nation.

Once they abolished those contributions so unfairly levied on certain social classes to pay for the cost of the festival of Corpus, and once they banished all the decorations and accessories unrelated to the rite and considered exotic in our present age, the zeal of the priesthood has been channeled to move the entire town to act with solidarity in serving and collaborating in the exaltation of the day of their unique and only Lord, and to come together as a single family in endeavoring enthusiastically to make the festival of their father and their God shine with splendor. On the eve of this last Corpus, no one failed to do something, to contribute something, or to offer something in honor of this great mystery. In one way or another, God has been celebrated by all those in our town who worship him on this occasion, without making us look ridiculous to those who adore him in other ways or who bless and exalt him on different days and in other languages.

It would be difficult to describe the innumerable scenes and circumstances that embellished Thursday's festival. The military parades, the huge crowd, the religious hymns are, in truth, worthy of mentioning, but they were nothing new, to me or to anyone else.

The impressive march of the procession along the route formed by the ranks of the civil guard, the religious restraint of the accompaniment, the sound of cannons, bells, and the music, the voices of the commandants and coronets and drums; this whole conjunction of scenes and the confusion of honors that towns render only to the Majesty of Heaven, certainly make up a poetic and admirable portrait; but neither do they represent a new spectacle.

The brush, not the pen, might offer an idea of the surprising beauty, the lovely effect of the altars that the matrons and young ladies of Copiapó set up in the four corners of our grand plaza. No part of them failed to shine, or detracted from the total effect, or clashed with simplicity and good taste. Only to God can such exquisite luxury, such lavish works, such resplendent thrones be offered. The idea of forming a tabernacle, a canopy for the Supreme Dispenser of all virtues and graces, constructed of everything a woman appreciates, all the jewels and precious stones she so desperately needs to persuade herself that she's beautiful, is an idea full of religious poetry, is a high-minded sacrifice of the inoffensive vanity so indispensable to civilized woman.

That precious Jesus seated on an airy and vaporous cloud that crowned the altar furnished by the Argentine women, the palm branch and brilliant structure of the sacred host made in Chimba, the diaphanous brilliance of all the decorations on the third, and the clusters of grapes hung throughout the room, are works and objects that would have deserved the praise of the most intelligent spectators and the admiration of any public.

There's no way around it: it's necessary and convenient to civilization that women play a more active, less private role in society. Woman, with a heart more virtuous than man's, loves civilization more than man does, loves it instinctually and desires it anxiously, whereas man becomes civilized out of vanity, egotism. Misanthropy, which is merely a return to our savage state, hardly ever takes possession of women, but it seizes hundreds of men every day.

In the festival that inspired this article, two progressive features can be credited to the cooperation and participation women made to lend it dignity: first, the exhibition of four altars, models of delicacy and good taste, in place of all those indecent carryovers from the past that previously brought ridicule to our faith; and second, the abolition of a tax, which until this last year was collected unfairly and necessarily to pay for those monuments to backwardness, irreverence, and ignorance.

May the Divine Majesty heap blessings on our enlightened and religious matrons! May the angels shield the hearts of their daughters from seduction!

In the name of progress, I kiss the dust on their feet.

(*El Copiapino*, June 14, 1846)

Lent

A time of great delicacy and a subject that's also delicate, if you're interested in going beyond doctrinal chitchat and sermons in considering it. And it's a great pity, because Lenten customs would provide material for all sorts of articles if it were possible to publish them under the name of some free-thinker, some Lamennais[1] or some . . . how should I know what name to give these courageous progressives, my contemporaries?[2] Because I want you to know, dear readers, that I'd rather rot with the reactionaries to whose party I have the honor of belonging than work to correct doctrinal flaws at the risk of my own skin: if that's the only way to make progress, let everyone remain as God made him and let me proceed with my usual circumspection so as not to fall into temptation in the process of writing such a perilous article.

Moreover, just in passing, I have a way of thinking that's not at all common regarding improvements and social reforms. I believe that this race toward progress into which its ardent apostles want to hurl us at bayonet point is an endeavor that will eventually be realized, not by them with their appalling petulance, but by our cemeteries with the tranquility and steadiness of hand they display in instinctively swallowing every obstacle. Let them do their work on these establishments with the freedom of expansion or contraction given only to doctors, and from one day to the next the regeneration will be accomplished automatically, without spilling blood or coming to blows.

Don't fool yourselves, missionaries of progress: the cemeteries, not you, will work this miracle. Cemeteries give a more powerful push toward civilization in a single season of scarlet fever than all your dramas, diaries, poetry, pamphlets, orthographic reforms, and propensities do in a year. Cemeteries pull the triumphal chariot of the new era; you are but the multitudes singing the Hosannah and escorting it on its triumphal march.

What we call men's sepulcher
Because their ashes lie therein
Is the cradle where begin
New life, redemption, and rebirth.[3]

To return to my topic, Lent is the commemoration of an epoch in which humanity beheld the unfolding of an event as stupendous as creation itself: it is a memory of a time when God walked the earth, promising his blessing to men and women in return for heeding this simple precept: "Love each other, forgive each other." But I, Jotabeche, would not presume to try to offer counsel in a matter so serious, even if I were up to the task, which of course I'm not. I'm merely going to take a look at how they celebrate Lent in my town. I'm going to write down a few observations made during this period in which, in order to appear to be Christians, we declare a kind of war on our old friends the world, the flesh, and the devil, and engage in hostilities against them similar to those our government sustains against the government of the Argentine provinces, forbidding any transaction between the two countries other than contraband.

It's been said that the world is a stage: I quite agree. But this analogy is based not on the notion that the world is fun, but that, to one degree or another, we all pretend to be what we are not, or that we are what we pretend not to be. Moreover, I've fallen into the sin of believing that Lent as it is practiced in our time causes us to behave more like actors and pretenders than at any other time of the year. (I hereby declare, for whatever profit it may bring me, that in what I've said so far and what I'm about to say there are many honorable exceptions, among whom I include all my readers without regard to social class, age, or gender. My intention on this occasion is to march with depth-probe in hand to avoid any shoals.)

The last hour of the rowdy days of Carnival sounded. Concluded are those nights whose traditional craziness has constituted for centuries a revered custom, a family treasure conserved and passed on from generation to generation of Christianity. What comes after all this delightful confusion? A contrast as surprising as a sudden death. After the sweet-smelling dew that the lover sprinkles across the breast of his beloved come the ashes the priest scatters on bowed heads; the harmonies of the orchestras are followed by the tolling of bells; delicious idleness by homework; declarations of love by mumbled confessions; the brightness of the theaters by the mute opaqueness of the temples; sighs of tenderness by sobs of repentance; orgies of gluttony by spare and indigestible repasts; and finally, the path of false roses is replaced by another sown with real thorns. The proud attorney shows up as a penitent, the thief turns into an honest man, the aggressor atones for the harm he did, the most fashionable dress is now a scandal, the dance an abominable den of sin, a sermon whether it's good or bad the prettiest thing you ever heard, and even the lovely daughters of Eve stop being what they are and degenerate into dry shoots on the vine of Christ. The forte of modern theater is to offer a similar counterpoint from scene to scene.

It's true that *good taste, fine tone, the new school, progress, liberty,* and all the other Aryan and Satanic phalanxes of the nineteenth century have brought Lent to a miserable pass, along with all the customs and institutions that have survived to our times, after having received the homage of many centuries in succession; but this novelty isn't common currency, it's a secret we're all in on and that we talk about in whispers for fear the walls will hear us. Meanwhile, the war against the enemies of the soul continues, entrusted to public diplomacy; we wage this war against them in exchange for not having to wage it against ourselves, which would bring truly unpleasant consequences, besides which, all the gunpowder we expend against the world, the flesh, and the devil is little more than an obligation to the Church, and we all know how seriously we take our obligations.

It certainly isn't my intention to preach or harangue my readers to a more sincere observance of the fasting, flagellations, and penance practiced during the holy Lenten season, because I'm of the opinion (and many preachers and haranguers disagree with me on this point) that to do so I would first have to fast, flagellate myself, and do penance, and unfortunately, sinner that I am, I'm not in the mood to offer such a good example. I do recognize that the mortification of our irrepressible flesh is a work of some merit, just as don José Rivera recognizes that the killing of Rosas is a pious work,[4] but I'm no more inclined to let my belly stick to my spine to satisfy some persistent itch tingling through my body than don José Rivera Indarte is to work up the resolve to kill don Juan Manuel, thus earning indulgences and being canonized on the spot. Ah, the anomalies our moral weaknesses visit on us!

If some reader has stayed with me this far without incurring the tedium he'd experience reading an article on American orthography,[5] pick up your cross and follow me: I'm on the prowl for some of those Lenten types.

Look, there's that group of smug-looking young men, aspiring to the reputation of progressives. They walk out of the café, where they've eaten meat because the elders in their house observe Fridays. Now they're entering the church, still complaining about the custom of fasting. As they stroll unceremoniously through the naves of the sanctuary, they giggle and smirk, everything they see astonishes them as if it were all new to them; they cast leering eyes at all the females, exactly as if they were picking out a partner for a dance. They never miss a procession or matins, but only as spectators, leaning against the back of a pew, sneaking looks at the reformed Magdalenes, or following the rhythms of the ecclesiastical chants with feet, hands, and head as if they were complete amateurs. The only religious ceremony in which the novitiates of progress take part are the matins of holy week, solely for the pleasure of knocking over a missal-stand or a confessional onto some poor devout soul unobtrusively absorbed in profound meditation in a corner.

Look over there. Isn't that a preacher on the warpath? Go, and you'll be enlightened by the revelation that *the world*, first among our souls' enemies, is the corset, the latest popular dance, the short sleeve, the long sleeve, this hairdo, or that decolletage. You'll learn that enemy number two, *the flesh*, is actually all the scandalous women on whom the orator vents his evangelical indignation, and that enemy number three isn't *the devil* but the fop—heretical, impious, atheistic, iconoclastic, and so on. The heavenly doctrine of the crucifixion, if you believe this holy warrior, is simply a matter of staying away from dances, the theater, the public promenade, the *tertulia*, all profane festivals, and any place else that isn't the church, its functions, or its auspices. All we derive from the sermon is the consoling news that, except for the sanctuary of the temples, there's nowhere to look, or stand, or sit without committing who knows how many mortal sins.

Isn't that another minister rising to explain the Ten Commandments to his flock? He does so under the entirely reasonable assumption that in the entire congregation there's not a single man or woman who doesn't, purely as a matter of course, violate every single one of them at every opportunity. And assuming that there can't be anyone in this wicked century whose innocence doesn't go up in smoke at the first spark of reason, he opens a public forum on the theory of sin that is bound to arouse the infantile curiosity of thousands and give rise to others far more serious. It's for this reason that on leaving one of these performances, you'll hear several young people saying: "What a fine preacher! Such clear explanations!" And he has indeed developed his topic as the most intelligent professor would, though to make sure ordinary people understand him, you'd have to admit that his language wasn't all that pure.

Just as there are men who are good all year long for the sake of God, there are others who tone down their wickedness just for Lent, because it's then more than ever that they fear the devil, whose existence they never question. And it should be acknowledged that this redounds to society's advantage, because they wouldn't care a whit about whether there were a God or a Heaven if it weren't for the possibility of an eternity in Hell with its fire ants, its white-hot pincers, and its molten lead. For them, confession is nothing but an inexpensive way to unburden their consciences, in the same way they use a wine cellar to load it back up again.

Here comes one of those good Christians leaving the church; it's what's-his-name or whatever you want to call him, who has just reconciled himself with God and is now readier than ever to fight with his neighbors. He's walking along sanctifying himself with holy water and sprinkling some all around him to scare away Satan, whose image he never stops carrying in his imagination. A beggar asks him for alms as he passes by: "Please, sir, for the love of God," and he keeps walking, muttering to himself: "Lazy good-for-nothing!" Further on he meets a friar, one of those ever out fishing for benefactors of the monastery: now his heart does indeed melt like butter; now there's no mention of good-for-nothings, as he falls all over himself to hand over the best coin he's got in his pocket and win thanks, kissing as much of the holy habit as he can get his hands on and stuff in his mouth. The hypocrite works hard to convince himself that by doing this he earns the remission of the sin he most regrets. He goes on his way. The postman who was looking for him hands him a letter; the good Christian takes it and pays the postage due with a counterfeit coin. He goes into his house; a servant asks for his pay, and he chases him away with kicks and blows with his cane. That's how his day goes. Is that the call to evening prayers? Back to church. It seems to him that his conscience is at peace, but why does he always see Satan at his side? Hell started early for this poor wretch!

Do I need to keep drawing sketches, imperfect ones of course, of the infinite Lenten types I've got in my inkwell, or shall I conclude my article right here? I opt for the second. Our catholic society is so *vulnerable* during those forty days, that even gossip, its most habitual activity, becomes an unforgivable sin. Things that all year long are regarded as innocent and delightful turn out to be grave sins during Lent. Damned if I can understand this; but then there are many things I don't understand and keep quiet about, and then they happen again and I keep quiet again.

(*El Mercurio*, April 6, 1844)

Copiapó: *Today's* Tertulias

This custom of people gathering to spend the evening must not be very ancient, since to tell the truth it's not all that bad; neither could it have been invented yesterday, because there are men so addicted to it that they're only alive when they're attending a *tertulia*, and when there isn't one, they sleep. It's also true that it's only over the last thirty years that there's been anything to talk about here, and some among us have so much to say that when they get the floor they seem to think it's their job to get the mail through come hell or high water, and pity the poor fool who gets in their way, because he and anything he tries to say will be swept along in the torrent of words. Until modern times, the nightly *tertulia* was regarded as a privilege of the elders, who would gather in the house of the neighbor with the most clout, or actually the one with the worst gout, to drink a glass of punch or to play rummy or pinochle. The teen-aged boys and girls would stay home with the door locked, the girls hearing from grandma the story of the children of Noah, who were Bran, Bren, Brin, Bron, and Brun, and the boys waiting until the old man came home for a late snack and then off to bed, then they'd slip out to leap over walls, run through vacant lots, maim dogs, and visit their sweethearts without provoking gossip—a far more moral, far more Christian practice than the one currently in vogue, where right in the middle of a crowded room and in full sight and indulgence of fathers and mothers a hulking adolescent boy sits down beside a child with milk still on her lips and starts prying her ears open. The elders of the church do very well to declaim against the corruption of the times.

This attendance at social gatherings, then, has become alarmingly widespread, and there isn't a town in the Republic, whatever its category, without two or more houses where people spend the entire evening in a semi-comatose state, which up to now is the best use we've learned to make of it.

But there are *tertulias* of all kinds.

Pernicious tertulias is what merchants have always called those who assemble in their own shops, much to their dismay considering that such a gathering must inevitably lead them into bankruptcy. Since in these gatherings the scissors are unsheathed and wielded primarily against the weaknesses of one's neighbor, the owners of the shop, as much to assuage their conscience as in a vain effort to nip the *tertulia* in the bud, are in the habit of posting alongside the license that allows them to practice their trade the following warning in large print: gentlemen, *tertulias* are harmful.

Courtship tertulias are those attended daily by as many men as there are daughters in the house where they're held. After a certain time dictated by public prudence, marriages ensue, and, even if they don't, they're regarded as done deals in the neighborhood.

"So-and-so's marrying what's-her-name."

"Excellent decision."

"They say she's decided against it."

"Smart girl."

"Her parents are against it."

"They should stay out of it."

"They got married in secret."

"Didn't I tell you?"

"They're making the wedding dress."

"He's out buying the ring."

"He's taken out a loan at interest."

And all of this ridiculous machinery of gossip is more likely to dissolve a planned engagement than to verify it. And that's when the suitors at the *tertulia* are bachelors, because when they're married men looking to incinerate their marriages . . . Lord help us! The wooed girls would be better off wooed by some priest or friar, whose vows of celibacy, insincere as they might be, have the virtue of stifling any slip of the tongue.

Terrible tertulia: this is where one of the regulars regularly regales us with a solo performance to keep us up to date on everything concerning his person and talent and on how sensitively and honorably he knows how to manage his affairs. A recently fired employee, a litigant who's just lost his lawsuit, a sick man who's been ordered to take *quimagogo*,[1] can turn the best *tertulia* into a terrible one, if the first two start revealing the barbarous injustice of which they are victim or if the latter starts pontificating to you about the prodigious benefits of the laxatives and rivers of emollients, stimulants, and chemical precipitants he pours into his body every day.

The *gambling tertulias* aren't really *tertulias*. They're a bullring, a cockfight pit. Here, men have turned back-stabbing and inflicting maximum injury on each other into a sport. Since they can't ambush each other on some dark highway without running the risk of ending up on the gallows or in prison, they agree to let chance dictate the business and decide which one loses his shirt and which one wins it, so that everyone goes away with his reputation intact.

The *friendly tertulia* is one attended every night by a certain number of men with no other object than to chat for two or three hours. If they're young, it rarely ends up being permanent or entirely benevolent; if they're old, its importance never goes beyond an archive of worn-out protocols; but if the gathering is made up of young men and men of experience, it's impossible for young or old to keep from learning something from it.

Party tertulias admit into their ranks individuals of both sexes and all ages and feature a great variety of entertainments. Men of a certain age can vent their spleen talking about politics, silver strikes, the old days, or their respective businesses. Respectable ladies will talk about anything, as long as it doesn't unearth some remote imprudence, because then they won't pick up the cards, they'll feign deafness, and if they whisper into someone's ear, it's to ask them to sing, dance, or do something else fun. For young people of either sex the possibilities are inexhaustible. Beyond the latest stories or jokes, or a tune on the piano or guitar, or memories of high school or of how certain marriages got started, there's always a story about someone who's been a member of the *tertulia* from the beginning, some sweet guy with a flat or maybe a long nose, or maybe a swaggering fop, or some dried-up old fellow or insipid sentimentalist, or some other poor guy to provide the fun for the evening. Naturally, after he leaves, the whole group exclaims in unison: "What a guy! Poor guy, he's O.K. He's got his heart in the right place."

Have I described the *tertulias* of Copiapó as they really are? Frankly, no. And why ask, or why answer such a question? Well, sir, it's to put to rest any suspicions my countrymen might have about whether that

Jotabeche has a malicious tongue, which, even if it were true, you shouldn't be all that surprised since it's no worse than anyone else's.

Now I am indeed heading out to visit this evening's *tertulias*. It's seven o'clock. Covered with the dust thrown up by every beast galloping down the streets (allow me to make a few honorable exceptions: donkeys never exceed a moderate rate of speed and are in fact the only beasts who obey the speed limit to the point of fanaticism)—covered, I say, with dust—I arrive at the house of a friend where several other friends are meeting. When I walk in a servant hands me a feather duster to dust myself off with, an excellent measure not only for the preservation of the carpet but also because now I won't have to resort to the custom of wiping my shoes with my handkerchief, which I'll have to use later to wipe my eyes, nose, and mouth. While we drink our tea, each person speaks to the person next to him or else he may decide to talk to the one he wants to talk to rather than the one most conveniently located; but whatever the case everyone ends up talking about the same thing— someone initiates the topic, others pick it up, they tell anecdotes, they laugh, they smoke, and it's all done without pretension. For me, this un-pretentiousness is what I like best about *tertulias*, just as I prefer to forgo formalities and flattery and to avoid eating garlic or any dish containing it. I've observed on numerous occasions that the preferred topics of discussion have to do with the needs of the town, the sicknesses of the social body that, as in almost all the social bodies of the Republic, are harder to cure than a liver condition or the chronic flatulence of the French. When they bring up problems they generally suggest remedies too; but they always run into a hundred or more inconveniences, of which the least is always that there's no money, because the municipal treasury is as clean as if it had been conceived without original sin. In matters such as these, hours go by until it's time to leave.

But since it's still not time to go to bed, I go from here to some other gathering, at the risk of falling into the water as I tightrope across a bridge or just a plank forming one of the crossovers, or turning a corner and running smack into a pack of dogs who, not having to avoid the lasso or the butcher's club at such an hour, are out on a *tertulia* of their own in the cover of darkness. I arrive, at last, at the house I intend to visit; from the patio I can preview the innocent entertainment going on inside.

"Number 41."

"Flat-nosed Alonzo."

"That Villalobos guy's selling whistles."

"Who'll pass me some beans?"

"On Independence day."

"Hit number 18, girl."

"How you doing, Jotabeche?"

"Watch it, don't sing so high."

"Now, there's a man's voice."

"If I don't get a ball!"

"Number 30."

"Have a seat; what breeze blew you in here?"

"I heard there were girls."

"We need a fourth."

"You want another card?"

"I'm O.K."

"Keep drawing."

"Well, sir . . . and he drew . . . a loser."

"Pontius Pilate's eyeglasses!"

"Number 84."

"He drew Carmen Pino."

"Silver! I drew the silver!"

"He got it, he got it!"

Before the game is over, I've taken cards for the next one, hoping for the pleasure of getting to be partners with one of the friendly girls attending the *tertulia*. Partnering up is the romantic part of the lottery. Besides, it's as classic as the Pythagorean table, and as insubstantial as the last page (forgive me, my dear editor) of the Valparaíso *Mercurio* ("Leaving for Liverpool." "Interesting Observation." "The High Fashion Prototype." "Advances in the Art of Dentistry." "Mr. and Mrs. Zapata's High School." "Bowling Pins from Armenia." "Soap from Mendoza.") and all that nonstop monotony that fortunately never arouses anyone's interest enough to read it.

When I don't feel like having any fun at all, I stop in at a *gambling tertulia* where the name of the game is *Malilla* and ill will is indeed the main event. When you're in a bad mood, sometimes the only remedy is a fight, and that's what gambling amounts to. You lay out the felt tablecloth, the cards are dealt, everyone passes, and more cards are dealt. The hand speaks for itself, the best hand wins, and you take your losses. Someone lays down a bird, saying *bola* so no one can trump it; but the horse is in its stall so they trump it anyway. And that's the way the game goes; the electric fluid builds up, and then the storm breaks out.

"What a game we lost! They stole that hand! And you, pal . . . !"

"You're the one who blew it. You had a run in clubs and didn't pass your joker to me! How stupid!"

"But I needed to get rid of the small trump . . . . If only you'd dumped your hearts, we'd have had a different game."

"You didn't even pass me your horse, and you had the jack along with it . . .! Why do you even bother to play?"

"I've met some stubborn men, but never any like you. You wouldn't admit you were wrong even if . . . !"

"You held on to your horse . . . ! We'd have scored thirty-seven points. Playing cards with you for a partner is like throwing money away. You've been playing *malilla* for years and you still don't know when to go down!"

Over anything at all, sir, you argue until you win; so the hostilities are suspended and then they break out anew whenever anyone feels like it, and no one has the right to interrupt, because if that was allowed the whole basis of this diversion (i.e., the well-known principle that grumbling is free) would crumble and fall like a house of cards. Frequently I quit while I'm ahead, sometimes when I'm behind, but always satisfied that I bickered to my heart's content; that way I keep the friends I started with.

Other times, for the sake of variety, an excellent reason when others are lacking, I go to the cafe, a place where the Argentine *tertulia* is forever in session. Rosas,[2] Oribe,[3] Benavides,[4] and Aldao,[5] these are the standard topics of conversation, with the usual sub-topics of beheadings, massacres, hangings, rapes, pillagings, public whippings, and banishments. Tired of listening to such horrors, I fly home, go to my room, climb into bed, and bless this humble nook where I can give myself over to sleep, the peaceful sleep the cannibals of the River Plate will never know, not even on the night of the day of one of their many victories.

(*El Mercurio*, June 4, 1842)

Afternoon Walks (First Article)

I've rarely felt sad while fasting. The table predisposes me to melancholy to such an extent that at times I think my soul is opposed to the liberal tendencies of my stomach. Of course, when it comes to pleasure, the poor thing has never gone in for a fancy table. In order to reestablish the good harmony between it and my body, I have to take them both out for a walk every afternoon, which happily produces a fusion that, though temporary, at least resembles the merger between two political parties that had previously sought only to devour each other.

Hence, after eating, there's nothing to keep me from leaving the house. I stealthily button my jacket, be-hat and be-cane myself, and plant myself in the street. (I was going to say be-curb myself, but the two previous verbs suffice to demonstrate that if I add my own efforts to the process of enriching the language, I'll end up becoming the most savage of all those who set out to assault the Royal Spanish Academy of the Language.) Humming a little waltz, I set out walking toward the outskirts of the town without paying much attention to the bit of spleen discomfiting me the way a slow toothache does, and confident I'll be able to ward it off with my singing if the mouthfuls of dust don't force me to close my mouth when I cross the streets.

Without meaning to, I come to a point from which the cemetery can be seen, a neighborhood that, in every town, I've always enjoyed visiting because of the pleasant sadness produced by their crosses, their sepulchers, their silence, and that mute eloquence with which religion promises paradise to us there, thus pointing out to us the irrefutable proof of our nothingness: incomprehensible contrast, consoling mystery, accepted without hesitation by this powerful instinct leading my soul to seek and pursue happiness, the very shadow or ghost of which intoxicates me with its illusions. Those were my thoughts as I directed my footsteps toward that solitary mansion of the dead, letting myself imagine, through a mild twinge of romanticism, that the friends resting there were happy to see me wandering in a state of tender empathy around the cradle of eternity. Perhaps from one day to the next, I said to myself, they'll open in that section a rectangular hole for Jotabeche, a hole where they can bury with me an entire assortment of hopes, memories of happy moments, the satisfaction of never having published my poems— because I've fallen, like so many others, into the temptation of writing them, but distinguishing myself in this from our neighbors to the east, who write so many so badly and publish them without remorse—and above all the deep-felt regret over the worst of my sins. . . . Shall I mention it? The fact that I was on the other side of the Maule River during the recent elections. (Dear Editor of *El Mercurio:* My dear sir and publisher. If it bothers your conscience to publish this confession, you can omit it by substituting a few hundred of your own, as long as it doesn't throw my own repentance off balance.) When that happens and they bury me, it's true, I won't be alive, I went on saying to myself, I'll have passed on to the other world. Think about it, sir. To pass from this world to the next, however unfortunate that may be, will be the same as emigrating to Chile from the United Provinces of the River Plate, about the same as becoming widowed and then marrying again, that is, shedding three or four tears bidding farewell to some snippy woman, promising her that in memory of her we plan to stick a piece of black crepe on our hat and console ourselves for our grievous loss by taking on some sweet thing. Could there be a more comforting resolution? For instance, if it's necessary to have friends there the same as here, that shouldn't bother me, because when the word gets out that I'm *in tempora nubila*, I'm sure that will be like opening Pandora's box, and just as there's still hope left in the bottom of it, there'll be two or three friends down below testing the water. If a pair of pretty eyes, the lying eyes of some beauty, for instance, should try to play one of their tricks on me, I'll just tell them "beat it, go play in the dirt," because thank God I've learned my lesson and am immune to temptation from this day forward. In the other life, they can't ask me to serve my country any more, and it's likely they won't do those other things to me . . . that's right, *other things,* and I know what I'm talking about . . . .

Such were my thoughts as I approached the cemetery, and just when I thought I was about to enjoy to my heart's content the sweet sense of abandonment that my sympathetic response to the idea of eternity would impart to my ideas, I felt all these illusions vanish when I suddenly found myself besieged, as it were, by filthy objects scattered all around me. Try to imagine a hospital sitting-room in which several hundred patients suddenly go out of their minds, which is a lot easier than imagining someone had finally managed to square the circle, and that teaming up together they organize a revel and start throwing anything they can lay their hands on, including doctors and pharmacists. Such a battlefield would be less vilely littered than the space around our cemetery, which is covered with mattresses, pillows, rinds, blankets, baskets, breeches, poultices, bandages, tumblers, and other such "instruments," clothes, and fragments of broken pots that, in our final moments, put the finishing touches on the end for which we were created, which, say what they may, I regard as a matter resolved, condemned, and sentence served, the end referred to being, surely, martyrdom.

My first impulse was to cover my mouth and nostrils to keep from inhaling that poisonous atmosphere, and as quickly as I could I stepped over the wall into the place where they have to take you when you're dead to keep from despairing. An enormous cross standing amid thousands of others that had fallen, or were about to fall, or that had been raised back up, are the only monuments adorning this place, unless we count a heap of earth covering grave after grave until finally the scene reminds you of the hills around Teno. The ground being covered with fragments of human bones, each step you take between those four walls can be nothing but a profanation, an impious affront to the ashes of those who no longer exist, ashes that, due to a custom contemporaneous with man, have been and still are venerated religiously.

The first thing I notice are several skulls placed in battle formation; I look to one side, and I see a pile of teeth; I try to take a step, and I step on a shin-bone; I try to retreat, and I make a piece of someone's cranium leap up. My God, is this what we call holy ground? Isn't it more like the area surrounding a fire where cannibals celebrate their horrible banquets? Is this the place where my friends allow the beloved remains of their parents and spouses to be buried? In a place like this, what value does an entire discourse on materialism have? Because if it has anything at all to say to the heart, it strips it of any consoling hope for a happy and eternal future. I wonder, do catholic priests, enlightened priests, come to such an obscene place to beg the Supreme judge for mercy for those who, with such indifference, they see suffering the impiety of the living? I don't know where these reflections would have ended up if it hadn't occurred to me that maybe all my countrymen were secret members of the cult of Diogenes, and that to prove themselves even more cynical than the philosopher of the drinking cup, they preferred that after their days were ended they be buried, exhumed, scrambled, and stepped on in that filthy burying place.

If a grave had no other object than to hide from the living the decay of our miserable humanity, and to prevent its exhalations from poisoning the breathable air, it's clear that you wouldn't have to wait for a lot of them to die before dumping earth over them; in that case, it would matter very little where you stuck them, since the operation would consist only in consigning them to the worms. But religion has consecrated tombs, philosophy respects and consults them as it would a book of truth and consolation, and civilized man embellishes them, likes to make them lively, surrounds them with objects in whose contemplation he feels his passions subsiding, and ends up persuading himself that death is another life consisting of blissful rest.

In our enlightened age, then, we don't keep faith with the dead by tossing them onto a dung-heap we're loathe to rest our eyes on. Without proscribing responses and solemn exequies, although everyone knows that generally the bank account of the deceased has more to do with such observances than the hearts of the survivors, the Enlightenment chooses to dress up our graves, and in memory of the dead it insists on more sincere and expressive manifestations, less hypocritical tributes. Perhaps the ecclesiastical canticles can rise to the feet of the Almighty even after He in his mercy has pronounced an irrevocable sentence against the culprit, but the tears of gratitude and tenderness that an orphan sheds over the tomb of a mother will always be the purest offering the Creator can receive for the work of his hands. The Enlightenment does not necessarily object that a silent gathering be invited to provide an air of solemnity to a funeral and to witness the sacred ceremonies celebrated by the priests around a catalfaque bedecked with black crepe, which is in most cases an image of our sorrow, but that same Enlightenment evinces greater satisfaction and pleasure when the rosebush, the weeping willow, and the sempervivum sprout from the dust to which the father, or the brother, or the wife has returned.

If when I die they still insist on burying my countrymen in such a demeaning place as this, I hereby formally protest, just as I might petition that the results of an election be annulled, the effort expended to drag my body there. And I request forthwith that my friends carry my body in the middle of the night, just as if it were the worthless leavings of a mine, to that isolated little hill situated to one side of precious, picturesque Chimba. I want to be buried at the foot of the willow you can see from its crest, a willow that will be from that moment on my universal heir, because I intend to bestow my name upon it. I make this declaration so it will be public knowledge.

I'll be very sorry if anyone complains about my "Afternoon Walks" or if they, with greater malice than any intended by my humble pen, discern in this modest defense I've just addressed to the dead any aggression calculated to annoy the living. No aggression intended. If on occasion I have the misfortune to displease a particular social group, it will never be the case that in my heart of hearts I stop loving them as individuals, because I always regard such groups as consisting entirely of exceptions. But if, in spite of everything, they choose to be irremediably offended and to seek revenge, I'll show them how: have them ignore me and treat me as they would the dead, or let them imagine that I've simply wanted to write concerning the application of law to matters concerning the mines.

(*El Mercurio*, June 13, 1842)

Afternoon Walks (Second Article)

Here I am again on a rampage, seeking some poorly developed vein to denounce, or certain wasteful practices to attack. Where will all these wanderings end up? Where will my walks end up? Don't worry about it, unblemished sir, because in all likelihood they'll end up where all things do: they'll end up nowhere, with God's help. The colossal power of Santa Cruz, in no time at all, found its Waterloo,[1] and was reduced to nothingness. That duel to the death between the sons of glorious France and the Illustrious Restorer of the Laws[2] ended with a lunch *à la fourchette*, and the blockades and fleets and ultimatums amounted to nothing. But without even leaving the house, let's consider our own antics. Do the projects formulated last evening come to fruition in the morning? How many plans for reforms are filed away every day with the intention of realizing them in due time? Our public servants, do they not all return to private life? Our heroes, are they acknowledged as such before rotting in a grave? What do we see every day but some building toppled to the ground, a life ended, a flower with its petals fallen, a hope frustrated, a friendship destroyed, a fortune in bankruptcy, a reputation lost; and an endless succession of events disappearing like the hours of the day, like the shadows from a magic lantern? What becomes of the beauty and charms of a woman? Is she any longer-lived than her promises of love? And this love, this omnipotent feeling, this torture of delights, don't we all believe, in good faith, that it will outlive our hearts? Don't we swear so at the feet of another mad creature who also believes it? And yet, isn't it clear to us that love, formidable love, vanishes like youth or like a paroxysm of fever?

If everything dies, if everything ends up nothing, should I worry about the consequences of my innocent writings? "They'll make people hate you and want to get even." And I answer, if I didn't write them, would I be spared that lash? Do you think there's some cure for the plague? "But who are you," they'll answer back, "to want to correct mankind?" Are you out of your minds? I, *correct mankind?* What a slander! Far more likely than that would be for an auditor, on going over an account, to forget to submit his bill for expenses, or for someone to try to persuade one of my countrymen to drop his lawsuit; it would be far less crazy, say, for me to get it into my head to call a meeting of pious, hypocritical churchwomen to consider the abolition of nunneries. Correcting mankind is like grabbing the sky with your hands, or trying to get wool from a donkey or sermons from a horse. Do you think I'm going to waste my time on such a foolish enterprise? Not in my lifetime! I'm just doing what half the world does with the other half, what a dentist does to the wretch who entrusts him with the remaking of his mouth, or what a hairdresser does with the bald woman who wants to bedeck herself with the remains of a corpse: I'm just trying to have fun and make use of my idle moments, as the poet calls his busiest hours, to exact fair and legitimate reprisals on the enemy who authorizes them with his own hostilities.

This being said, bring on my hat and the street. But in this burg called Copiapó, where it doesn't rain except for the death of a bishop, it's as cold as it is in the southern provinces. And that's very cold! I can't remember those climes without shivering. Happily they passed as all things pass, or to say what I really mean, I passed them by, and as sure as God has a place for me in glory, I'll never navigate such altitudes again . . . .

So bring on my cloak and let's get under way . . . .

You're in for it now! Now we've got another digression . . . ! My cloak . . . !

Sublime invention of some philosopher tailor who, when he offered it to man, tried to give him a single stone to kill two birds: the bad weather of Nature and of Society; the attacks of the cold and of public calumny! From the days of Noah to our own, the cloak has hidden the flaws of Adam's descendants, who having been created even more morally fragile than their father, perhaps because there are so many tempting Eves, there wouldn't be enough fig-leaves to cover their peccadillos, and they'd find themselves obliged to feel shame, which nowadays it's necessary to avoid at all cost. A cloak gives us the audacity to wear a jacket that's had the misfortune of having been worn before, a circumstance that suffices to make its owner scorn it, considering that wearing it makes him a man like any other; a cloak lets a fop commit the unpardonable sin of walking around in comfort, freeing his shoulders of the pressure of suspenders. A cloak makes an old man's stooped posture less perceptible, and though the weight of the cloth stimulates hip-gout, that's nothing to him if the world, in trying to guess how many winters he's survived, omits a few by mistake. The nocturnal Don Juan, hiding himself up to his eyes in this spacious garment, pulls off feats that would immortalize him if the arenas for these displays were as public as they are customary. No unsavory-looking street is left unexplored by him, no intrigue unconcluded, no broken marriage alarms him, and without the least fear of being found out, or having his reputation smirched, though for the rest of it he doesn't come out so clean, he manifests the lustfulness of a Heliogabolus with regard to susceptibilities. The next evening he shows up at the *tertulia*, confident that no one will say to him, "May you rot where you sinned!" Was there ever a cloak that didn't cover up some bad example?

Which street shall I go down? Let's try Calle Grande, where at least there's not so much dust. It's paved. It doesn't matter: it's daytime, and you can step around the holes. At night it's another matter, people keep falling, getting back up, and cursing as much as is proper.

I was walking along a little path so narrow it had nothing in common with people's consciences these days, when . . . Crash! [Another article for *El Mercurio*!] . . . a gang of men armed with clubs are shouting, running, jabbering excitedly, and chasing . . . a thief? It might well be, and if he's a *cangallero*, a guy who'd steal ore from the good people who do him the favor of letting him work himself to death in their mine, the miners union will celebrate his capture with a dance, even though that very night the culprit will walk out of jail a free man, leaving in his place several ounces of silver ore. But it doesn't happen to be one of those they're chasing, but a poor dog with a rope around its neck, barking, attacking, whining, snarling, and tearing itself to pieces trying to break free and escape the inevitable torture. Barbarous torture, a bloody spectacle the butchers offer the town so the police won't fine them. Long live civilization! Now I'm sure we're heading down the path of progress, the way of the conquerors. Yes, indeed: let the masses experience the benefits of the Enlightenment; let our customs become more refined; and meanwhile let gangs of murderers roam the streets with their cudgels, their stones, their knives, and their mongrel souls, playing the role of mutilators, so they won't blow it if tomorrow they're promoted to executioners. This way the town can get used to seeing how eyes, brains, and anything else a head contains can be crushed by a club and scattered all over the street

. . . . Long live the dog-slayers! Long live the police! (It's natural for us to have dog-slayers and cops, since we live among animals.)

Amazed to discover that even for animals it's a curse to have to live among men, and to see men repaying evil for good just as if they were dealing with human beings, I went on my way, trying to shoo with my cane the dogs I met along the way, to scare them away from a place where they were being summarily prosecuted as usually happens when the health of the nation is at stake.

It wasn't long before I was standing in front of the alley leading to the smelter. The sight of those chimneys amid a forest of tall willows swaying in the wind as if to say to the romantic among us: "Come hither, you rake, if you want to have a good time"; the sight of that row of houses where industry flaunts its wonders, and where the miner, depending on his salary, can try to figure out if he's married to a mine or to a wife with mother-in-tow; that sight, I say again, is too enticing not to succumb to the call of the willows. It's true that Chimba is also calling to me, and Chimba is delightful, but that ancient temple of San Francisco, looking more than anything else like an old hermit, those enormous struts placed there to prove that it's not some saint's miracle holding up the church, and then that sand-hill you have to climb that's heavier than a mortal sin . . . those are obstacles you don't want to have to deal with when all you're looking for is a little exercise. Let's go, then, to the smelter.

There comes Patarata to meet me, expressing his affection with his wagging tail, a tail with more sincerity than many tongues can muster. A fair-sized slash over one eye testifies that he too has had a close call with another gang of dog-slayers; but the poor beast, despite how badly he's been treated by men, doesn't hate us all; his instinct knows how to distinguish a true friend, something all the power of reason of a misanthrope can't do. Patarata probably says: "A mad human injured me," just as one of us might say "A mad dog bit so and so." Neither we nor Patarata see anything extraordinary in that.

Now I've reached the door to the establishment. I'm standing in front of a little fountain that's trying very hard to pump out into the air a trickle of water, an element as precious in that process as blood to the body. The water that enters there doesn't come out without first having circulated through a complicated labyrinth of canals, pipes, and tubes, without having run through all the veins of that body that owes its activity and life to it. And, in fact, that is a stupefyingly noisy activity, a dizzying noise, a French inn hosting *la Jeune France*, a patriotic society on the eve of an election, an orchestra of Argentine verse . . . . Here they cast girders and pound steel; here they extrude metals; over there they refine and transform silver nuggets into ingots; here's the room they store them in; in that one they make troughs for washing ore; they get quicksilver from that small room there, mud from all those holes, and where you least expect it you step into one. Wheels turning that way, this way, horizontal and perpendicular wheels, wheels to stir the water, water to turn the wheels; wheels, finally, that turn backwards so others can turn forward, an entirely natural contradiction in this world where some go down so others can go up, where these lose what those gain, where these weep what those celebrate, circumstances that, taken in their entirety, constitute *social harmony*, as the hurly-burly of human interaction is so mockingly called.

Amid all these machines set in cacaphonic motion by the mere opening of a floodgate, there's a windmill for grinding metal whose canvas wings remain utterly still, which has led them to give it the title of *mayorazgo*[3] of that hard-working family. If now and then it takes a notion to spin around a couple of times, everyone celebrates its grace, and as if they were trying to spoil a pampered child they assure it that in time it will be a useful windmill. But if Copiapó is ever going to produce the hurricane needed to set that imbecilic apparatus in motion, it won't happen without burying us under what's left of the sand-hills of La Bodega, Chamonate, and Ramadilla.

Night surprises me in the middle of this pleasant visit. It's so easy to get caught up for hours watching the continuous movement of a wheel, or the steady flowing of water! They say this is the favorite occupation of idiots, and I take that personally, because on several occasions in that building I've caught myself red-handed amusing myself that way.

The irresistible fragrance of fresh-ground Yungas coffee usually snaps me out of my state of ecstasy, and I automatically gravitate toward the little café from which that balsamic odor is emanating. Let's have another cup of coffee, for I've put away my mean scissors until another afternoon.

(El Mercurio, June 7, 1842)

Outings

To tell the truth, this business of going out for walks still isn't anything more than an imported activity in Copiapó, a way to overcome the general inertia of the people here. The *siesta*, that drowsiness brought on by overeating, still has its devotees and proselytes: it's our way of keeping up the good fight against effective digestion by not going out for a little stroll right after eating.

It's also true that, with regard to digestives served during and after the meal, we're on a par with the most civilized countries: sherry, port, San Vicente wine, and other strong medicines help us ward off colic in the same way that an orderly society keeps us safe from anarchy, a democratic society prevents despotism, and the sign of the cross immunizes us against the spirit of both these plagues.

So you aren't likely to bump into strollers everywhere you turn late in the day: if around then you see three or four gentlemen heading this way or that and you think they're out for a walk, follow them and you'll discover that they've set out walking because only by walking can they get to where coffee is served and a *tertulia* is in progress.

That young guy who, at sunset, climbs on his horse and sets out riding along the city walls, he's not out for exercise either; he's scouting; he's a falcon looking for prey.

And what about those people walking toward Chimba in the cool of the evening?, you'll ask me. No way! Nobody would go to Chimba, at any hour of the day, if there weren't all those girls to look at, all that *mate* to drink, all those flowers free for the picking.

After a certain age, a man doesn't walk below San Francisco, even if they invite him to a picnic without having to pay. "That's O.K. for young guys, but I'm not up to it anymore," he'd reply to the one suggesting he make the trip.

If a stranger comes to Copiapó without knowing what day it is, which could very well happen if he's coming from the port and gets crazy from all the dust in Ramadilla; if he comes to Copiapó, I repeat, and sees a lot of women coming and going with white hats or handkerchiefs on their heads as if they were out for a walk, he should say: *today is Sunday, today is a festival*, because it's sure that he won't see them in the streets on any other day. To take a walk on a workday is an absurdity, you risk catching a cold, or worse, *having someone see you. Jesus, what would they say, we're walking for no reason, like people with nothing to do!*

In light of this lack of enthusiasm, this non-custom of taking a bit of fresh air, our illustrious municipality has decided not to include plans for an alameda, a public walk, among the many projects for improving the comfort and appearance that have been drawn up so far, improvements that, thank God, have got Copiapó looking like a jewel for anyone with the imagination to appreciate them as if they'd actually been constructed! The roads alone, for instance. Just look at them. There they are, in good shape and getting better under the Conservative regime. Since it's such a joy to travel on them, the owners of the deserts they traverse charge a dollar for each mule, donkey, or horse that has the privilege of dying of humger and thirst in those barren wastes.

Our hospital is the best in the universe: the odds are eight to one that no sick person will ever die in it. And although it only has one bed right now, it was an excellent decision to include it in the municipal plan.

The forest of willows that was planted on the plain, a deal that, in the opinion of one of our oldest governors, is going to produce, within a very short time, an annual revenue of ten thousand pesos in wood, is about to pay off; it's only hoped that the burros don't eat the seedlings.

The town of Chañarcillo and its market, that's a done deal. There's no more planning to think about in the town, except for those who got everything ready to build on the sites allotted to them.

The reform of the water rights has been a great success. No one complains about violations, and each person continues to draw off all the water he can, using the ingenuity God gave him.

As for the new cemetery, we've got the main thing: the rules and tariffs for burials. The rest is yet to be done, including the choice of a site; but that's the least important part. The important thing is to know how much they're going to charge to bury us so that, if we don't like the price, we can go die somewhere else.

Having said this, let's get back to the subject of my piece.

But if there's no one out walking in the streets, there's hardly anyone who doesn't like an outing in the country. At the present time, it's all the rage, even among our most stay-at-home merchants, to take a few days off for such a pleasant vacation. Springtime has got the people moving, wanting to see what a generation almost never sees more than once in Copiapó: the fields, hills, and valleys covered with innumerable flowers. Our arid peaks, this dead nature that if it inspires anything, if it expresses any moral idea, it's the nakedness of disillusionment, the despair of a frustrated administration or a lost election, to see it now adorned with all the colors of the flowers and exhaling rich perfumes, it could only be caused by some enchantment, like a government that decides to shower with pensions, honors, and medals some poor wretch who's lost both legs.

The standard signal that a family is heading out for the country is a cart with an awning overhead and curtains over the door. The curtains should be quilts, or old bedcovers; if not, forget it, the ride's no good. This cart, what a warehouse of things it holds! It's an arc, but instead of carrying every kind of animal it carries one each of every sort of kitchen or garden utensil, furniture, vegetable, candy, table service, snack, plus one each of domestic servant, housekeeper, cook, child, maid, dog, piglet, turkey, hen, lamb, and every other domestic animal. The woolen bags, leather chests, trunks, baskets, sacks, and packages represent a bottomless accumulation, a scrambled ocean, a labyrinth, a lawsuit over a copper mine in Freirina, a political association that decides to support a minister because they think he's not close enough to being thrown out of office for them to stop sucking up to him.

However, the mistress of the house is on top of it all, and, like the minister of state, she's the only one who can see her way through the confusion to thread the needle:

"Look, driver, these chests, put them on first; they're full of breakables."

"Leave that bag, it goes on top."

"You'll have to move those sacks of vegetables."

"Take it slow, that basket's got eggs in it."

"Children, stay clear of those oxen . . . !"

"Have them bring those jars of candy."

"Girl" (to the maid), "bring the children's clothing."

"Juana" (to the cook), "don't forget the grill."

"Ah, I forgot; that little box with the syringe in it . . . ."

"But, no; I'll take it in the carriage, we don't want it to get . . . ."

"But, woman," says the husband, "what about the cold stuff for lunch, where does it go?"

"Oh, what do you know, the boy can carry it up front."

"We're off!" shouts the driver, grasping the long goad.

"Hold up a minute . . . ."

"What are we forgetting?"

"Girl, check and see if we forgot something."

"Nothing, mama; everything's fine."

In the meantime, the individuals mentioned above have already piled into the cart. The servants are shouting, shrieking, and laughing loudly; the children are quarreling, no one pays any attention to the voices of authority, and the oxen, who think the confusion is the signal to start, jolt the cart forward. Ah, the fright, the cries of alarm, the noisy exclamations. Amid the hubbub and confusion, the curses of the driver crash like thunderbolts. The poor fellow curses the oxen, the mother of the oxen, and his own, curses them all equally; and so loudly that the cries of "Jesus!" and "My God!" can be heard all around.

Finally the oxen calm down, the travelers get comfortable, mother issues her last instructions and recommendations, and this first battalion departs, to the sound of happy goodbyes and the squeaking of the cart.

All these noisy preparations have caused the whole neighborhood to come out to the doors to the street and the passers-by to stop and look.

The departure of your own family and family friends doesn't provoke such a democratic fuss. Seeing these faces beaming with happiness, that excess of life stirring all those individuals who are preparing to leave, those jokes exchanged between them and witticisms invented on the spot, you feel tempted to call for attention, ask for the floor, and give a little speech, saying: "Ladies and Gentlemen: this spontaneous reunion, this crowded gathering inspired by the purest sentiments, etc., etc., etc."

I cut short the speech, afraid that my enthusiasm will carry me away and make me force my readers to *sit down under the lush shade of the tree of liberty, which grows upward with such vigor, always laden with abundant fruit.*

Nor do I follow the family that passes by in carriages and carts. I only meant to talk about their departure. Now let's talk about a ride on a donkey.

Without a doubt, the donkey is an orderly animal, despite the fact that his misfortunes and services, always ill-paid, have given him a certain reputation for stubbornness. Here, I'm speaking about donkeys from other towns. As for those in Copiapó, they enjoy so many prerogatives and such consideration, and inherently display such a sober character, and have received from the climate, or from who knows where, such brilliant endowments, that they constitute a separate class, an aristocratic family of the species. Is there any town other than this one where donkeys are given honey and honeycombs to eat with their alfalfa and barley? Where other than here are they cared for, loaded, and led by certain women who, although in many respects they seem not to belong to the fair sex, never inflict any punishment on their droves but pinches and kicks? Where except in Copiapó do you hear a drover say that he's hired out his asses, not to carry firewood or garbage, but for happy, good-looking girls and elegant fops to ride? Was there ever a more delightful amusement, a more rollicking party, or a wittier and more sprightly entertainment than a donkey ride?

No sooner do we propose it than we start getting ready for it, because all those involved start laughing out loud. Generally, these rides are episodes of what we call country outings; they are the ride of rides. In them people make up their minds to laugh at each other without ceremony, to run a few leagues and subject themselves to no few knocks and falls with comical consequences.

At dawn on the pre-arranged day, the ass-keeper enters the patio of the house they'll be leaving from with his drove. The braying, that happy song, that energetic and unmistakable voice like a "Long live the people!" ringing out in chorus from all the bums in Santiago, awakens those who are going on the ride, who, half dressed, come out or look out their windows to see or select their respective mounts. Everybody wants to ride on the best ones. Impossible! One is no better than the other, all donkeys are equal before the law. Even so, the gallants examine, interrogate, and discover those who are recommended for their good temper and eagle-like gait: the ladies will ride on those, each on her own saddle, which if they aren't old and moth-eaten won't do for the ride. The donkey who's liveliest and most liberal, who it's suspected may interrupt public order and attack public morals, is assigned to the best horseman and the one with the best fists, so that, in his capacity as judge, he can opportunely restrain him if he acts up: donkey-carousers such as these are distinguished from the rest by their heads with only one ear, their truncated tails, or other mutilations inflicted for their excesses.

Once the preparations are completed, the necks of the donkeys adorned with jingle-bells, the saddlebags stuffed with food and bottles, the mouths of those who are going filled with laughter, the eyes of the children staying behind filled with tears, the moment comes for mounting those mild animals, who let themselves be saddled, loaded up, and led with the charming deference of a battalion of civil guards on election day.

The male riders, as they leave, divide into two groups; some ride ahead to serve as guides, others ride in the rear, urging the girls' donkeys forward with stimuli that aren't always that innocent or decent. There's a carnivalesque craziness to the general sense of revelry: everyone shouts out of sheer habit, everyone laughs more loudly and readily with each step they take, each look they exchange, each donkey image that occurs to them: no one sees anyone else except in caricature.

Here comes one with long legs riding a burro with short ones, forming a portrait, not of donkey and rider, but of donkey with six legs. Over there another donkey fell down because of the law of gravity of the one riding him. This one's saddle, having slipped back and offended with its cinch the privates of the jealous animal, obliges him to demand with incessant bucking that they treat him more respectfully and only make him perform functions he was hired to perform. The girls buy some real estate every so often, falling, never to their own liking but always to everyone else's; never like a cat, but always like a carriage tipping over. The rogue donkey, which out of prudence they make march in front, brays constantly one of his memorized tunes and gives unmistakable signs of his anarchist intentions. Everything provokes the party to go crazy with pleasure.

Next come a few gulps from the bottles and the pleasant state of fermentation into which they put young heads: moments when man finds paradise in his life, another self inside his self, that a few drops of liquor arouse; when we dream a thousand wonders without falling asleep, but they all disappear when we really sleep.

The drinks in the saddle are followed by drinks at lunch, which has to be laid out in the shade of some enormous boulder, on a table at mouth-level, the diners bellying up side by side. The sandwiches have come apart, the ham is smudged with dirt, the bread's gotten soggy, and you can't tell whether from water or burro sweat; but everything is delicious, everything's perfect. Obviously, their appetites, since there was nothing to treat them with, got carried away on one of the burros.

It wouldn't be so bad, I told myself while walking one day, if you were forced to take an outing, as long as it was on a donkey.

(*El Copiapino*, November 29, 1845)

Letter from Jotabeche to a Friend in Santiago

If you hadn't sent me a letter on the steamship *Peru*, do you know the punishment I had lined up for you? I was going to dedicate one of my articles to you so your name would appear in print like an ECCE HOMO at the head of some columns of *El Mercurio*.

You've escaped a good one, escaping that dedication, and in this you're more fortunate than some ministers of state who, barely appointed to office, are already being heaped with celebrations of their enlightenment and virtue, proffered to them by virtue of ancient custom in that ancient act of homage. But be forewarned: if I don't get a letter from you on every steamship, I'll do you in, I'll shame you publicly, planting an obsequious dedication in terms such as these: "Dedicated to my friend the brilliant and virtuous young poet So-and-So." This "brilliant and virtuous" bit are compliments exchanged among friends, and, as for the "poet" part, though in truth I'm not sure if you are one, it's enough that you aren't entirely stupid for me to confer that honor on you with my eyes closed.

I also want to warn you that I don't like getting letters by sailing ship, or ships with sails, as you call them, because they lack tone, and you get no credit here reading a letter from Santiago posted more than four days ago. And please don't send me any newspapers or other public papers, unless by addressing them to me you want to give them to the administrator of the post office of this port, who has turned into a confiscator of newspapers, declaring them all undeliverable because practical jokers have started inserting their names on things with guano. Is there anything they haven't done with guano . . . !

Happy are we, born in a time when we know the supreme importance of this stuff, which characterizes our century so perfectly! The century of Napoleon, the century of liberty, the century of light, the century of the romantics, the century of *guano* . . . !

But getting back to your letter, is it possible that you still haven't come to terms with romanticism? What a reactionary! But, you know, I don't believe you, and I'd be willing to bet you're a romantic and don't even know it, haven't eaten it or drunk it or understood it, as is the case with many of us. As for me, I can tell you that I'm one by instinct, by habit, by practice, that is to say, without it costing me any work at all. Could anything be easier? All you have to do is let yourself relax, and willy-nilly, *papam habemus!* Ever fall in love? Then you're a romantic. Never fall in love? Then you're a romantic. Do you live *fashionably?*[1] How romantic! Are you *lazy in fashion?* Ditto. Do you wear a corset, trousers *in this style or that*, such and such a jacket, and a hat that matches? Romantic. Do you wear a moustache with a tuft on your chin, or a tuft with no moustache, or *sideburns in the old style?* A refined romantic. Do you carry a thick, knotty cane *like a drum major's?* That's all it takes. Do you comb your hair *in the plain style?* That's all it takes. Do you smell of jasmine, or just smell, but not of jasmine? Do you wear shirts without collars, or collars without a shirt? Can you say hello in French? *Il suffit. Tu es fièrement romantique.* There's no escaping it, my friend; romantic and more romantic. Because if Plato and Diogenes, Heraclitus and Democrites, or Aristotle himself, had lived in this epoch, they'd have been romantics whether they wanted to or not. If not, we'd just ostracize them as being *too literate,* that is, as *reactionary absolutists;* or to say it more clearly, as *harmful anachronisms,* and for lots of other reasons *that I'd rather not go into detail about here in order not to delve more than necessary into the arcana of language, or to pause too lengthily over the exteriorities of thought;* in a word, so you won't understand what I'm saying.

Don't wear yourself out, dear friend; don't waste your time resisting romanticism, this flood or fad that's the cheapest thing we've ever gotten from Europe, with a stopover in San Andrés on the River Plate, where the national intellectual class welcomed it with open arms, expressing through it their *sensitivization* and their spirit of *socialitism,* and vowing that, from May 25[2] forward, they would devote their lives to humanitarian progress. Become a romantic, man of God, resolve once and for all to make this sacrifice. Look, it's as easy as opening your mouth, striking out left and right against the aristocracy, praising democracy to the stars, giving lip service to literary independence, writing so only the devil can understand you, marinading yourself in arrogance, declaring yourself on a first-name basis with Hugo, Dumas, and Larra, speaking of them as if they were high-class rakes with whom we have a mutual understanding *sans compliments.* Get yourself ready to receive this sacrament of penance by reading the article in the *Revista de Valparaíso* on romanticism and classicism,[3] and let me know if the Spanish language in which it's written is the same Spanish you and I speak, or if it's a different Spanish, just recently arrived on the planet, because I swear to God that around here we haven't been able to get our teeth into it, even though a committee of linguists was convened to that end.

You ask what's up in the love department? If you're asking me personally, I'll confess the truth: it no longer attacks me so fiercely; but if you're asking about Copiapó in general, I can assure you it's proceeding here exactly as it is in Santiago. These days, thank God, people don't fall in love, they just fool around. It's regarded as a pastime, an opportunity to lie without taking responsibility, to perjure yourself without sinning, to talk just to keep talking, to promise what we're under no obligation to deliver, and to ask for what we know will never be given. This is a point on which men and women are totally in agreement and about which we understand each other amazingly well, as if we had of necessity been born men and women so that eventually we'd agree on something. On this question of love affairs, then, we're as progressive in Copiapó as in any of our towns where people regard it as their solemn duty to live fashionably and to adopt, among other customs and practices, the ridiculous fads that come to us from Europe purely for the sake of hair-dressers and dressmakers, or for the sake of some Baron whom the brothels of those great capitals have banished. They tell us in Paris that it's stupid to actually fall in love with a woman, that a Lovelace[4] is a *person of consequence* in the societies of the *grand monde;* so here we are offering a caricature of the hero, determined to represent the role of se-ducers in our pitifully burlesque fashion. It's quite true that those we mock for this we also mock for a thousand other fatuous and stupid acts from which young girls looking for a good time derive enormous advan-tage, but the bad part is that there are many of us, and that others will inevitably copy us so as not to stand out as originals among the crowd.

There are young men who if they seem to be in love, if they visit some young lady assiduously, it's only to get people to talk about them, for ostentation, so people will see how busy they are courting, so every-one will know they've made a conquest, and they don't have to do a thing if gossip takes a seduction for granted, or if not a seduction at least a relationship that they may not even have sought.

There are young men who wait until witnesses are present to display their talent for making insinuations to their beloved through gestures, glances, and secret smiles in order to hint that there's some mysterious understanding between them. They're delighted if in this way they man-age to arouse envy in all those they're trying to have observe them.

There are young men who just in visiting some girl, without their eyes or their tongue ever having expressed anything but the usual com-pliments, if you should happen to see them and congratulate them for the progress they're making with the young lady they'll squeeze your hand, smiling maliciously as if to say: "You're very observant: she adores me, it's true, but don't tell anyone."

There are young men who spend entire years sweating out their love for a pretty girl, adoring her, seeking her out, pursuing her, harassing her, spying on her as if she were already theirs; but if with the passing of time they meet some rich older woman, they'll forget the pretty thing, cling to the old woman, and they'd climb down a sewer just to get their hands on her fortune.

In view of all these *young men,* and many others who exist even if I don't describe them here, it's easy to imagine what it is the other part has to put up with when it's time to fall in love. It is, in fact, an almost im-possible negotiation, a lost cause, a business that can only lead to bank-ruptcy. Go ahead and fall in love. Here's how it works:

"Look, honey," you say to the sorrow of your life, "believe me, I truly love you."

"Oh, really? What do you mean, you love me? And where do we go from here?"

"Yes, I love you. I swear it on my honor."

"What a lie! It doesn't show on your face."

"You're really mean. Always teasing!"

"Who told you that? Damn, it's cold today!"

"You, who are snow personified, are you really capable of feeling cold?"

"Thanks a lot. Were you at the theater on Sunday? They say the play was ancient."

"To tell the truth, it has no connection to modern times . . . *The Faithful Wife!*"

"Yeah, but boy, did that guy know how to love! You're right, that's got to be from the old days."

And she'll joke around and lead you on, and irritate you and try your patience, without you ever being able to get anywhere with her, or get beyond the status quo, the place where the relationship started. Go ahead, fall in love.

That's about it for my first letter. If you find it short, don't be surprised, because I've no talent for writing long. Wait for the next, but watch out for dedications.

(*El Mercurio*, July 23, 1842)

Letter from Jotabeche

Copiapó, November 12, 1842

My dear countryman:

It's time to write you a letter, and I intend to amuse myself as I write, hoping it won't bore you when you read it. I have to confess: I'm as keen to write letters as Argentines are to emigrate, Peruvians to suffer, soldiers to fight, *Pelucones*[1] to influence fashion, and the children of my land to litigate. The thing is, I can't resist this propensity, just as a woman can't help being deceitful, the poet can't help lying, and the whole human species can't help gossiping. For me, the pen is all there is in the world: without the pen, the world seems like nothing to me; without it, I don't know what I'd do, there'd be no occupation left for me. This John the Baptist of yours would be in that case a most unfortunate being, quite useless, of no use at all, the man most suited for a monastery, unless the ministry were to recommend my aptitudes for the position of deputy.

If they still cast spells in these times, I'd be afraid some warlock, seeing my extraordinary fondness for writing, would turn me into a pen, which as you know wouldn't be much of a job for him, because he'd find more than half the metamorphosis already done. However, I wouldn't mind all that much if he turned me into a bird. If it was a parrot, I'd emigrate, and wherever I landed I'd take up journalism. If a canary, I'd go warbling off to the other side of the Maule, where the cages aren't the sort that make a bird desperate for freedom if through misfortune or destiny, which are synonymous there, it should end up in one. And if a hawk, I'd head north so when I got to Peru I'd be a bird of great distinction: worthy sir hawk, supreme hawk, hawk of the nation, third hawk of discord, or whatever other title they gave me, though it could never be a new title, since they wouldn't be able to find it in the dictionary.

But let's get down to the letter I mean to send you. You probably know, then, that since your departure for Valparaíso, there've been all sorts of developments here, among them an earthquake as strong, terrifying, and sudden as a well-planned coup, which around here is called high politics, from which I pray God save us just as he'd stop a falling house from crushing us. The quake struck at midnight, an hour when even little scares are magnified, including those the members of the *Pipiolo*[2] congress and the administration sprang on each other in recent years every time they turned a corner.

Following the earthquake there was a change of administration in Chañarcillo, a novelty that, if it's always a cause for celebration wherever it happens, this must be because of the fall of the old, because, as for the rest of it, I can't see why we should be cheered by the fall of a government when we know that the next morning another one will rise. Speaking in confidence, on this question of administrations I hold the same opinion as I do regarding women. Some are younger and prettier than others, this one seems like an angel of mercy to us, that one is sheer modesty and sincerity, the one we have today is a little piece of heaven, tomorrow's is as lovely as love, but in the end, my friend, they all end up being women, which is a desperate hard thing to convince yourself of.

All ministers end up wearing wigs, which is another disappointment we have to bear.

Back to Chañarcillo. The subdelegate Mardones fell, because after all he wasn't elected minister for life. He takes with him back to private life, among other things, the pleasant satisfaction of having served his country and his conscience, etc., etc. I don't mean to upset you: the fall of a public man is a very sad event. In consequence, either because of the earthquake or the fall of the subdelegate, the funds that had been anticipated at 4 percent per month plus an additional four *reals* in marks, at one *real* per *peso*, to be paid in seven-*peso* silver coins, after discounting 6 percent for the cost of taxes and the legal reduction of eleven dollars and twenty-three cents, all budgeted for personal expenses and interest, have suffered a considerable diminishment, and they continue to diminish as the costs incurred in insuring against ore-theft go up. There's been much sadness in Chañarcillo over the deposition of Mr. Mardones: as we know, he was a benefactor of the poor, and apparently he was moving forward on the very liberal plan that everyone should own their own mine. In his place we now have Captain Palacios, a young man with no defects other than his many illnesses; but his temperament is magnificent, so if the problems of the mines are not resolved, at least the problems of the subdelegate will be, which is quite an accomplishment. To complete the reform of the Chañarcillo police department, for two months we've been expecting at any moment a reinforcement of Hussars to relieve the force we now have, a force made up of men who, just as they were shanghaied for service in Copiapó, could well be rounded up and, without it weighing on anyone's conscience, sent to prison, and even that would be like giving them a pardon.

It so happens that during these days of earthquake and the removal and installation of subdelegates we've nearly died of hunger, because the police who have talents and spare time for everything arranged that there should be no meat in the market, not even enough to make meatball soup. What happened was that the butchers hadn't supplied the quota of dead dogs the abovementioned police demanded, so the police came, rounded them up, and stuck them in jail for two days. The crime could not be overlooked, and the judgment of the police should not be overpraised. The butchers believe it's unfair to subject them to such a vile obligation, because there's no longer a statute requiring them to serve as dog-catchers and executioners; the police tell them that that's pure romanticism, basing their argument on custom and the threat of incarceration, a gigantic and, if you will, a stupid argument, but one sufficient to persuade you there was no God if He were standing right in front of you.

This was followed up by another energetic measure taken by the police, not against the butchers now, and not against the dogs, but against the girls who, like them, had taken to walking the streets with rabies. So now there's not a one to be seen, not even if you're in dire need, which should make us happy because the men here were barely earning enough to buy root beer. We've been assured that measures will be taken to prevent these unfortunate creatures from disembarking at our port and that the zealous customs inspector will be ordered to inspect this traffic as if it were a matter of rigorous fiscal concern from top to bottom. Get the word around in Valparaíso as you see fit.

As for new discoveries and mineral wealth, every day several pretty lies spring up, and then like certain flowers they wither and die as soon as the sun heats up the soil around them. Still, I'm convinced that there must be many good mines, because there are plenty of bad lawsuits. It's well known that when a miner makes a strike, a silver strike I mean, the one who makes out is not the miner but the notary executing the deed. Not two weeks ago a miner from Chañarcillo wrote to a lawyer: "My dear sir: after two years of coming up dry, day before yesterday I struck a subvein that brightened up the one I'd been mining, and I have good claim to it. Based on what it may produce, I give you broad power of attorney to represent me in any lawsuit anyone brings against me." The lawyer wrote back: "My dear sir: I'm regret very much not being able to serve you by accepting the power of attorney which I hereby return to you, because when I received your kind offer, I had just agreed to defend N, who intends to sue you, alleging his claim to half of that mine; X came in yesterday claiming the other half; this very day Y has charged that it was stolen from him, and Z's children are now looking for a lawyer to claim a third. Their creditors will be meeting tomorrow to claim the mine as collateral." The miner had made a single strike, and the notary five.

The news from the trans-Andean provinces of San Juan and La Rioja is promising. The war is about to come to an end in that part of the Argentine territory, and all we're waiting for now is for them to finish killing off the few who are still disputing the ownership of those cemeteries. El Chacho,[3] the commander of the unit, is now occupying Binchina, after having passed through Jachal where he unfortunately found it necessary to shoot a few citizens of the federation in order to redistribute resources: however, there couldn't have been more than ten victims, though it seems that the entire population of the village couldn't have been more than ten. It's being recommended to company commanders that they kill decently, kill in a manner that is more in keeping with the enlightenment of this century; they can shoot citizens, but they shouldn't behead them the way that barbarian, the cannibal Rosas, does.

So much for my letter. Now all I need to do is close it where I should have started it, wishing you good health; as for *pesetas*, no matter how poor we are here, there are always a few left over. In case your liver improves as much as our *Colorada* mine, don't show your face around here: they're likely to sue you, thinking you're holding it as an asset.

Your countryman, JOTABECHE

(*El Semanario*, November 24, 1842)

An Illness

I don't ask God to spare me from sickness as intently as I beg His mercifulness to spare me the horror of a cure. The afflictions of the body would be, more or less, about as tolerable as the rabid frailty of an anti-*Pipiolo*[1] administration, except that it would garner us the compassion of our neighbor and make us the target of the cruel solicitude of infinite relatives and acquaintances who, insistent on restoring our health, would torture our sad corporality and try our patience far more than the debilitating effect of the humors, fevers, or attacks of nerves. Such is the urgency everyone exercises in visiting a patient morning and afternoon, hovering around him day and night, that you have to convince yourself that falling sick isn't a terrible misfortune, unless of course you compare sickness to a suspected bankruptcy, since in that case as well there's no house so burdened with visits, nor any person more surrounded and pampered than one assumed to be on the verge of financial disaster. In this world everything has an explanation, even the policies of the current administration. If we need the commiseration of others, if we need someone to do us a favor, everyone knows we'll never find them, but just let us fall sick, and then you'll see that a gripping pain won't leave us breath enough to do anything but beg them not to attend to us, care for us, or help us, and they'll kill you with concern and diligence, hovering over you, running their hands over you, consoling you, turning you over and around. Even when the patient is poor he doesn't get off that easy, unless of course there's a hospital in his town and they take him to it, so that when he passes on to a better life they transfer him to the autopsy room and only then do the doctors discover what disease he died of.

But what really turns into a circus is the house of a patient who's fairly well off. Then you should see the pantomime of exclamations and silent consternation, that running through hallways, that popping in and out of the patient's room. In no time at all the place is converted into the back room of an apothecary shop: flasks, gallipots, jars, cups, teakettles, drugs, and herbs crown the tables, occupy the chairs and corners. Everybody runs into each other, all the while gesturing for a silence that's inevitably interrupted by a chair falling over, a servant bumping her head, and the prolonged shushing of the nurses and curious onlookers who, crowded together behind the curtain around the bed as if they were attending a farce inside an embroidery frame, produce with their whispering a sound like rain on a quiet night. And the worst part of this crowding together is the solicitous concern lavished the whole time, robbing the victim of the right to complain or vent his rage, which up to a certain point generally calms any pain.

A case of sickness, then, produces a revolution throughout the neighborhood, a notable alteration in the domestic behavior of the nearby families. The mother who spends the whole blessed day carrying things from the pantry to the kitchen, from the kitchen to the servant's quarters, from there to the dining room, from the dining room to the garden, from the garden to the coal cellar, always extremely busy and always forgetting something she meant to do, on hearing "So-and-so is very ill," she drops everything, calls her oldest daughter, gives her the bunch of keys and her instructions, takes off her apron and her slippers, fixes her hair, and goes off to let a friend know, who also undoes herself to comply with the unavoidable work of mercy. Another woman, who spends her time not just in sewing but in stopping periodically to shake herself to look for needles, thread, and thimble that are always getting lost among the patches and strips of cloth inundating her, when she hears the same news, shouts for the servant and for instant providence, tells her to carry a funereal consolation to the unfortunate family, a message that, even if it doesn't reach its destination, the carrier well knows she'll have to bring back the thanks proffered and the news that the patient "is doing better now." In short, no female friend of the latter, after learning of his condition, proceeds with the tasks she was doing when the news interrupted her, and the fact that they were neither summoned nor needed is all the reason they need to take flight, carrying chaos to the place where suffering has set up house.

One day the servant of a friend of mine knocked at my door, advising me of the perilous state of his health and begging me to come see him.

"What's the matter with your master, Pedro José?"

"Who knows, sir. The poor gentleman is complaining a lot, the wife doesn't know what to do, the kids are running loose, and the house is filling up with people."

"And what does the doctor say?"

"No doctor has come yet, but lots of ladies are arriving, and I think they're preparing some remedies."

"You run get don Guillermo.² Tell him your master is ill, and take him to the house. I'll be along in a bit."

And so I did. The first person I met when I entered the rooms was the desolate wife who, taking my hand and weeping, said: "Please help me, for God's sake." Six or eight friends stood around her, ten or twelve were running in all directions, not counting many others who kept arriving, who like those who got there before them set up their meeting space right there in the patient's room, where addressing each other mysteriously they begin exchanging remarks such as these:

"How did this happen?"

"It came on all of a sudden."

"Yesterday he looked perfectly well."

"No, girl, he was already coming down with it."

"What a terrible thing!"

"Holy Mother of God!"

"With so many children!"

"Has he asked for a confessor?"

"Such a good Christian!"

"Someone send for a doctor."

"No, dear friend. The salvation of his soul is the first concern."

The unfortunate object of all this compassion, on surveying the swarm of Veronicas,³ makes a strenuous effort to turn toward the wall, in the same way a condemned man already on the scaffold turns his eyes away from his executioners. In short order the discussion turns to what remedies should be adopted. One of them had suffered the same ill and was cured, after God, by a certain ointment she describes ingredient by ingredient, application by application, and by enemas of very complicated composition. Another decides that the sickness consists of a rising fever: she prescribes mustard-poultices, sudorifics, and of course enemas to bring the temperature down. Several others think it's a concentrated chill: warm, damp cloths across the stomach, rubbings, ointments without salt, and this or that remedy. Over there they say it's a touch of delirium; another group decides it's indigestion; in that corner, measles; those women think it's parasites. Finally, the opinions vary as much regarding the sickness as regarding the remedies, though they all agree on one point of attack: enemas. One heartless woman prescribed them with such a lack of concern that you might have thought she was acting as prosecutor in a court of last appeal.

While this debate was going on, other sisters of mercy closed all doors and windows so tightly that neither light nor air could enter. Once again curtains are drawn around my friend's bed; they pile over the poor wretch every blanket they can find in the house and place several miraculous images at the head of his bed so that from there they can work their magic to greatest effect. All that formed a veritable oven. The heat and exhalations of the medicines and lady doctors threatened to suffocate us all along with the patient who, in despair, was cursing the ruthless concern with which one by one they leaned over him to ask: "How do you feel, poor fellow?" His discomfort was diagnosed as delirium, leading them to redouble their fervor in caring for him, bewildering him, and eating him alive. Irritated by all this officious attention, I made so bold as to observe that it was necessary to wait for the doctor, and that meanwhile they could clear out the room, let some fresh air in, and make a bit less noise . . . . "What do you know?" "Men are of no use in cases like this." "You're just in the way." "Run along, now." These and other similar compliments were all I got for reply.

The happy arrival of the doctor suddenly paralyzed the maneuvers, brews, applications, and preparations of the inflexible Aesculapiuses who, shadowing the new arrival right up to the sickbed, began to echo in chorus his findings and questions, now on behalf of the lady of the house, now for each other, now on behalf of the patient himself, so the doctor was left starving for information and I in a state of despair. The doctor asked for pen and paper; they all shouted, "Bring pen and paper!" They all wanted to know if they should take a glass or a bottle to the apothecary; at what time and how often should the medicine be administered; should they give dried potatoes or broth to the patient; and not a one of them thought to ask how serious it was. You could tell the doctor wanted to break free of this swarm and send them home, but many of his regular parishioners were among them, and he didn't want to be thought discourteous or unfriendly. He conveyed this to me when I begged him not to go, leaving my friend in such imminent danger of dying in the care of the devil or the women.

A happy inspiration saved the day. The doctor confided to one of those charitable ladies that the sickness of my friend was smallpox, of the worst kind. Within thirty seconds the secret circulated throughout the house, passing from mouth to ear and from ear to mouth. Mute with terror and leaving behind their ministrations, handkerchiefs, and cloaks, they practically knocked down the doors trying to get out, as when in a fire someone shouts "There's gun-powder in there!" or when they register the first quiverings of an earthquake in a *tertulia*. Up in smoke went the ardent charity of the neighbor women, who dashed for their houses to fumigate, wash, and shake themselves vigorously in case the least bit of the contagion had landed on them. My friend recovered his health attended only by the doctor and cared for by his wife.

The greatest drawback to polygamy, as I see it, would be that if the husband got sick, six or eight wives would set about curing him.

(El Semanario, October 20, 1842)

A Word about Fools

The faculty of reason that man is so vain about, on which he bases his superiority over the other creatures of Creation, and which constitutes the pride of our species, the glory and honor of the human family, is this not also the source of all our ills, the cause of that slow, continuous pain, that discontent gnawing at us for most of our lives? Isn't it reason that takes from our lips the cup of delight, that watches over us like an impertinent pedagogue, that reins in the delightful propensities nature endowed us with, that diverts us, finally, from a path of roses, leading us down another sown with thistles and thorns? Isn't it reason that has stripped us of the best part of our natural freedom, and isn't society based on reason for the purpose of dumping its load of necessary evils on the individuals who constitute it? Doesn't reason force you to forget the wrongs done to you at the same time it builds jails, prisons, and scaffolds to punish your frailties without mercy? Don't they tell you it's reasonable to endure existence no matter how hateful it seems to you, and that it's reasonable to refrain from cutting off the executioner's head no matter how much you'd like to parade around with it on your shoulders? Doesn't reason tyrannize you and don't they tyrannize you in its name in the cradle, in school, in society, and even in the grave? If you ever surrender to the flattering illusions of your fantasy, doesn't reason come running up like a jealous woman to destroy with its presence the sweet dream you were dreaming? Reason . . . ! A most dismal gift, master of deceits, ill-omened book whose most beautiful page is the chapter titled resignation! I suspect that reason wasn't born with man in the Eden of our first parents. They loved each other the way doves do and adored their Maker by joining the birds in their morning songs. Woman's first act of reason was a suggestion from Satan, and this act, this first glimmer of rationality, banished us all from Paradise, stripped us of the innocence of the Angels, and doomed us to Hell.

Without intending to I've climbed up to these heights trying to prove something that, perhaps, no one would even argue with me about, something that for me is axiomatic and that only in these times of polemics and controversies would there be any danger of anyone disputing, it being a maxim, as I see it, a central tenet of romanticism, to wit: "social happiness is in inverse proportion to the talent of the individual," or, to put it another way, "fools are the happiest of men."

This is so obvious that even nations are better off if they're endowed with a certain disposition toward stupidity; vice versa, a nation's stability is more ephemeral, its progress more delayed, if a brilliant talent, a passionate and lively imagination, and, finally, a valiantly clear rational faculty characterize most of the children of its soil. The anarchy of the Argentine people, in my humble opinion, has its origin in the infinite number of doctors, poets, economists, politicians, and eloquent judges who turn up there with the first warm rays of the May sun. That tree with thin trunk lifted its branches above the clouds only to break in half before the raging force of the revolutionary *pampa* wind. The Peruvian debacle probably cannot be explained in exactly the same way, nor any other way. The enlightenment has scarcely affected that hodgepodge of Negroes, but neither are the revolutions in Peru the work of anarchist peoples but rather of a bunch of vagabond soldiers who, fleeing battle, open and close their military campaigns with desertions. On the contrary, I am of the opinion (in conformity with the principle posited above) that without these accursed people, the descendants of Manco Capac[1] would be the happiest republic, the richest and most fortunate country of our hemisphere.

The prosperity of Chile . . . . But this panegyric shouldn't be expressed by one of its own children. Let's just remember that certain great talents, certain national men of genius, have produced pernicious consequences for us and dismal ones for themselves,[2] like exotic plants whose failure to adapt to the soil we've supplemented with nourishment charged against our account with fortune.

But none of this bears directly on my proposition. I'm going to return once and for all to the question; I'm going to describe how blessed the ignorant are. An invocation to the appropriate muse would fit perfectly here, but I don't want to stray a centimeter from the precepts of my school, which has included, if I'm not mistaken, this flower called rhetoric among its proscriptions.

All you need is an ounce of instinct to identify a fool. If he's poor, he never walks down the street without an entourage of boys who will point him out to you with their shouts and whistles. Without passions, without vices, with no past or future, his days are a stagnant pond stirred only by the breeze from the movements of his body. A few crumbs of bread are for him another Camacho's wedding,[3] a *peseta* his entire capital, and the ashes from a fireplace the soft bed from which neither nightmares nor regrets wake him.

The first-class fool stands out among a thousand others by his air of self-importance, by the meticulousness he puts into caring for his person, by the urgency he employs carrying himself everywhere so people can see him, examine him, envy him, imitate him, and praise him. There's never a festival or parade, never any spectacle where he doesn't make an appearance. The personal impression he makes is the essence of a fool, the center of his existence, the idol of his soul. Whatever would become of him if he didn't have a head to hold high, a face to show off, a trim waist to put a belt around, a firm and elegant foot to put forward! Usually he has no vices except for snuff or a fine cigar, both of which give him the opportunity to demonstrate his gentility and grace in using tobacco. His best friend, his intimate confidant, is the full-length mirror. At home he consults it at length for long sessions; if he goes for a walk and comes to a tailor's or a hairdresser's shop that's open, he slips inside, takes a quick look at himself front and profile, brushes himself off, glances at the latest figurines, and goes on his way. Does he stop somewhere for a visit? He addresses the mirror first, then the homeowners, under the pretext of adjusting his hat or folding his cape; at night, no one is quicker than he to snuff out the candles in front of a reflecting glass. He's a Narcissus hopelessly in love with himself. For this reason he's passionate about having his portrait painted so he can dwell at length on the contemplation of his image; for the same reason he buys and makes a gift to himself of a heavy ring on which his name is engraved: the name of a good fellow! And the pleasure he takes in all this is immense, because a fool imagines he's engaged in the noblest of careers just being generally acknowledged as a gallant fellow in the society he lives in. None of these individuals (another incomparable blessing) thinks he's lacking in wealth, even though he's invested his entire fortune in dress-coats, combs, canes, caps, and perfumes. It's enough that some uncle or distant relative owns or rents some rustic property for all the fools in the family to talk to you about the hacienda, the plantation, the estate, and to invite you to spend a few days in the country, saying: "Whenever you want: you'll be in your own house."

It doesn't matter that he was not at all fond of learning in school for him to forget everything he never knew. In literary debates he's as formidable as he is in any subject; because if you try to change his opinion, you'll have someone to argue with for the rest of your life, and he'll have energy enough to argue with your heirs as well. The motto of the fool is "Never give in."

Politics is the field of his passion. Although he has no stake in such matters, it would be a grave misfortune for him not to imagine his own interests intimately connected to those of the top leaders.

If his name should happen to appear publicly in some erroneous report, in some petty intrigue identifying him as the person who did or who suffered from the action, on the spot he publishes his vindication in the press and appeals to the court of public opinion to take a position between the delicacy and circumspection characterizing his person and the perversity and stupidity of his slanderer, whom he challenges to debate this matter in print. The other, if he's a fool too, as may well be the case especially in large towns, picks up the gauntlet, firing off a volley of letters to the editor, providing for days at a time intense amusement to the idlers and gossips attending the *tertulias* of the city. The polemic ends at last with each one of the writers saying that he doesn't want to carry things forward because the rogue, thief, and drunk who is his opponent has responded with insults, not reason, irrefutable proof that his cause was weak: both declare themselves masters of the field, and each one sings his own victory song.

Fools are so fortunate that if there's only one in a town, overnight the fool and no one else will get the job. And the lucky star of this lineage of men shines so bright that if they aren't recognized as such or if there aren't any fools in town, all vacancies will be filled by fools from the next town.

When the fool finally gets married, it's inevitably to a woman who's rich, young, sentimental, or charming.

I sing the happy career of my hero right up to the matrimonial blessings: I do more, I give him mine. And if it turns out that my little article is bad comedy, when I reach this point I play the flute, the curtain falls, and I exclaim: "Let's take off the mask, etc., etc., etc."

(El Semanario, December 8, 1842)

The Provincial in Santiago

The Muslim has to make a pilgrimage to Mecca at least once in his life and visit the Holy Places of his religion and traditions. The European painter isn't a painter if he hasn't visited the important cities of Italy and the landscapes of Switzerland. The antique collector, to transcend the category of hobbyist, needs to go steal something from the ruins of Athens, exhume mummies in the sepulchers of the Pharoahs, or make a journey to Peru to search for burial-grounds. The elegant citizen of Santiago who hasn't gone to Paris to study elegance at the source, to see in real life the fashionable types who come to us here in the form of lithographs, should abandon all hope of achieving celebrity in his career. And watch out, because those who dedicate themselves to fashion rarely shine in any other endeavor.

Just as indispensable as these visits is the one we provincials have to make to the capital of the Republic. Anyone who has failed to render this homage, unless there's been some powerful obstacle to doing so, is regarded as a poor wretch, like one of those automatons who have the sad distinction of never experiencing the joys of music or any of beauty's more divine impressions.

In fact, for a provincial to reach old age without having found it necessary or been moved by the desire to leave his village and go to Santiago, his days must have slipped by him in the most bestial, brutish fashion; he must have lived without being aware of it, without ever, pardon the expression, having surprised himself existing. Fortunately, we don't have in our towns but one or two such automatons, and those don't belong to the times we're living now. They are, in truth, the only foreigners existing among us, the ballast we drag along on our epic journey.

Young men and women from the provinces, who haven't been educated in the high schools of the capital, are eager to visit that happy precinct, where a stay of only a few months is sure to teach them more than all the courses they've taken in their hometown, and where the brightest lights of civilization, like the dazzling radiance of midday, pervade everything, infuse everything, inundate everything, and inspire everything with inexhaustible life. I may be wrong, but I think I've noticed in many of my friends from the provinces who were preparing to make their first short visit to Santiago, a certain happy faith, not about satisfying their simple curiosity, but that they were going to learn something useful, acquire knowledge they knew instinctively they were lacking, and clear their minds a bit of that inexplicable fog enveloping those who've neglected to cultivate them. They've noticed that this short visit, this modest aspersion of that Santiago essence has worked wonders in others: people who previously couldn't disentangle themselves from their habitual backwardness and shyness have come back endowed at one and the same time with gracious manners and a substantial intellectual development. These traits of backwardness and shyness, it should be said in passing, though fate has unfairly stamped them as characteristic of the provincial, hardly ever turn out to be irremediable, almost always turn out to be nothing but a thick cocoon inside of which precious talents are germinating. (Let this serve as consolation to anyone who pleases, and let's move on.)

Don't go looking for a type of this traveler of mine, because I tell you there isn't one. My creation is *sui generis*. He's not from Chiloé, nor Concepción, nor Maule, nor Coquimbo; he wasn't born in any place in any one of our provinces. And if there are any so malicious as to accuse him of being from one of them, that province can protest, saying what Quevedo said once about the son they wanted to claim was his, whereupon it will be clear that this creature is a miscarriage of mine, but that everyone contributed to his upbringing.

Once upon a time. It's a night of anxiety and insomnia, the last night the provincial will spend on his way to the capital. The following day will be a day of great happenings, wonders, and novelties, the mere anticipation of which is already beginning to confuse and oppress him. What he's experiencing is what we all experience when, as the thing we most ardently desired draws near, our heart and soul sink into a state of near-mortal suffocation. Accursed neuroses, they rob us of half our happiness, deprive us of the opportunity to savor it as soon as we see it coming toward us in the distance. One minute before hearing the soprano Rossi sing for the first time,[1] my heart seemed swollen and was pounding violently; when she began to sing I was nearly comatose.

The first impression our traveler receives as he approaches Santiago is the distant appearance of its white towers, rising above a confused blur of objects that cannot be identified by sight without magnification. Our queen city, situated as she is at the foot of the Andes, to whose startling massiveness the pigmy-like elevation of her groves of poplar trees and proudest buildings offers but humble contrast, the plains surrounding her not allowing one to contemplate from afar her vast extension or the symmetrical ensemble of her divisions or the variety of her picturesque locales, the provincial approaches her off guard, unready to meet the challenge of her endless streets, to endure without bewilderment the succession of such strange scenes, ill-prepared not to succumb to the noise and confusion of those boisterous, riotous multitudes.

His attention engrossed in the crowds of travelers of all classes whom he overtakes or meets along the narrow streets down which he's turned, he suddenly enters the suburbs of the city, those anthills of democracy, always abuzz with riot and revel, that commonly offer the same Sunday babel at the gates of the capital that we find in the fields where games of *chueca*[2] or horseraces are held in the provinces.

Being accustomed to the emptiness of the streets in his village, where a midnight silence prevails at midday, the traveler's surprise is indefinable when he comes, for example, to the place called El Conventillo[3] and finds himself surrounded by its tremendous tumult, its impenetrable cordon of animals and carts, of women and men, of quadrupeds and bipeds blocking his path, tugging at his poncho, making his horse skittish, shouting at him, greeting him: "God save you, stranger." "Where's your nurse?" "Didn't you bring your family?"—and other devilries, all aimed at spooking his horse and making the rider lose his cool before he finally calms him and gets him back on the road. Woe unto our friend if, because he's not holding on tightly, he falls to the ground to the delighted hoots and whistles of that bunch of bedouins, who applaud the fall, just as if it were a new equestrian maneuver, never seen before. Then everyone comes up to him to help, lifting him up and shaking him off, and just like that, they leave the poor guy alleviated, not exactly of the pain of his bruises but of the weight of his wallet, spurs, hat, and amen to various parts of his saddle that, like everything else, disappear by magic among that honorable crowd.

And then if the watchman shows up at the scene and begins to investigate what has caused that ruckus, the adventure usually continues.

"Look, watchman," exclaims the provincial, "these rogues jumped me. Make them give me back my hat, my money . . . ."

"That's a lie!" shout a hundred voices at once.

"Don't you believe him, señor Juan," says one.

"He wasn't even wearing a hat," swears the very one who's caressing it under his poncho.

"You want me to tell you what happened, señor Juan? What it was was, this fellow came galloping up and his horse fell down and . . . that's all I saw."

The watchman, who before becoming one undoubtedly must have graduated from scarer of horses and stripper of fallen gentlemen, knows from experience that matters such as the one under way before him are just one more Gordian knot with no solution except the tried and true. So declaring martial law in a loud voice, or, what amounts to the same thing, notifying everyone that he will resolve the problem of the aforementioned knot if they don't disperse, everybody scatters to their hiding places, except for the provincial, who still has to endure a lecture for having galloped his horse in violation of the municipal ordinances: "I'm not going to fine you," says the judge on horseback, "because I can see you're from the country." "Thanks a lot," replies our peasant, relieved at this favor, and he goes on his way with God and with this first lesson in the ways of the world under his belt.

But let us imagine now that he's taken lodging near the Alameda[4] in one of those house-buses whose owners have the audacity to call them inns and which, if they don't take it the wrong way, I prefer to call rat-holes. Yes, sir: that's what they are, rat-holes like the ones thrown together in Peñaflor by that kind gentleman, don Pedro Valenzuela, so the fops of Santiago who've decided to live the good life in paradise for the summer at economy rates can hole up for the night. I repeat, let us imagine our traveler lodged in one of those houses, which are available to provincials and which because of their general appearance seem as if they were built specifically for the acclimatization of their guests, that is, so they won't be too nostalgic about the houses they grew up in. Four walls covered with signs and hieroglyphics, a roof with spiderwebs for ceiling, wall-hangings of the same material, a dirt floor the color of lead, and the whole thing smelling like a kitchen; a table that's more than lame, a wooden cot that squeaks and grumbles, and two rope chairs: those are the furnishings doled out to a poor provincial in Santiago, perhaps because he doesn't know enough to look for something better. If you add to these his piled-up trunks and saddle, the chitchat of the servant, and the trappings for the mule that are also stored inside to keep the dogs from ripping the leather and the straps, you'll have a thorough idea of the commodities laid out for the convenience of the guest, so he'll think he's set up like a king.

His first night in this dump. After entrusting to his pillow that vague feeling of sadness that comes over us when we've just arrived at a place where nothing belongs to us, where everything is unfamiliar, men as well as climate, objects, and customs, the provincial falls asleep as soundly as an angel. But as soon as he's asleep, he has a terrible nightmare: the hoodlums from El Conventillo are assaulting him, grabbing him, scratching his face and arms, poking him and skinning him alive; and he can't scream, or cry for help, or break free of that swarm of murderers. He's trapped in those anguishing fantasies for a long time; the battle against his aggressors is long and furious, until, finally, he manages to wake up and thinks he's being devoured by a horrible fever. He jumps out of bed, lights a lamp, and discovers that lies are always the children of reality. It's not the toughs from El Conventillo but the bugs in his bed that have been tormenting him.

It goes without saying that this early awakening of our friend gives him every good reason to stay awake the rest of the night. By the time God turns on his lights, the poor guy's already put away twelve cups of *mate* and at least twice that many cigarettes. This done, he shaves and gets ready to go out and have a look around, killing some time until a more reasonable hour arrives for doing whatever he plans to do.

Large, thick, bristly sideburns framing a chubby, sunburnt face; two long, sharply pointed collar-bands, folded horizontally, forming a pedestal on which the whole head rests; a velvet cravat; a showy vest that opens to reveal a bright-pink, ruffled, lace shirt; suspenders with shiny buttons and embroidered tips; trousers with ankle socks attached; high-heeled boots with taps; a jacket with wrinkled flounce whose cut shows that the tailor tried very hard to imitate the fashion that hit the provinces six months ago; a black felt hat, tipped pretentiously over the right ear, and enormous gloves apparently made for hands that were still growing—there you have the notion of elegant attire the provincial likes to assert, shortly after dawn, on the streets of Santiago.

Half-jokingly, half-seriously, they've repeated to him a number of times before he left home the following admonition: "Careful, friend; don't go standing around with your mouth wide open at all the wonderful things you'll see, or they'll take you for a hick." So, as he heads out for the streets of the capital, the thing he's most concerned about is his mouth, fearing that the slightest carelessness will give him away irremediably. Everything he sees amazes him, astonishes him; the crowds, the hustle and bustle, the pretty houses, the impressive buildings, the high towers, the spacious, tree-lined alamedas, the good-looking girls; in short, everything is new and surprising for our innocent abroad; but thinking it's proper and cool not to let on, he wears painted on his face and mien an expression of utter indifference, total seriousness, and all the officiousness of a judge of the primary court of claims.

In most of the provincial towns of the Republic, the sight of a new face is a festive event that excites and perturbs people in the same way the aristocracy of Santiago is excited and perturbed by the appearance in their drawing rooms of some actual or apocryphal count or marquis. Our provincial, then, remembering how new faces affect the people in his town, walks around under the misapprehension that his face is also quite noteworthy in the streets of the capital and that everyone who sees it will want to have the honor of meeting it and the pleasure of knowing where it came from. So when he comes face-to-face with you he'll stare at you to find out what you think of him; for the same reason, in order to impress you, he'll keep his features utterly frozen, studiously taking on the expression a person who's posing for a portrait assumes; so, hoping to win your approval, you'll see him nod and wear out his repertoire of polite phrases—"After you." "Thank you." "Please don't bother."—on everyone coming or going, who aren't paying the least bit of attention to him or bothering to reply, except to say "To hell with you."

But of course, he never defers to deadbeats. He always walks blocking their path, shoving them out into the street, and cursing them as *dogs* and *thieves,* until in one of these confrontations three or four will gang up on him, attack him, pull him down, call him *hick from Colchagua* or *asshole from Chillán,* and our friend ends up with his second lesson about the world, which he won't likely forget for the rest of his wanderings abroad.

On this day he'll walk down many streets, go up to many churches, and take in many famous sites he's heard the folks from his village talk about. He visits the building of the Company of Jesus,[5] which since there's no room to expand it laterally, the clergy are adding on to it heavenward the way you'd guide a climbing passionflower or forget-me-not vine that's been growing up your wall forever. He also stops in to see the old Customhouse and Moneda,[6] buildings that are apparently being restored in such a way as to provide an accurate reflection of our progress: the new adjusting to the old, the old propping up the new, so that all the moths get preserved and perpetuated just as if they received daily blessings from heaven. Everything is progress. Long live progress!

The next day the provincial goes to the National Institute,[7] where he has a first cousin for whom he's bringing a bit of cash and messages from all the relatives. The doorman tells him "Come in, go down that corridor, and ask for him there." He goes down the corridor, asks, and a student tells him that this cousin of his lives in the patio in back. He follows these new directions, gets involved in further inquiries, and another jewel of a guy directs him to an open door, and when the provincial enters, half-running now, he finds himself in a room with forty or fifty kids, and it's a class, who no sooner do they lay their eyes on that exotic figure but they burst out laughing. He leaves there with a fresh wind behind him, and there are still a couple of cruel characters who direct him to the dining room and the chapel. The upshot is that he doesn't find the cousin he's looking for until after they've sent him to all sorts of places, purely on whims, like the guy who finally gives up in a guessing game, or like the one they send this way and that and around and around in an Easter-egg hunt.

He takes his leave of his relative and the house, embracing the first and casting a cordial curse on all the others who live in the second. Once he's back on the street, he takes the one leading to the Plaza de la Independencia,[8] whose fountain, gates, palaces, cathedral, and post office have been highly recommended to him. But the devil's got him by the hand. Because he's looking along the way at the innumerable trinkets in a French jewelry shop, he doesn't see the melon rind some boys have placed carefully on the path; he steps into the trap; his body lurches, and the slide is as precipitous as the fall is heavy, as their taunting is brutal and orchestrated: "Those things happen." "He almost fell." Here, let me help you up."—and a thousand demoniacal laughs are the only echo of the terrific and provincial pratfall.

As the days go by, one comes along in which my beloved compadre is walking along a different street, as they say, without direction or purpose. He sees a man coming toward him; he thinks he recognizes him, and in fact it's don Pedro, the good fellow from Santiago who was in our friend's province last spring buying oxen; the same one whom they put up in his house, regaled, and treated like a city father, not because someone had recommended him, and not for money, but just because he was from out of town and seemed to be a good guy. What a lucky encounter! At last I've found a friend, says the provincial to himself. And overjoyed, with his hand and arms outstretched, and walking faster, he goes toward the welcome guest from his father's house. The guy from Santiago has also recognized the rustic; good breeding won't allow him to be grateful for favors received in the provinces, nor would it look good for a man such as he to be seen stopping to talk with *that* character. Considering all this, his excellency pretends he's looking back at something and brushes past the newly arrived provincial, ignoring the effusive "Señor Don Pedro!" that the latter shouts out in a state of near rapture. Such an unexpected put-down is a fecund and precious lesson for my friend. From that moment on, resentment sparks his mettle and fortifies him so that across his brow there's now visible a new air of dignity that wasn't there when he arrived from the provinces. "Scoundrel!" he says when the shock has passed, "someday you'll come back to buy more oxen!"

Such are the falls and blunders that befall a child of the provinces who comes to Santiago for the first time. Not a step he takes, not a word he pronounces, not an article of clothing he puts on, not a situation he gets into, fails to lead to his ruin, fails to provoke laughter and derision from all who happen to cross his path. For this reason, I'd advise the provincial that his first act, as soon as he finds himself in the capital, should be to put himself under rigorous quarantine, not making his grand entrance into the world until after he's gotten that accursed period of isolation out of the way, which may be long or short depending on the character and experience of the individual.

Because, finally, it's true that this period will come to an end. If the new arrival makes contact with one of the many excellent families of Santiago, they'll provide him with his first reforms: the girls of the house, who can't stand to see a good figure hidden by an ugly outfit, will take a personal interest in fixing him up so they'll be able to take his arm in public without the risk of people pointing their fingers at them. And availing themselves of the frankness inspired by the kind of social inferiority all neophytes experience, they'll offer him counsel. Day one: people don't wear embroidered shirts any longer; day two: that jacket is a fright, and the trousers and vest are abominably tailored; later on: you need to take your head and your sideburns to the barber; and bit by bit they'll bring about such a revolution in the student that, after a short while, he'll look like a totally different person, worthy of engaging in any activity or work alongside his amiable protectors. The first job he'll get, generally, will be as a substitute, an auxiliary worker, or someone to fill in. Subsequently, he'll either rise or not, undertaking employment based on his merits.

(*El Mercurio*, April 6, 1844)

The Renegade Provincial

A mong the many things that must be explained to be understood, I should include the title of this article. If you go strictly by the dictionary, it means the provincial who gives up his faith in Jesus Christ, but this is not my topic, because, thank God, one of the most lovely efforts we all make in this world is to persuade each other that we're keeping the faith. Whether anyone believes it is another matter.

The provincial who goes off to live in the capital, turning his back on his province, the province of his parents, where he was born and raised by them: that's what I meant to say by my title, whether I said it or not: that's the topic I'm dealing with now.

The child of the provinces who's in possession of old money accumulated in the traditional way, little by little, either by him or by his ancestors, hardly ever abandons the land where he was born. His relations and business interests are roots that definitively bind him to this soil, and these bonds become invincible because of the money inherited or created by his own effort. The trees in whose shade he played as a child, the nurseries he's planted, the animals he's domesticated, the tenants who have served him, the gratitude of all those who received favors from him, are satisfactions that if he ever should renounce them, it would only be in contradiction of the strongest and most pleasant affections. For this reason we see, in almost all provincial towns, one or more of those old and rich families whose names have never been transplanted beyond the region, even by their descendants.

Neither does the middle class produce renegade provincials. No one from that class is likely to be unhappy with his lot to any degree; no one looks for a life horizon other than the one he has; no one has excessive ambition, and they all maintain their mediocrity instinctively, unwilling to risk anything for the mere hope of bettering their lot in life. If there are any happy men on earth, look for them among the middle classes of society.

Members of the proletariat do not emigrate to the capital unless they're suffering from hunger or have committed some crime in their province. The vexations resulting from their enlistment in the civil guard, which in our towns is run with all the rigor of a case of martial law, obliges them to desert their town and lose themselves in Santiago, where they won't be pursued by the commanders, sergeants, and officers of the battalion or squadron whose ranks they enlisted in.

Those who get rich quick in the provinces almost always emigrate. The reasons obliging them to make this renunciation are well known and quite justifiable. First of all, they want to do whatever they please; second to buy a ranch, a house, a farm, an estate; third, they want to ride in a coach; fourth, to show off; fifth to hide their money from the depredations of the governor, subdelegates, and inspectors of their district, who, if they aren't their friends, will declare war unto death against them, demanding "contributions," and imposing fines and penalties on them for any yawn or belch they fail to stifle.

But of all these reasons, and the thousands of others justifying such desertion, there's one, perhaps the most powerful of all, that it seems the curious have failed to notice, except for me. As I see it, this is the secret of these emigrants.

The man who gets rich all of a sudden does so after having experienced over long years the misfortune of being poor. Fortune mocks man, generally coming to him with full hands when hard work and years have already mistreated him so much that the pleasures of life are about as tasty as cattails. During years of scarcity, the man who's now suddenly rich needed someone to help him with credit, another to arrange extensions for him, another to lend him money. The man who's now suddenly rich before being rich, had comrades, had companions in misfortune, had friends who shared their bread and their purse with him. His brothers never closed their doors to him, though they were as poor as he; a number of relatives helped him, if not with cash, then with good counsel; and he had many elderly aunts who often repeated to him the prophecy that God would someday hear their prayers and give him a treasure when he least expected it. Like all of us who've been poor, the man who's now suddenly rich, when he finally is rich, finds himself burdened with that immense debt of gratitude, beyond the cash he owes, which is so difficult to repay with money. So what happens when a man like this betters his fortune, finding the treasure he's pursued for years? A final accounting, an assembly of innumerable creditors, an unprotestable asking and collection for unpaid services. Those he owes cash to are at such times like sheep; the rest are inexorable. The friend wants some money; the usurous boss, more money; his old partner and friend wants his company; his relative, security for a loan; his brother a share in the deal; his pals, largesse and free meals; and the elderly aunts, snuff, a hairpiece, a wig. He gives them all what they want, they're all satisfied, no one has anything to complain about. But before long, one goes broke, the other loses all his money and earnings gambling, the brother goes under, the relative takes off with the loan unpaid; and then they start asking for more and crying on his shoulder again until they get what they want, without the newcomer to fortune seeing the end of anything but his fortune before this onslaught of furious begging. It is this conspiracy, I believe, that causes so many provincial capitalists to emigrate to Santiago.

I'm speaking here of those who legitimately and by honorable means acquire their wealth: as for those who suddenly show up as millionaires, telling the neighbor that they've neither inherited, nor found any buried treasure, nor miraculously received a treasure chest—these lose themselves in the capital like someone hiding in the woods, fleeing from evil tongues, from the slander of some and the envy of others.

What becomes of the rich provincial when he finds himself in his new home? The first ones to visit him are the doctors. No sooner do we get rich when the infallible law of compensation of human life dumps into our other saddlebag some illness, an incurable fistule or some other servant of fate. If the above-mentioned compensation doesn't come to us by accident as if it were some living entity, all it takes is a change of climate to turn the renegade's body into the favorite dwelling of all the colds and endemic and epidemic cases of indigestion, colic, and rheumatism either known or unknown beneath the Santiago sky.

As soon as he gets better, and I say better because he never manages to get well, he buys the hacienda, the house, the farm, and the estate. The first he rents out; the second he settles down in with his family; and it should be noted that no matter how magnificent the building is, so intense are the gloominess and silence reigning there that it seems more like a magnificent tomb than a house. In the Santiago dwelling of a provincial, you never see festive candles shining, you never hear the happy sound of an evening party. Anyone would say that when these people go to the capital, they retire from the world.

If the move has included family and all, the children get used to the schools right away, but the other members of the family fade and wither like those tropical shrubs newly transplanted in a place where the snows of both poles prevail. The wife is always sighing for the relatives she left behind, for her childhood friends, for the open cordiality of the relationships she had to give up. The new friends she's made in Santiago torture her with their insipid, ceremonious ways. Each visit she has to make is a steep hill she has to climb; each drawing room she has to enter is a hostile and rigorous examination she must undergo. In the social life of her province, she occupied the first rank; here, some secondary rank, and many times it would be better for her to have no rank at all.

Once he's settled, the deserter of his province takes up the business of banking and starts down the road of usury, a thing he understands frightfully well for those who accept his capital. To conclude one of those contracts with any of them, it's necessary for the agent or messenger to show up at the hour when digestion is under way, to return two or three times to learn the resolution of the matter, to offer a litany of guarantors, and finally to be present at the redaction of a notarized voucher whose innumerable clauses and imperatives constitute a maze similar to the tangle of ropes, cables, pulleys, and riggings flaunted by a ship with three masts. There's never been a case of a renegade moneylender losing a nickel over any failure of stipulation. This is the reason they are regarded as the final enemy, into whose arms the desperate fling themselves on the eve of hurling themselves down the deepest well of all.

These rich emigrés, though in their provinces and their poverty they may have been more liberal than a patriotic society, as soon as they establish themselves in Santiago they become more conservative than the Liberal who rises to become minister. The cabinet never fails to give them the only public office they're suited for: the military commander who wants to defend the terrain he's occupying surrounds himself with them the way he surrounds himself with immovable walls and impassable stockades. As men of state they are true brick and mortar.

Along with this commendation, they have the defect of being very ungrateful toward their own province, which if they think of it from time to time, it's with the same sense of shame they feel when they remember they were once poor.

When one of them leaves the capital to vacation in the town he renounced, let all the peasants get ready to hear the story of the honorable role he plays at court, of the distinguished men who flock to his *tertulia* every night, of his powerful influence, and of the extremes the administration, the legislature, the clergy, and the courts of justice go to to please him. If there's a fool in the room, he promises to make him governor as soon as he returns to Santiago; he promises another that he'll appoint him customs officer, or keeper of archives, or whatever office he chooses from among the vacancies or nonvacancies in the district: there's no moron anywhere whom he won't take under his wing. Does one of his friends tell him he just lost, through a perversion of justice, his lawsuit in the lower court and that he's planning to file an appeal the next day?

"Appeal with all confidence, appeal," he repeats to him, furious: "I'll teach that pissant judge how to make rulings. I'll write to Novoa,[1] to Vial del Río . . . ."[2]

"But, my dear Don Timoteo," the litigant interrupts him, "my case will go to the court of appeals, and those gentlemen are from a different court."

"It doesn't matter, I have jurisdiction over both of them, they listen to me. You'll see the reprimand that's coming to that judge. I'll skin him alive."

And in fact, through the influence of this provincial *crow*, the appeal is turned down, and the appellant was ordered to pay court costs.

Except for that, he's a guy you can get along with pleasurably. Because if you don't spend any time with him, or see him, or bump into him, or conduct any kind of business with him, or pay any attention to him, or expect anything of him, he's incapable of harming anyone or doing you the least damage.

(*El Copiapino*, April 25, 1845)

Gossips

They are a species of poet-people, whose Apollo is the devil. The devil inspires them, the devil has made them stand out among us: they're geniuses, they're nothing at all. If you come across one of them while you're out walking, make the sign of the cross and start running, as if you'd run into a spy just when the Conservatives, finding the water has risen up to their beards, have declared the country in crisis.

The gossip is an animal that's raised among us, just as ray-grass is raised with the wheat. Like the cat he comes rubbing up, then scratches us, like the mouse he digs holes in our house, like the moth he devours us, like the fly he buzzes in our ear, like the bedbug he keeps us awake at night, like the crow he pecks out our eyes, and like the donkey he gives us a mean kick, precisely when we've given him no reason to do so. Invisible in his maneuvering, he's the source of the goblin in old-wives' tales: from his hiding place he upsets and alarms an entire neighborhood with his stone-throwing; he fills a whole family with fear and anxiety.

He's a ventriloquist, who makes his own voice, his own lies, his own slanders, pour out of the mouth of your friend to persuade you that your friend is the one tearing you to pieces; next, he slips his voice inside you and poisons your friend.

He's an entire postal service, whose bag is always stuffed with contagious correspondence. With a single "My Dear Sir" that they pull out for you to read from what's inside, you've got pus in your soul. Pity the man who receives letters inspired by malicious gossip. If they concern some friend, you'll know he's betrayed you; if they're about your wife, she's deceived you; about your debtor, he's defaulting; about your sweetheart, she's sleeping around; if they concern an employee, he's robbing you; a Minister of State, his conduct is suspicious; if they mention the doctor, start writing your will; and if they come to you from heaven above, poor wretch, you'll learn that it's impossible to get there, because the demons have blocked every avenue. What the gossip brings you takes all your hope away: that's his instinct, his gift.

It's useless trying to escape him if he persuades his victim to listen to the first installment: in this he's like a venereal disease, which, once contracted, gets into the bones, and there's no medicine to get rid of it. And there's no mystery about this, because in most cases the gossip or gossips who turn their attention your way are your most intimate friend or friends, who are with you constantly, the ones who brush the loose hairs off your jacket, who know what you're thinking before you do, and who ultimately erode the trust people have in you. The gossip mesmerizes his target, as the fox his prey, as any demon our souls: this is why I said he's a genius, at villainy, of course.

If they ask you, which one's your gossip?, you should answer: "Not the friend I love most, but the friend who seems to love me most." No soothsayer could say truer.

But what are the distinguishing marks of the gossip? Nothing could be easier. Is there someone who tells you *in private* (this is the essential part) things that after you learn them you wish you hadn't, or things that profit you nothing to know but that bring harm to another? That's your gossip. Do they tell you in secret news that upsets you, spoils your peace of mind, and alarms you without providing the means to avert the harm, eliminate the risk, or flee the danger? Those are your gossips. Do they show up at your house looking upset, at an inconvenient hour, to tell you that so-and-so said terrible things about you? Gossips. Do they hurry you into the bedroom to warn you, *for your own good*, against trusting yon Juan, that skinny friend of yours? Do they keep you informed, for no apparent reason, of the vices and defects of your neighbor? Do they do you the great favor of informing you, as a friend, of the terms of such and such a deal, *so you won't be taken by surprise?* Do they try to get something from you by excoriating, under protest of impartiality, some friend? All of these are gossips, of the most devious sort.

Are you the head of a province? God help you. If you fall into the misfortune of falling into their good graces, your peaceful days are over; they'll eat you alive. If you reject and despise them, Man Overboard! The minister will immediately learn that you can't be trusted, that you're betraying him, that in your house everyone says terrible things about the administration, that you're hand in glove with the Liberals, and that those scoundrels are up to their old tricks. The minister, on whom gossip is never wasted, lets you know indirectly that he knows everything and that you need to change your ways, that is, appoint at least one gossip to a position of trust in your office. Because it's well known that nine out of ten town gossips are as conservative as donkeys, and as aspirants to some post in the administration, they constantly strut around the ministries.

Are you the head of a district? Well, every day you'll receive official rumors. Subdelegate number 67 tells you, *in fulfillment of his duty,* that in the house of neighbor Perejano (the subdelegate abhors him cordially because the poor guy is from Cuyo)[1] there have been a number of late-night disturbances, the covering up of robberies, drunken parties, illegal gambling, and other suspicious behavior, but that since it isn't possible to catch him in the act, he asks you for authorization to block all the doors and windows of that house, leaving only a single opening in the wall so that, having access through it and nowhere else, the comings and goings of this dangerous neighbor can be monitored.

The next subdelegate informs you officially, *to unburden his conscience,* that in his jurisdiction don Manuel and a certain Juanita (disdainful nymph, it happens, vis à vis the subdelegate) are having illicit relations, that the scandal is appalling and the neighbors' complaints constant: he asks for the power to prosecute, out of charity, of course, not envy, that lucky don Manuel and salvage him from the road to ruin.

The third subdelegate, who also has someone he wants to do in and who isn't all that pleased with a number of others because they don't tip their hats to him or kiss his feet, informs you that the whole precinct has fallen into a state of siege, that the thieves, drunks, and vagabonds constitute an invulnerable army of thugs subject only to the ineffectual local police, and that it's necessary to place the subdelegation under the rigorous jurisdiction of Chañarcillo; in other words, to declare martial law. All these cases, of course, consist of nothing but rumors. If you were to give in to the nonsense they're demanding, the subdelegates would spread the word in their jurisdictions that you were the one clamping down; they'd be the first to protest against your barbarous persecution of the people.

You're not in a position of power? I'm happy for you. That way it's less likely that these buzzing flies will make you their honey and get stuck in your hair. But rest assured, they'll find some way to be of service to you. Sooner or later they'll bite you.

There's no need to ask anyone in Copiapó if he's involved in a lawsuit, once the word gets out that he owns some property. There's bound to be a gossip running up to tell the judge that this or that part of the case is going to require his involvement; and he walks out of the judge's quarters to assure both sides that they're in danger of losing the lawsuit and that he knows it inside and out: he insinuates to both of them that the judge has told him this or that in confidence, or that he infers from something the judge said . . . and that he has a bad feeling about things. This is all it takes for the lawsuit to continue to be aired not so much between the litigants as between the judge and the litigants.

But someone's sure to say to me: "I'm immune to characters like that. I don't fight with anyone; I don't visit anyone; I go to bed early . . . ." You say you go to bed early? You don't have to say anything more. The neighborhood gossip says you've been out carousing at night, so no wonder your business is failing. If you get up very early the next morning, and leave your house for any reason, God spare you an encounter with the gossip. Right away he'll start joking around:

"Come on, admit it, you fell asleep at her house! . . . That's exactly what our neighbor told me . . . and me, so dumb!, defending you . . . ."

"But I just came out to bring in the milk!"

"Don't come to me with that milk nonsense . . . I know all about it . . . the whole town's talking about it. You've got one sharp-eyed neighbor . . . !"

It's no use trying to defend yourself. By twelve o'clock noon the whole town will know that you came out of such and such a house at dawn, or that they saw you jump over the wall and recognized you, even though you tried to lose them walking down the wrong streets.

If the gossip can't do his dirt personally, because he's worried about exposing himself, he'll post a lampoon in a public place to make sure his lies get a hearing. If they ban him from a house, he'll let a few days go by and then show up again there under any pretext at all. If they catch him in one of his intrigues, he'll grovel like a dog, ask forgiveness in the most demeaning way, thus calming the waters and coming out of it as cool as can be.

In short, gossips hate the printed word the way bats hate daylight, the devil hates the truth, and a number of hapless fellows hate, with all good reason, the *Copiapino*.

(*El Copiapino*, May 9, 1845)

The Liberal

There are two things you can brag about mercilessly without fear of offending God with a lie, or aggravating modesty by exposing yourself as a fool: the first is being honorable, the second is being *liberal*. It's understood that no one is going to deceive anyone about these two points. *Anyone who says he's more honorable than I, lies:* such is the challenge every son of a neighbor makes to everyone he meets. *Anyone who says he's more liberal than I, lies twice,* replies the administration to the opposition and the opposition to the administration at every run-in they have in the newspapers and gazettes. So honorableness and liberal ideas are like everything else we all have and which we enjoy without taking them from anyone else: the air, the wind, the vacuum, and other attributes common to the honorable and liberal human species.

With regard to honor, if we're pushed to speak about the amount we have in circulation, this is a touchy point: social propriety has declared this matter a mystery that should not be profaned, a *sancta sanctorum*, because if truth be told, the less said the better. It has, however, been clearly ascertained that we have honor in abundance, and always will have, thanks to the strict economy with which we use it.

Let's skip quickly over this topic, then, as if we were venturing down a road swarming with thieves or crossing a filthy and pestilential alley, and I will now address the notion of being liberal, sure that I won't fail to give due respect to anyone. Because it's my desire to let everyone, including ministers of state, be as liberal as they want.

Liberalism, if it is a virtue, is a virtue of our time; it is the vow arousing fervor in this century the way taking up the cross did during the crusades. In those days men swore to behead Turks, visit holy shrines, the holy land of miracles. Today the goals set by Liberals are not so Christian, it's true, but more humanitarian and socialist. We vow to attack the Conservatives, those grim-browed and renegade Turks who are in possession of a thousand precious relics, which, if we possessed them, would redound to the honor and glory of *progress*, which is the life everlasting we seek in the holy war we wage.

In those times, the Christian world was moved and excited when the popes or their emissaries preached a new crusade, however diabolically badly Christianity had fared in the previous campaign; these days, the Liberals are moved and excited when, in each electoral campaign, some

Bernard or *L'Ermite* shows them the banner of the cross of 1828,[1] on which the Conservatives were crucified only to be resuscitated shortly afterwards to rule over us until the end of time, apparently.

Liberalism is a virtue that we profess the way Franciscan monks profess the vows of mendicity and poverty, until such time as they attain a guardianship or a province to govern. It's a temporary vow we take, like the promises of those hypocritical churchmen who vow to dress in coarse sackcloth until they are cured of some ill. Generally, the ill we wish to cure by dressing as Liberals is the longing to serve the country in an appointed position and other conditions, which, because they are categorized as secret illnesses, we're ashamed to mention.

The Liberal and the office-holder are mutually exclusive, like the elements of an exclusive disjunction, an either/or with no middle ground. An administrative appointment kills liberal ideas as a fingernail a flea, a trap a mouse, a mortal sin a soul.

However, like the butterfly that flutters around the flame until it ignites and dies, Liberalism flutters and roosters around the job it wants until it falls into it and is consumed by it.

Employment is to the Liberal as matrimony to the Casanova: his reformation, his seat of judgment, his death. The past administration, and may God keep it so, thought it could silence Liberalism by jailing it, frightening it, and wringing its neck; impossible: the Liberals nearly ate it alive. The current one, with a better knowledge of the Liberal heart, which is no different from the human heart, as long as someone was there from the start to stand around admiring it and nourish it, in which case, case closed, Liberalism kaput: the Liberal slogans are put on hold while they live (employed of course) allied with men of sound judgment, free of any odor but the stench of employment.

It's true that our administration, no matter how conservative it may be, has not of late observed this rule except to apply it in certain cases. For lack of party hacks it resorted to the fresh wind of extraordinary appointees, who are capable of preserving order, along with the ministry, and even the devil in our midst.

Withal (a sad digression), the healing power of the conservative regime is unable to keep our great men alive, could not keep the eminent EGAÑA alive.[2] There are losses so truly grievous that at times we wish the truism so oft proclaimed by social egoism were false: *no one is indispensable.*

Back to the matter at hand. Liberal ideas are nothing like innate ideas that flit in and out of our heads as the times change, the way swallows migrate or return to our rooftops with the change of seasons. When there are no elections, there's no reason to go looking for liberal ideas; they're out on the ranches, in the mines, sleeping like humming-birds in winter, or maybe they're nowhere at all. But scarcely does the electoral sun start warming up, God save us!, when all the Liberal ideas and principles and goals come swarming over us from one district to the next in a hellishly noisy fermentation. Then each Liberal head is a garden in the breeze of beautiful and patriotic thoughts. Liberty in all its manifestations, the heroes of independence, democracy, progress, the blood of Chacabuco,[3] the masses of the people—the people who are victimized by the military police, the people who have no reason to wax nostalgic for the founders of ancient Rome, especially in regard to honor—the enlightenment and everything else that's grand, noble, and de rigueur for the prosperity of societies, everything, everything gets pounded into our craniums, and the devil has his way with us. Even the clergy and the holy-apostolic-Roman-Catholic Church get in on it, and Liberalism sits down with them for tea and crumpets despite the nagging concern that they're ultimately incorrigible.

The Liberal is rigorously orthodox: he adores some image, he idolizes some flesh and blood principle. A Liberal without a candidate is a contradiction in terms; it can't exist, just as a Portuguese can't exist without his Saint Anthony, a body without a soul, or a hypocrite without her spiritual advisor. It's also quite true that there are Liberals who regard themselves as candidates; but the main thing is that from the start we say, *I'm for so-and-so, I'm supporting what's-his-name, long live you-know-who.* This is what we call tipping our hats to a flag. Not uncommonly, the candidates of the Liberals are characters who were miraculous saints once upon a time, who suffered martyrdom under the administration in power ten years ago, but who are better suited to Plutarch's age than to ours.

It isn't absolutely necessary that a Liberal be poor: there are rich Liberals. But the poor man must necessarily be a Liberal, and this is what discredits us, this is why our party will never die, unfortunately. Does some merchant go broke? . . . he leaps into our arms. Does some employee get fired on suspicion that he's a crook? . . . he becomes a Liberal ipso facto. Do they strip the insignia and medals off the uniform of an officer because he's gone over the edge? . . . we'll welcome him into the fold as a frenetic Liberal. Is there a corrupt friar? . . . he appoints himself our chaplain on the spot. Do you have a son who's a good-for-nothing Casanova? . . . we've got ourselves a preacher for the rights of man. In short, our party is the rendezvous of all the hapless, a complete collection of every variety of human aberration.

Happily, in this latest electoral crisis, the majority of these types allied themselves with the men of order, which is why Societies of Order.[4] have sprung up all over.

The strength of the Liberal is the press: his pen wreaks devastation. Generally, he opens his campaign by developing his principles and theories in long, sempiternal articles, which aren't read by those who understand them, nor understood by those of us who see it as our obligation to pore over them. This all starts a year before the elections. After that the Liberal makes a direct assault on the arbitrariness of the administration and a personal attack on some particular minister, who is committing the atrocious tyranny of maintaining himself in power through underhanded maneuvers, exactly as the most liberal minister on earth would do, if there were any liberal ministers on earth.

A bitter polemic ensues with the writers from the administration over violations of the most basic laws, and over the undue influence that the authorities exercise in the elections. But up to here neither side can claim victory; both sides are right, both sides are on the side of reason; they know this because morning and afternoon fickle public opinion assures both of them that this is so.

This kind of uncertainty is unacceptable to the administration; it's necessary to remove Liberalism from the field and draw it into another fray that is more likely to lead to conviction and jail. To this effect any one of the champions of the administration takes up the pen and says in the most distinguished newspaper that *writer so-and-so, an anarchist by profession, is a thief, because on such and such a day he robbed in such and such a place this that and the other.*

So long, Liberal cause! With this new ploy our writer loses his focus and expends all his energy on the vindication of his name. The principles— liberty, the people, and the Catholic church—are pushed to one side to make room in the press for the biographies of the patriot of 1810[5] and, of course, the honest man.

This administrative diversion brings reprisals, and anything goes. They publish the lives and miracles of the government writers, the lives and miracles of the ministers, the vicious blasphemies against the tyranny of power. The administration loves to see all this in the press.

The license of the press is frightening.

"The Conservatives are afraid."

"The Society of Order is holding a meeting."

"The people are hooting."

The devil's got his foot in it, and when they least expect it the Liberal writers wake up in jail, whose doors in times like these are wide open, like those of the temple of Janus in times of war and insurrection.

Once the state of emergency is declared, it's time for the state of siege, and the Liberals go off for some fresh ocean breezes and to publish their manifestos abroad. These writings are of serious concern to our ministers.

Keep moving, keep moving, says fate to the wandering Jew. *Write, write,* says the Liberal cause to its champions. So every day our defeats are more horrific, thanks be to God.

(*El Copiapino,* July 8, 1846)

III

JOURNEYS
AND EPISODES

Items of Interest

What country doesn't have its curiosities? Go to the province of Concepción and you'll find the lost paradise, nature decked out in its most splendid attire, the creation during the first days of its virginal existence. In that garden of Chile you'll see the most beautiful and picturesque landscape, experience the sweetness of country living and the delightful solitude of those forests where the poet dreams a fantastic future of happiness. There you'll find the fields of Chillán and Roble, the heights of Quilo and Curapalihue, Talcahuano, Gavilán,[1] and a thousand other sites of glorious memories, soaked in the blood of our liberators, where the star of the military exploits of the Republic first began to shine.

Go to the north of the Itata river, and you'll be in another territory whose vast plains are gouged by two different systems of rivers running in opposite directions: the Perquilauquén, the Longavi, and the Achihuenu that drop down from the Andes; and the Purapel, the Tutuvén, and the Cauquenes that, having opposite sources, run toward the east until they merge with others that head north, emptying into the Maule.

Come to Talca. Talca has the most gorgeous little tower in Chile. They'll bring *pejerrey* to your table, that fish from Río Claro that is more delicious than anything you'll eat for the rest of your days. You'll get to know a community that's so enthusiastic about progress, so passionate in its desire to move forward, that it doesn't like to waste time learning and stays awake nights looking for something else to imitate. This is the town of women with pretty eyes. Nearby is Cancha Rayada, the site of three bloody battles, consecrated now to the growing of wheat, *chala* (the husks of maize used for fodder), and the raising of cattle.

To the north of Lontué extends our Cossack province, Colchagua, object of so much ridicule, and its capital the dilapidated San Fernando. Nothing noteworthy here but the huge sombreros of the farmers, the Teno Hills, and the Mountain of Mud Flats *(Monte de los Barriales)*, with its wild-animal caves that formerly served as dens for highwaymen. Are there men anywhere more filled with pride than those *hacienda* owners? Are there slaves anywhere more slavish and stupid than their *inquilinos*? But there's a charming spot in Colchagua, a delightful place, the

". . . lovely field
and pleasant olive grove . . . ."[2]

Wade across the Cachapoal; Rancagua's PLAZA OF THE HEROES OF 1814 greets you. Turn down any street and you'll see the name of some martyr of liberty: Campos Street, Cuevas Street, Gamero Street, State Street. The State was Rancagua's first martyr, but happier than the State, the others weren't resuscitated to suffer further martyrdoms later.[3]

Let's continue northward. The Capital, the Law Courts, the Congress, the Aristocracy, the *Mayorazgos*,[4] the army headquarters and general staff, the government employees, the hangers-on, the Canons, the Provincials of the Religious Orders, the Economists, the Literati, the Lawyers, the Monks, the Romantics, the *Pipiolos*, and an ocean of small-fry never taken into account except when a census is conducted, when someone wants to overthrow a government, or when electoral qualifications are being auctioned off.

Here's Aconcagua, the *refugium pecatorum*, the port of redemption for anyone shipwrecked crossing the Andes. When you enter that valley enriched by art and nature, the warriors of the River Plate throw the bloody lance and pluck the lute, sending up those melancholy threnodies in memory of the absent fatherland, songs whose grace and inimitable expression can only be found in that nation of troubadours.

La Serena, with its money exchange, high school, library, and printing press, is a lot like a widow whose rich haciendas have gradually fallen into ruin since the skillful administrator who once farmed them died.

Finally I reach my town, this beloved Copiapó that also has its curiosities of no little importance, which I now wish to publish in homage to its devotees.

There still exists, as if it had been recently constructed, the road down which the people of Peru traveled across the desert and the Andes to conquer the savage and nomadic tribes of our valleys. Tradition has preserved until today its name, Inca Highway. The stones forming it and tracing its path don't seem to have budged at all, and it's sure that for many centuries this Indian monument will remain intact, a colossal project of a spirited, brave, enterprising people, a people proud of their power and their origin, subsequently humbled, then mutilated and demeaned by the conquistadors, preachers, liberators, protectors, regenerators, collaborators, and restorers who have taken them under their wing in succeeding generations.

Walking a few leagues north of this valley, after crossing the mountains of Chanchoquín, you come upon the old Cachiyuyo gold mine and the ruins of a town, apparently quite large, surrounding the rubble of its chapel. But its famous bell tower is still standing and will continue to stand until the end of time, a monument formed of two enormous boulders that, when you strike them with smaller stones, produce a dull, lugubrious sound that can be heard two leagues in any direction.

In the *hacienda* of Ramadilla you can take refuge in summer beneath a shady carob tree of such obvious antiquity that you may be lying in the same spot where, more than three centuries earlier, the natives held their war councils and decided to behead the Spanish soldiers who had recently appeared among them with the suspicious intention of offering them their friendship. The weight of the wood from this tree has been estimated at a thousand pounds, its shade can cover an entire battalion, and despite its ancientness it's still as fresh and green as the young oak tree grazing its branches across the currents of the Maule or the Bío Bío.

Take a walk to the port of Copiapó, on a day in August, and there you'll see them selling in a single place grape juice from Penco,[5] brandy from Pisco, corn liquor from Valdivia and nougats from Cuyo, raisins from Huasco and the fruit of the *lúcumo* tree from Coquimbo, potatoes from Chiloé and dates from Guayaquil, cheeses from Chanco and coconuts from Panama, oranges from Quillota and pineapples and chirimoyas from Ecuador, chickens and turkeys from Valparaíso, and dried eels from Paposo, sweet potatoes and plaintains from down the coast and onions and gourds from up the coast. You'll see a town managing to survive even though they pay half as much for salty water as people in Santiago pay for corn liquor, where a hen costs eight *reales,* a pullet four, and a ton of firewood six or eight; where the innkeepers will charge you a fee even for the air you breathe each minute.

In Copiapó a famous Argentine poet wrote the greater part of his fables and poetry, which were published in two volumes and are now circulating throughout the literary world.[6] Although another country gets the credit because of the nationality of this poet, Copiapó will always claim the glory of providing the beautiful sky beneath which he wrote some of the most brilliant images gracing Argentine literature—a literature as blessed by the inspiration of patriotism as it is precocious and susceptible to proclaiming its intellectual emancipation, freeing it to take genial flight.

But among these and other curiosities of my land, none is more important than the existence of a little town[7] in which more than a thousand men live out their lives without the burden of the cross, I mean, without women. Thanks be to God, we've resolved the problem: a person really can live without these amiable storms, without feeling the bitter enchantment of their gaze, proof enough that the gaze of the basilisk is not entirely mythical, without seeing their voluptuous figures, without the soul becoming corrupted on beholding them, without loving, finally, which is the true and supreme happiness.

My countrymen, then, utterly convinced that, in general terms, there's no good woman under the sun, since it is they who corrupt us poor men who, if we steal, drink, and fall in love, it's because of the above-mentioned women, who oblige them to steal, drink, and of course fall in love; completely satisfied that single males behave better than fathers of families, and considering the feminine sex guilty of being the cause of the disorders in our rich mines, the owners got the police to cleanse them of women, and in fact, so it came about, for the honor and glory of God, as I could easily demonstrate. After all the goodbyes and farewell hugs had been exchanged between the wives or mistresses who were leaving town and the innocent oresmugglers who were remaining, things changed. Ore was no longer stolen as it had been in the past, but rather as it is in the present, which is more than yesterday and less than tomorrow. They no longer steal ore to give to a pretty young woman, but to buy brandy from the smugglers or to silence the treacherous subforeman with bribes. If a mine is rich, its owner has to maintain on the work-site a detachment of armed guards to scare off the thieves swarming through the mine like birds through a grape arbor someone forgot to harvest. Everything was remedied by banishing the women from Chañarcillo and declaring them contraband, *personae non gratae*. Moreover, what we have now is a real social portent: men sweeping, men doing laundry, men boiling stew, men making beds, men frying *empanadas*, men dancing with men, men singing the *extranjera*, and men doing everything that needs to be done: it's a colony of fairies, a body without a soul, a monster repugnant to look at, and certainly not the object of least interest in our Chile.

(*El Semanario*, September 8, 1842)

Letter (Visit to the Maipo Canyon)

Maipo, April 23, 1841

My Dear Manuel:[1]

I'm back now, and I can assure you that I'm up to my eyebrows in mountains, as they say.

On the tenth of this month I left here with all the excitement we feel when we set out on a journey hoping to see new things and visit places we know nothing about except their names. As soon as I entered Maipo canyon my curiosity began to be satisfied. The sluice of the canal named after the canyon,[2] the obstacles overcome at its source; the considerable torrent of water it contains before dividing into its many branches, and the tiny settlement made up by those in charge of maintaining and repairing this important project, are at the outset worthy of being visited, worthy of a stopover to examine them in detail. To this point the road from the capital is magnificent; and, given this advantage, the sluice of the canal would make an interesting and entertaining hike for anyone fond of going out into the country during one of our beautiful springtimes or taking an early morning stroll in summer. Although the enchantment of the landscape continues to increase as we move inward, with the imposing spectacle of a nature vast in its elements and in the variety of its vistas, the difficulties of the road are considerable, at least for those accustomed to enjoying a leisurely outing and riding on horseback through familiar fields they visit on a regular basis. If it weren't for that, I would recommend to you the little town of San José and points between here and there as the best in the vicinity of Santiago, good places to amuse yourself and take your leisure without the discomforts of Colina, or the dangers and dust of Renca, or the mystical sadness of Apoquindo, and with all the attractions we seek out madly in those first two Babels especially. The craggy ridges through which the crashing Maipo has ground its path; the forests greening and enhancing the beauty of the gorges opening up parallel to each other in infinite succession; the abundance of delicious fruits, the fecundity of the cultivated soil; the abundant, crystalline waters from countless arroyos; the many huts scattered along our way, and the freshness and beauty of the girls who live in them, a leisurely hike through this landscape almost unknown to the inhabitants of Santiago wouldn't be a waste of time. San José, in particular, offers all a family could want for spending a short summer vacation happily and comfortably, if what they're looking for is delightful temperature, excellent spas, and pure air in a natural setting that is noble, picturesque, and bright, with affectionate neighbors whose simple customs know nothing of corsets, ties, and other such torture devices imposed by etiquette.

Farther on, that is, farther toward the mountains, I must confess that in my opinion the country holds little of interest except to those who make the study of nature their profession, or those who for reasons of sentiment or for the quality of their souls take pleasure in contemplating the most imposing, the grandest spectacle proffered by this immense machine on which we're moving through space.

About twenty-five leagues from Santiago, leaving behind the little settlement of San Gabriel, the landscape begins to change and become denuded of all vegetation, offering only crags, enormous boulders, abysses, precipices, torrential rivers, and whatever else cannot be witnessed without experiencing an involuntary shiver and an alarming melancholy. There, there's no gentle silence of the forest to soothe us, filling our drowsing imagination with a thousand pleasant illusions that make us remember past joys that seem poised to pleasure us again, or to paint for us as if it were present the faraway glow of hope, nothing to intoxicate our soul sweetly and soothe the ardor of the passions ruling it. The heart fills with sadness, but it's the sadness of the misanthrope, which causes him to indict mankind, bringing back to his memory the persecutions of ingratitude, the sorrows in which calumny and vengefulness have sunken him; that species of sadness that obliges us to reject all movement toward reconciliation with our enemies, or with happiness itself, if it means we have to give up our hatreds.

Manuel, don't be thinking I'm painting what I felt as I passed through those bleak vastnesses; you know very well that the few friends I have don't make me miss any less those I've lost and those I'll lose in the future since it will become harder to hold on to them. But when I found myself in the midst of those deeply wild places I started wondering what some fugitive from over the Andes would feel after fleeing the butchers from his own homeland and thinking himself safe on our soil, as he stopped for the first time to reflect on his fortune and that of his family and friends (those he hadn't seen trudging up the scaffold) and what they might be undergoing at that instant, and about the irremediable misfortunes of the country of his birth. I imagined that the echo chambers of those horrendous solitudes must have echoed again and again the curses of those unfortunate fugitives, their horrible oaths of vengeance, and the passionate expression of their rage and despair. The memory of a wife abandoned or a loved one exposed to the brutality of those barbarians would never bring tears to his eyes in that place. The abysses and crags surrounding the traveler in those places strip all feelings of tenderness from his heart.

After two-and-a-half days of hiking, we arrived at the slopes of the largest mountain, at the point called Volcán, because it's the base of a high peak at the top of which there's a volcano named San José. It was even at the time in a stage of modest eruption, and from below we could make out the small puffs of smoke that emerged from its crater approximately a minute apart. This was on the 13th at noon. The air seemed perfectly calm, not a single cloud in sight, and we felt quite warm even though we were standing in snow. We saw some cows grazing in a meadow even higher than where we were, and in order to see them better, in case some of ours were among them, we began to climb the peak, seeking the most accessible spot to look down on the place where we had seen them, not being able to get to where they were due to the ruggedness of the terrain.

From there we began to shout almost in unison to get the cows to come down through the break, but one of the seasoned vaqueros who was with us quickly cautioned us: "Don't shout, you'll make the volcano mad," advice that at the time I felt needed some explanation, though shortly afterward I saw the gaucho's fears realized. Before five minutes had passed the calm in which we found ourselves turned into a gusting wind that raised whirlpools of dust on all sides and whose chill became more and more unendurable. Volcán peak was covered with a thick mist more than halfway down, and very soon we had to vacate those rocky slopes, fleeing the sudden squall beating down on us. I don't have to tell you that I can't explain this truly astonishing phenomenon, though I've seen it and observed it with great curiosity since I first noticed it.

There's not much vegetation up on those mountains, that is, no forests or even any bushes, but as soon as the snow disappears with the summer heat, they're covered with abundant grass and can then pasture animals until the cold season starts to return. The passes and small tablelands form so many pastures that they've been given different names; almost all of them are so naturally enclosed that communication from one to another is very difficult, and perhaps even the cows' instinct, so well developed for finding gaps in fences, is insufficient for locating them in these places. I've seen pastures with more green grass in April than the most fertile plains in springtime, and the cows grow as fat in them as they do in the famous pastures around Santiago.

There are also silver and copper mines still in operation, although I can't tell you if they're producing or just running on hope. Among the owners, there's one man who seems to be tied to bad luck and who, since forever, has been the target of misfortune's arrows. His hair has turned white from failed speculations, followed by the death of his children, the playing out of his mines, the burning of his houses, the imprisonment of his surviving children for political reasons. Welcome, misfortune, if you come alone! A man capable of surviving so many blows, is he not as impressive and respectable as the massive granite outcrops in the mountains I've traveled over? Is he not the proper barometer for measuring the misfortune of those who weep and wail when they stub their toe in life's race?

I've seen, finally, my dear Manuel, what I only wanted to see because I hadn't seen it, and which I'd like you to see now, because it deserves to be seen. Sky-high cascades; hills carved away by the constant grinding of water for who knows how many centuries; the immense Maipo, which fertilizes so many lands and spreads so far and so wide, squeezing between two crags that barely leave it a space so narrow it has to leap to get past; rivers born suddenly at the foot of a mountain, then disappearing into the abysses covering the base of another mountain; entire hills broken loose and thrown down by impulses of some power superior even to the calculations of man's imagination; and all of this in a vista so vast our sight can scarcely embrace it. Accustomed to knowing nature only in its ordinary functions, if they can be called that, of producing, resting, then producing again; of seeing only forests, plains, gentle rivers, hills scarcely rising above the ground, where a monotonous and unchanging order can be discerned, we are staggered on seeing ourselves surrounded by all the imposing majesty of creation, in a theater that nature seems to have wanted to adorn with its own ruination, displaying surprising proofs of the immeasurable power it can squander in wrenching forth revolutions and upheavals.

On leaving these sites behind, what lofty and noble ideas we carry with us! How wretched and puny we find everything we return to! I feel a deep incapacity for expressing to you, as I would like to, what I've felt, what I've thrilled to, and what my soul said to me during those moments in which, with such pleasure, I began to question it up there.

(*El Mercurio*, May 16, 1841)

A Little Journey by Sea

It wasn't that long ago that taking a journey was the same as readying yourself for sacrifice and facing imminent dangers courageously. Ten days walking or sailing was an entire career finished, constituted an epoch, an epoch fecund with memories to last the rest of your life. Around winter fireplaces, people would listen in astonishment to what someone would tell them they'd seen in Negro Ravine, on the way to Santiago, or coursing through the waves in the English ship that brought him to Valparaíso. Ah, to have sailed on an English ship was only for certain daring souls who would be secretly stigmatized by the common folk as not comporting themselves in strict conformance with the holy fear of God and the beliefs of the Church.

Long before the departure you could already hear the sighs of imminent absence. The eyes of the mother, the sister, or the wife would fill with tears whenever they met the eyes of the one who was going off to be among strangers, experience romantic encounters, and see other lands. To distract them, the traveler would try to feign happiness and calm their fears about the risks to come, and as he got his weapons and luggage ready he'd promise to bring them a thousand things on his return, though there was always a cautionary "If God brings me back healthy" as an express condition of his plans and goals.

The hour of departure could without exaggeration be called the hour of despair. The son would receive kneeling the blessing of his parents, a patriarchal ceremony that the poor boy would not be able to remember without sighs and tears for a long time. The husband, his courage abandoning him then, would sob louder than his wife; the children would hang onto his neck; the servants would become undone weeping; the entire neighborhood would show up to share in the tender and sorrowful goodbyes; and even the watchdog would howl in despair over not being able to break his leash and follow his master, whom he could see mounting his horse and riding off. The family would be praying fervently and continuously for the life and health of the traveler: the mother of God would listen for hours at a time to the Salve Regina, Our Hope imploring her to watch over that young man who, far from home, would surely be surrounded by all of life's dangers and all of death's menaces.

Nowadays, what a difference! A voyage is a stroll, a recreation, a *tertulia*. Everyone travels: this fellow on business, that one for pleasure, others so as not to waste their lives in a single place, many for cures, and hordes of others because they were born in Peru, Bolivia, or Argentina. There's hardly any business deal that doesn't require skipping around from town to town and from market to market, shipping aboard steamships and winging across country in carriages and horses. In a two-week period one departs and returns to his country after having covered hundreds of miles, visited dozens of cities, and made countless conquests, after having, in remote places, liquidated and canceled accounts, made sales and purchases that, if they don't increase the fortune of the individual, put him on the road to bankruptcy. Today a voyage is such an inconsequential thing that you can file an appeal in Copiapó, set sail for Valparaíso, stop off in Santiago, set the case in motion by hiring the pint-sized lawyer most in vogue, send off a couple of *mercuriazos*[1] to the presiding judge, sell a shipment of ore, and be back at the point of departure before they can accuse you of the least delinquency in the other lawsuits pending against you.

It's true that steamships have involved us in a state of hyperactivity as sudden as it is noisy. It's customary to go out to meet them when they dock at our ports and a cause of shame to have to confess that we've never taken a short trip on one. Marriage contracts have been drawn up with the stipulation that the bride would immediately be entitled to make a trip by steamship to Valparaíso.

As the days draw near for the arrival of these ships, coming from Peru, it's amazing to see the state of excitement that envelops us. Friends and whole families place orders for one port or another, offices certify shipments, businessmen would make a pact with the devil for an order of payment against don Diego Duncan,[2] collecting without consideration and paying without mercy; the litigants solicit liens against property, silver marks pass from hand to hand like the key in the entertaining game called Piña; open carriages tear off in all directions; mule-drivers lift luggage, smelters pollute the streets and rooms with their foul-smelling, poisonous fumes, the police do nothing to stop the emissions, because they look at everything with the philosophical eye of the inseparable companion of Sancho Panza; the girls send by the departing friend potatoes and flower seeds, each one, finally, entrusting him with mail and items to pack in his chest for so-and-so, and whether he wants to or not he has to become postman and smuggler so his friends can save a couple of *reals.*

This was the scene in my town only a few days ago; and one day I awakened with the whim to take a little trip by sea. Without stopping to think about it I packed my suitcase, requested a passport from the police, who issued it to me in the friendliest of manners like someone who sees an unwelcome guest putting on his hat to leave, and not expecting any further obstacles to my departure than one or two broken or fallen bridges, I left Copiapó by way of the barrio of Chimba at an hour when those living there were restoring through sleep the energy they'd used up dancing the *resbalosa,*[3] almost epidemic now.

Before the burning rays of the sun could bear down on me, the cool ocean breezes began to whistle sweetly in my ears. The port came into view shortly afterwards with four little boats, each one sporting on its stern the fluttering tricolor flag of good omen, and further out an enormous Swedish frigate with a yellow flag unfurled its sails, determined not to furl them again until they reached the far, stormy coast of Norway. A ship weighing anchor in a bay and heading out into the immensity of the ocean, that's what a man is when he's born into the world, being engulfed in life's storms, steering close to the wind, then tacking, then plying windward, always menaced by reefs and rocks, always driven and beaten by his own passions or someone else's, and sooner or later rounding the Cape of the Sepulcher. What will he find on the other side of those mysterious narrows? The Maker's hand placed thick, dark fog in that spot, a darkness penetrated perhaps by the imagination of certain privileged men who at last discern the paradise shrouded there and hold the torch close to the image of Santa Barbara so they can fly to the mansion of peace they glimpsed in their dreams. Larra, illustrious Spaniard! A harebrained writer from my country, whose works and *zamoraidas*[4] are as noisy as the jingling bells of a comic actor on a public stage, has distorted your latest thought, turning it into a dirty joke. However, he only offends your memory in Chile. I respect your dying days as the brilliancies of the divine genius who inspired them, and I believe the radiant spark bequeathed to human beings by the Light of heaven at your birth has not been annihilated.

My readers, if I have any, will forgive me for this digression and for any others I make on my journey.

A few hours after my arrival at the port, a floating structure made its appearance in the distance, belching a plume of dirty brown smoke, like a volcanic island recently smothered by the waves. It was the *Peru*, one of the two tireless agitators of our coastline, and to which that coastline owes almost all the animation and life displayed here in recent years. In an earlier letter, I had the occasion to sketch the excitement and confusion produced in our small ports by the visit of one of these ships. The moment of embarkation never approaches without the heart beating more violently: it's a novelty one cannot enjoy without experiencing a certain embarrassment, a certain conflict of impressions and feelings that take control of the soul moment by moment.

When the steamship cast anchor, we on shore had everything ready for boarding. Two hours later the sailors weighed anchor, singing farewell to the land in songs as monotonous and sad as the plaintive cries of birds announcing a storm. The shore began to flee from us, that shore on whose steep cliffs our friends were waving their handkerchiefs in the air, knowing they could be seen from the deck of the brigantine cutting sailless through the wind and the waves with the violence of a chariot pulled by enraged horses.

Seasickness quickly began to drown the slight sadness the recently embarked experience following any leavetaking. Faces that only moments before had been beaming with the flush of life gradually took on a deathly pallor. Huddled astern, they no longer cast toward the receding land gazes filled with poetic melancholy; their half-closed eyes seem not to stare intently at anything around them but glaze over with a moribund indifference. Meanwhile the ship is lifted seaward on the waves, and when it drops back down with all the force of gravity, those who are seasick feel as if they were suspended by their hair, their stomachs rise, and one or two throw up into the water in violent convulsions, like a ship lightening its load during a storm.

Night falls, and the bridge of the steamship is almost deserted. Here and there a couple of friends are still walking in the fresh air, but they're English, and their bursts of speech come to my ears sounding indistinguishable from the noise of the machinery dragging us over the surface of the ocean.

Two Frenchmen have also remained on deck, waving their arms up and down to the rhythm of the brigantine, and while one debates the question of the regency, the other curses *l'abominable Bordeaux* served with the meal that has ruined his stomach.

In a comfortable and gaily lighted drawing room tea is now being served, a tea whose harshness could not be neutralized by all the sugar attributed to the first kiss of love by the most ardent poet. This is where people gather to spend the night playing a lively game of chance, or a dull game of chess, reading newspapers, having a few drinks, talking of their hopes for the Almendral,[5] their memories of Lima. So the room looks a lot like a crowded café, with the difference that on board there's no thick cloud of tobacco smoke, but there is a certain odor of gas from the coal that more than makes up for it. The low hum of the *tertulia* is interrupted only by the violent vomiting you hear from time to time from the cabins, but the anguished cries that precede or follow this sound make no more impression on their traveling companions than the complaints heard in an infirmary make on the soul of an apothecary, or the hysterics of a woman on the soul of her heartless husband, who sees nothing but manipulation in this excess of sentiment.

The absence of a single letter-writing papist among the polemics and scandals of our press would be more conceivable than the absence of an exiled American on board the steamship. Not long ago they said the *Chile* had sailed by here carrying a hundred thousand Peruvians from Cuzco who had boarded in Callao bound for Valparaíso on a search warrant for one of the insatiable patriots of that Republic. When I took my cruise several Bolivians were bound for exile, whose physiognomy reflected the interesting humility of the slaves of the ancient Incas rather than the republican arrogance of the sons of the great Bolívar. There exists among the individuals of this nation such an air of family that it seems as though they must all be very closely related.

At eleven at night there were only two Germans left in the room, finishing a game of chess, but since one of them had fallen asleep while the other prepared to launch his decisive assault with typical national phlegm, the hostilities were suspended, both muttering a few unpleasantries and perhaps good night. Then, wrapped in my cloak, I lay down on one of the sofas toward the stern, not wanting to box myself into one of those beds and have to breathe the bilious atmosphere of the tiny cabins. Sleep cut short my meditations, and my sleep was in turn violently cut short at three in the morning by the blast of a cannon fired by the steamship on dropping anchor in the port of Huasco.

My sailing trip was coming to an end. Farewell, pretty ship, I said as I climbed down its ladder; may the waters of the Pacific always be as friendly to you as the arms waiting on shore today for *Jotabeche!*

(*El Mercurio*, March 13, 1843)

Excerpts from My Diary

Speaking on behalf of my species, there's no locomotive machine like man. I say this on my own account, because with only a few ounces of impulsion I've run, for many days, step for step with another machine moved by the force of a hundred or more horses, including its captain and subjects.

Back in the village of San Francisco de la Selva[1] now, and recovered from my wounds or tribulations after a pleasant dream, which is all my journey amounted to, I publish the following excerpts from my diary, a work that of course I want to dedicate to anyone willing to waste his time on such insignificant reading matter. Here's another compliment in the same spirit: *my regards to anyone who asks about me.*

July 4

Precious view . . . ! On rounding the point of Teatinos we come upon the bay of Coquimbo in all its vast extension, its circular beach, the expanses of cattails looking like fields of wheat from a distance, and the hills and heights serving as background to this lovely landscape. We can see La Serena nestled there against the hills. Just then, the last rays of the setting sun were glancing off the towers and façades, highlighting their dazzling whiteness against the shadows cast by groves of *lúcumo*, orange, and chirimoya trees. Wisps of smoke rising in delicate columns in the calm of the afternoon seemed scattered across the fields to bring to life the enchanted scene laid out before us.

We left the arid coastline of Copiapó and Huasco, the small, bare islands of Choros, Chañaral, and Pájaros; we had sailed past that region of Chile where you're more likely to discover a rich vein of silver than a flower or a drop of water, and now the hills and plains coming into view were lush and verdant; fields as green as that always amaze one sailing toward the coast, especially if he's come there as I have from another coast where man is the only thing vegetating in all of nature. If it were true that liberty is a tree, you would despair of ever seeing it sprout and scatter its seeds beneath the sky of my country . . . . But no, liberty isn't a tree; liberty, if that word has any meaning at all, is a mine like any other, always playing out for everyone, temporarily bringing riches to a few, though even they have to share what's extracted with a swarm of workers smuggling out whatever they can.

The sight of such a picturesque coast, if it provided a pleasant diversion to all the other passengers, sent me into one of those fits of ecstasy whose delightful melancholy would be worth its weight in silver to the poets of this epoch. The pretty city we saw there is the homeland of my earliest years, the land of the friends and protectors of my childhood: there I turned fifteen, a year spent building festive memories for the rest of my life: a time of life a man comes to with no other ambition than winning awards in school, with no other love than that of his parents, not yet having aroused the ire of a woman, loved by all and hating no one. A thousand times happy he who hates no one! Why should he; no one's slandered him yet, or ridiculed him, or broken his head, or done him any harm at all, which is all the happiness possible in this world of sinners.

These old ties to La Serena made me desire passionately to walk its streets again, and in fact, knowing that the steamship wouldn't set out again until midnight, several friends and I decided to go ashore. On disembarking we saw the wharf crowded with young women, but we were prevented from looking them over by the boatman collecting his fee for bringing us ashore, another offering us a good coach to get us to town, and a passel of others importuning us simultaneously — "I'll hook up those horses for you." "Fine horses!" "Take it slow." "Give this one his rein." "A gallop like a rocking chair." — all of them touting the fine qualities of what they were offering with such an air of sincerity and gentility that I thought I must be dealing with a dentist, a hairdresser, a horticulturist, or even a French dressmaker offering the latest Parisian designs.

A few minutes later, four of us were bouncing helter-skelter along the shore in a silver-smooth stagecoach on the way to the city; two of my companions murdering the well-known song "Tossed from remote climes" (it should be said that murder is an attribute peculiar to all our national music) while I pointed out to the fourth the progress that had been made in coach travel in the capital of my province. Fifteen years ago, more or less, when an open carriage dashed down the streets of La Serena, all the neighbors came to the door to admire it. In those days you never saw anything on wheels except for the wheelbarrow of D. Manuel the Englishman[2] and the enormous, four-seat calash driven by the town bigshot. Nowadays, four stagecoaches run nonstop between this town and its port. However, let's say it right now: there hasn't been any progress in the north, where it's regarded just as civilized and toney to break your leg when the coach overturns as when you fall off a bucking horse.

It was already well into the night when we entered the main square of La Serena, a truly dark and empty plaza covered by the rubble of the original old church and the materials for constructing, God willing, the new cathedral.[3]

From there I set out walking, guided by my memories, which I can tell you were growing more and more fermented by the minute. Here's a house I don't recognize, further on there's a homeowner who doesn't recognize me, though I embrace him like a madman. This street seems new to me; I turn down it and after a few steps find myself fooled by my memory; I ask in a store about the family that used to live nearby, and the shopkeeper turns out to be a friend, a schoolmate who welcomes me. I keep walking; there's a church in front of me; it's San Agustín!, with the marketplace right beside it; I had no trouble recognizing it; it's in the same state of partial construction I left it in fourteen years ago, not an adobe brick added, not a stain removed. What remarkable stability! It's just like the pantheon in Copiapó, just like a governor in Maule Province.

Then I headed toward the high school I'd attended, and for a long while I wandered among the willows now growing in front of it. I felt my soul stir joyously, mysteriously, as I imagined those days had returned when the whole world is our plaything, quite the opposite of now when we are the plaything of everything around us. May God bless you, building so sacred to me, as he blesses the cradle of the just, as he blesses the temples where we worship his name!

Many years have passed without my memory erasing that time of my life when I ran through the streets of this beloved town, caught up in such beautiful feelings. How much more valuable a single hour of that existence than the half a lifetime I've endured and overcome since then!

At eleven at night I rejoined my companions at the agreed spot, and we set out for the port again, after having just one last drink for the ditch and then several more in the house of a friend whose obsequious hospitality has become famous in the towns where he's lived.

Adios, Serena. I never got a good look at your pretty girls, and I'm glad. Pretty girls are like missteps, tripping up everyone in the race they're running.

July 6

At dawn, the hills of Valparaíso directly ahead! The chill on deck was unbearable, but who could tear their eyes away from the beautiful view about to unfold before our eyes in scene after glorious scene!

There's the lighthouse: the light from the lighthouse is the only light a brave sailor seems to appreciate. Not even the light of the sun matters a whit to him, because his entire wellbeing depends on not seeing the sun.

The telegraph office; the cliffs above the port and their windmills, the winding roads that go to Santiago and Quillota: a forest of masts, and amid all this confusion, all the bright, proud flags of the earth; ships spreading their sails to head out to sea like birds taking flight; the barrios of Arrayán with their houses as close together as the numbers on a logarithm table; all those ravines and canyons where man has stuck his dwellings the way shellfish planted their conches in past millennia when these heights were covered by the sea; the elegant little towers that crown the Planchada and the Almendral or some other section, huge new objects gradually coming into view as we approach by sea this dazzling city that time must mean to symbolize by the white star on our flag.

Our entrance into Valparaíso was like a festival to me. While we stood on board absorbed in watching the most glorious vista that had ever unfolded before my eyes, the steamship was drifting into the waters of the port, where at eight-thirty in the morning we came aground without any problems, as everyone knows, except that Captain Holloway can't explain why, so contrary to custom and in peacetime to boot, he tried to bring the ship aboard the forecastle of the *San Antonio*, God forgive him and also spare the inoffensive Pacific Ocean from captains such as he, who inflict more dents and scrapes on these poor steamships in three years than the basic law of the land suffers reinterpretations in ten.

But the fact is the steamships always manage to survive, the law of the land suffers these interpretations without complaint as if it were on salary, and I came aground in Valparaíso, though it was mud, not ground, a condition I attributed naturally enough to recent rains and not to the authorities, as certain solemn journalists try to prove each winter.

Let's move ahead. But who the devil can move ahead in this Valparaíso? Where can you go without running into obstacles? Where does a poor provincial go who's used to walking down the streets of his town without the risk of being crushed under a load of freight, without having to stand aside for some cart, without some gringo giving him a shove this way, a second gringo pushing him that way, a third elbowing him, a fourth knocking him down, and a fifth and a sixth trampling him underfoot?— a "Careful, sir!" here, a "Careful, sir!" there, another "Careful, sir!" in front of him, a "Step aside!" in back of him, and they assist you with a shove; "Get out of the way!" and before long they've knocked off your hat, which rolls down another street where the hooves of a horse or the wheel of a public carriage happen to run over it. There's no time for anyone to be courteous; everyone wants to keep moving, everyone is running, rushing, muttering; no one's standing still, no one thinks of anyone else, but only of himself and the business he's about, flying to the post office or the customhouse to deliver papers or pick up papers, or to the police station, to the dock, to board a ship, to the money exchange, or just rushing about for no reason. And the center of this anthill, the focus of this mindless activity is a tiny plaza, perhaps the only place in all of Valparaíso where a newly arrived traveler can stop among the bundles, boxes, sixty-gallon casks, and luggage stacked everywhere.

There's nothing to do here if you aren't buying or selling; in order to have dealings with human beings you have to sign a contract. If you want to walk along the streets, woe unto anyone who uses his eyes for anything except looking where he's going, or at whatever is coming his way. There's no way to accompany anyone or for anyone to accompany you: the only thing in Valparaíso that doesn't travel alone is the air you breathe, which is always laden with the social smell of tar and the breath and body odor of others. The smell of tar pursues your nostrils everywhere, the way the night watchman pursues the poor, the way the poor pursue the night watchman, the way packages pursue fashion, fashion pursues your purse, poets pursue stale tradition, and pedantry pursues poets.

Amid this babel, an elegant dresser is an exotic plant, the absent-minded philosopher a suicide, the provincial a ball rolling every which way, and the poet just another wanderer through the crowded desert, a desert without illusions or mirages to nourish him, beauties to inspire him, or (and this is the worst lack of all) any other cross to make him melancholy but the Cross of Kings on coins he'll never own. I who, thank God, am only a humble provincial with nothing elegant about me, with none of the attributes of the philosopher or the poet, though if truth be told the romantic genre or gender is, next to the feminine, the one most to my liking—I, who never saw the people of my town run about in such a tremendous tumult and hubbub over any business of this world, was nearly suffocating in this terrible plaza; perturbed, maimed, and oppressed by its bustling, rude multitudes, it seemed to me that the prophecy concerning the gathering of the dead on Judgment Day in the Valley of Jehoshaphat must be coming to pass, a gathering in which, more likely than not, we'll be similarly piled on top of each other, three to a shoe.

An angel shook me out of my predicament, an angel in the form of a coachman, a disguise usually worn only by the devil.

"Do you need a coach to Santiago?"

"Yes, my friend."

And in fact I needed it like Ariadne needed her thread, like a shipwrecked man needs a plank, like a steamship run aground needs a better captain, and like my country needs a better leader; for even if it hasn't actually run aground, it certainly looks as if it had, because it's moving forward about as much as a buoy.

For two hours I was a spectator to the mercantile frenzy of Valparaíso, after which I becoached myself and headed for the Almendral, one of the sprawling barrios of that city, but not as diabolically European in its construction as the ruins of Planchada fortress where it starts. Here it's easy to see that people go about their business more calmly than in the port, without that commercial zeal bordering on frenzy that proves that money-making is a passion as violent as any other. In the Almendral I saw lovely buildings, a public walk lined with *luma* trees in place of poplars, and above all I spotted pretty women looking out from windows and balconies, with whom, by all indications, those merchants or Phoenicians would most likely be doing some business. By the staff of Mercury!, if these men proceed as swiftly in matters of love as they do in delivering money orders and drawing up invoices, they'll sweep up all the Amazons and Satan too in a grand conquest!

Satisfied that I'd lived a day as agitated as any I ever hope to experience even in a battle ending in a rout, I took a room at seven in the evening at Casablanca, a well-known island in that lake of mud you have to plough through to get from the Ovalle pass to the Zapata hill.[4]

"In twenty-four hours," I said to myself then, wringing my hands, "I'll be in Santiago!"

And this future of delightful intoxication vanished . . . ! Today I ask myself: "Will it ever return?" If I didn't think so, I'd surely commit suicide.

(*El Mercurio*, August 27, 1843)

More Excerpts from My Diary

The child of the provinces always loses something when he arrives in Santiago, and I don't count among his losses the red handkerchief they steal from his pocket the first day he takes a stroll through the plaza. If he goes looking for a job, he very quickly loses his patience and his hope; if he goes to complain to the military leader governing his district, the trip is a waste, a total loss; if he enters into litigation, he loses the lawsuit or its equivalent in hard cash; if he decides to make his home here, unless he's very old he'll lose his provincial accent; if he comes here to have a good time, he'll lose the desire to return home; if he goes carousing, he'll lose his health; and if they appoint him delegate, he loses his sense of shame about discussing certain issues, and on other occasions his ability to speak at all. I arrived in Santiago and immediately lost the thread of my diary, though thank God I didn't lose even five minutes trying to recover it.

Set before a child all the toys that strike his fancy, all the sweets that arouse his voracious appetite: offer them to him and watch as he grows confused and hesitant, lacking the resolve to head down the road to ruin, not knowing where to start. It's the same with the writer of customs, as my good friends have taken to calling me; when he suddenly finds himself in the noisy capital city of the Republic, dropped down into the middle of that brilliant society that justifiably aspires to the title of distinguished alumnus of the society of Paris or London, he freezes up and becomes mute on seeing so many objects and scenes, just one of which might inspire ten articles, and knowing that with each day, each hour, there'll be new occurrences no less fitting for this genre of composition. Ah, Santiago is an inexhaustible treasure, a veritable mine for the writer-tailor. In it there are fashions, *tertulias*, duels, theater, newspapers, and cafés; there are poets, individuals both elegant and unique, pretty coquettes by whose side if you don't manage to win a heart, you'll win ideas and pleasant inspiration. Pretty coquettes are the muses invoked by modernity, and in Santiago entire choruses of them can be summoned; it must be so there'll be enough muses and too many poets.

You'd rather talk about something else? Bring on the politics of spineless expediency, in fashion ever since our current Cabinet adopted it as theirs, demonstrating the popularity it enjoys. There sit the Ministers: that one pretends he hasn't a clue about the continuous resignations offered to him by the governors and mayors whose hair has turned white (among other greater and lesser disasters) since they were appointed to their positions; there's another who promotes some and demotes others, who distributes jobs and beatings arbitrarily, conferring many titles but hardly ever a salary, who likes to see a Liberal sitting alongside a Conservative with a wig, and vice versa. There's the Minister of the Treasury, looking as hard-working and unministerial as possible, always sincerely motivated by the national interest and concern for policy; the Minister of War ever occupied in his arduous task of sucking up to the military, which in our march toward progress consists of the baggage section, the hospitals, and the munitions; by some strategic anomaly he prefers that these awkward nonessentials bring up the rear as we advance.

There too sits the Chamber of Deputies, that political pianoforte whose keys, when plinked one at a time, sound distinct from each other, but when some intelligent professor plays them together always produce harmonious chords.

And if you aren't inclined to write about matters such as these, we still have the employees, the job seekers, the weavers, the police, the Intendant,[1] and so on and so on, which, if they aren't customs, do bear a striking resemblance to bad habits in the difficulty we have ridding ourselves of them. An Intendant is an entire warehouse full of cloth for our scissors. And I'm not referring particularly to the Intendant of Santiago, whom I don't even know, and who's done me no harm at all though I've given him every good reason to do so, for I was a great supporter of the *pipiolo*[2] party back in those days when said gentleman was a bit less liberal than he is now, precisely when we're all a bit more conservative than we were then.

You don't like politics? There are also monastic customs—virgin territory, intact and uncultivated and consequently full of thorns and thistles—though it would be difficult to go very far down that path because right away my contemporaries, whoever and whatever they are, would start shouting at the writer from all sides: "Hey, man, don't start that," and so on.

O.K.: if that subject is off limits, no use poking at it. Go stand by the corner of the jail (anyone can do this without being accused of sedition the next day), and to get them to let you observe in peace the confusion reigning there, without scrutinizing you too closely and ganging up on you thinking you're the flunky of some litigant or merchant, pretend to be reading the winning numbers in the public lottery that's run by the municipality in collaboration with the founders of the savings bank: they display the numbers on one of the balconies of the courthouse so everyone can see that the council is playing fair and not cheating. What a fine article will come to mind as you stand there! Top it off with an epigraph, it doesn't matter which classical source you use: *Scylla and Charibdys* or *The Notaries and the Agencies*, and straight into the drop-box of *El Progreso*,[3] which accepts articles pleasing to the public ever since they changed their politics.

More customs? What's that huge crowd doing by the town gate on a Saturday night? Are they selling? Buying? Not exactly: their principal occupation is showing their wares to one another. The merchant is showing his rich weavings and cloths; the clerk is showing his finery, his spiffy haircut, and his white teeth; the French peddler his fake jewelry, the old woman her girls, the girls their soft, tinkly voices and their charming disdain, the beggar his rags and sores, the craftsman his crafts, the dandy his beard, the lover his sweetheart, the writer, *a genius of this court*, the article that was published this very morning, the pickpocket his skill; the cop his vigilance, the shoppers the description of the item they're looking for; in short, the purpose, the common interest of this lively, amusing fair, is to exhibit your wares or yourself.

More customs? You'll find good and bad ones whichever direction you go: the good ones singing victory, the bad ones going along with the reforms. Everywhere you can see the regenerative fermentation of our times, the struggle of reason between the new and the old, between the passionate innovators and the tranquil golden mean, between athletic young patriots and gouty old ones, between those who cry "Forward! Down with all obstacles!" and those who reply "You don't have to knock it down! It will fall in due time!" Meanwhile, the administration says to everyone: "Think carefully what you do," and things go on as they are, the government with its point of view and every madman with his. Ah, the value of a well-bred administration!

Yes. Santiago is a town that's progressing admirably, that's beginning to fulfill its mission of shining above the earth: the pity is that there's not another like it in all of Chile, that only here do we find enlightenment and grandeur, and in every other town ignorance, wretchedness, and rabble. However, we Chileans can do with Santiago what the citizens of a southern city did with the only pretty girl in town who managed to grow up there with any talent and charm. Every visitor from out of town, before he saw anything else, was introduced in the house of the pretty girl, and naturally the guest was captivated by her green, talkative eyes. As he was about to leave, the one who introduced him would ask: "What do you think of the fair sex we've got here in this town?" We, after the foreigner has seen and carefully observed Santiago, should ask him: "What do you think of these towns we've got here in Chile?"

(*El Mercurio*, August 28, 1843)

A Practical Joke

I

"They murdered him right there on the corner where the house you're living in stands."

"But . . . how?"

"As for how, all we know is they stabbed him, because you could see the stab wounds clearly when they examined the body. He had three fatal wounds; the ugliest was in the back."

"What savages!"

"I remember it well," said a third man, "because the morning they discovered the poor fellow murdered, the women in the house made me get up early so I could go out and bring them back details of that sad event. Apparently they chased him for more than a block, because some neighbors declared they'd heard shouts and a scuffle at midnight, the time the deceased left the *tertulia* several *pesos* ahead. The poor guy was stripped totally naked after he was dead, but his murderers didn't leave a clue."

"A horrible thing! Happily, the day has passed here when they kill men as casually and openly as they beg for alms in my country. Although I haven't been here long, I think I know this town well enough to believe that crimes like this aren't committed any longer."

"You really think so? By God, you're wrong. Here's a man right here who'll tell you what happened only a few nights ago."

"What? They tried to kill you, too?"

"Well, I won't swear to it, since thanks to my legs they never got close enough to me for me to be convinced of their intentions. But three masked men tried to stop me on the street two weeks ago tonight. When I saw them coming toward me, trying to surround me, I turned right around and ran until I got to the plaza, shouting to the guards for help. The masked men ran after me for more than a block and a half."

"And you weren't able to recognize them?"

"What do you mean, recognize them, man? It was as dark as it is tonight; I couldn't even see my own hands!"

"Christ . . . ! Weren't you even carrying a weapon?"

"Just the ones that got me out of that fix."

"Well, I can't even count on those right now. My pistols are back in my apartment. I never carry a dagger; you can't carry a cane with a rapier inside when you're traveling abroad; and then my legs, I swear to you they'd just be in the way in a situation like that, like heavy artillery when a division's in retreat."

"Night before last," said the owner of the house, "I went to bed around 1 A.M., and on the corner by the whiskey stand, two women with their shawls pulled over their faces, both of them gigantic, started calling to me with those whistling sounds boys use to lure goldfinches into their traps. The idea of a pleasant little adventure almost tempted me to acknowledge them, but the size of those figures made me suspect a *quid pro quo* with respect to their sex. I started walking really fast; those treacherous sirens came after me with huge strides, so I ran as fast as I could until I reached my house out of breath. Yesterday I discovered a cave almost finished on the corner where the women . . . . "

"Come on, they were men disguised as women," interrupted the foreigner. "This town is a nest of murderers and evildoers!"

"I tell you, you can't get careless, especially on nights like this. Listen how that north wind is blowing!"

"You're right! But you should insist they post nightwatchmen. In Santiago, that's where there are scoundrels everywhere, you can still wake up and walk through any neighborhood in the city, confident that the nightwatchman on duty there, and any within the sound of a whistle, will be right there by your side at the slightest indication of danger. Here, from everything I've heard, there's terrible insecurity, an abominable police force."

"That's as true as a tower. And then, these dark, stormy nights give thieves such an advantage when they're on the prowl. It lets them jump you without warning so the first indication you have that you're standing right beside them is the gunshot, the blow to the head, or a ferocious stab-wound."

II

In conversations such as these, four companions were whiling away a winter's night a few years ago in a small town in the south. The site of the *tertulia* was the room of one of the speakers, a bachelor like his guests, all of them great fans of what are generically called *calaveradas*, adventures encountered while prowling the town at night. It's said that around the table that night, prior to relating the events referred to above, they had already covered the usual topics of good reputations and bad, pretty girls, impertinent old women, jealous husbands, husbands who didn't care, and everything else going on or not going on in the town, whose name I choose not to recall. Among the four was a young man recently arrived from out of town for the purpose of buying some oxen and sheep from one of the nearby farms, as it's very well known that the southern part of the Republic produces them in great abundance and of unsurpassed quality.

The events that we have just heard had upset him greatly: the night was as dark and stormy as the usual mood of the provincial authorities; he had no weapon, and he had to walk six gloomy, muddy blocks to reach his house. These considerations made him taciturn and pensive, as the others continued telling other similar stories that were hardly designed to calm his fears. It was then that he remembered, more vividly than ever, what he had heard since his childhood about the many thugs and bandits in the country he was visiting, the land of the face-peelers.

He would have gladly stayed to spend the night there or asked one of those present to accompany him, but his vanity preferred not to put up with the ragging that would ensue, so he rejected both remedies as equally embarrassing. His watch showed half-past midnight, too late for even the usual Don Juans to be roaming the streets. However, he had to leave despite his very real trepidation and his lack of a weapon. What a fix! He gets up from his seat without having made a decision, and the owner of the house asks:

"Are you leaving?"

"I'm leaving. Do you have a weapon you can lend me?"

"What, still worrying about those women who accosted me night before last?"

"I'm not afraid of anything; even so, a weapon inspires a certain confidence that never does any harm. They say that prudence is the mother of safety."

"That's probably so, but unfortunately there's not even a club to offer you. The only weapons in this house are this gentleman's legs, and as you can see, it's a bit drastic to think of cutting them off. Come on, don't be afraid; in five minutes you'll be there, safe and sound."

While this good-humored teasing was going on, the stranger stood thoughtfully for a few moments; then as if he'd made a sudden, bold decision he headed for the door, bidding everyone good night.

III

As soon as he left, one of the locals said, "He's scared to death, just like a northerner! We set him up perfectly. Let's not waste a second; bring the ponchos, the hoods, and let's do it. Tomorrow we'll have a great time listening to him tell about it."

And talking and slipping on their disguises at the same time, they take out their daggers and head off running down a side street. It doesn't take them long to get to the corner next to the room of the pal they're planning to give a tremendous scare. They spread out and crouch down so that at an agreed signal they can leap on him, grab his cloak, watch, and hat, growl for him to stay silent, and vanish into the darkness.

They'd been waiting a quarter of an hour in their uncomfortable positions, and the only thing you could hear in the streets was the wind. Coming out of their hiding places then, it occurred to them that fear must have given wings to the northerner's feet and that since he had come by a more direct route, he was probably in his house already when they thought they had cut him off. They were annoyed at having to go home without their fun, but just then they heard hurried footsteps at the end of the block . . . .

"It's him . . . ! Back to your places!"

And indeed it was the poor victim hurrying their way, paying no attention to the puddles he was splashing through so as not to be caught unprepared in some ambush. He had his cloak folded over his left shoulder and his hat pulled down tightly on his head, but in such a way that his broad forehead was completely bare. When he reached the fatal spot, the terrible cry of "Stop where you are" pierced his ears like a bullet . . . three men were coming toward him . . . "Stay back, you . . . !" he yells, accompanying his shout with the most violent of Spanish expletives and covering his back as best he could against the nearby wall. The aggressors surround him, then attack: one of them is just reaching out his arm to grab him by the neck, when the victim shoots him with a pistol from point-blank range, causing him to fall back onto one of his companions, who also falls to the ground but then quickly gets back up. The other lying there can't do that.

IV

Two days later the young northerner was brought up on charges before the local magistrate.

"Night before last a man was shot on the corner near your lodging. It is true that you killed him?"

"I killed him, sir, thinking I was defending myself from a murderer."

"You think he was trying to attack you or harm you?"

"I no longer think that."

"Do you have anything to say in your defense?"

"Yes, sir. Until twelve-thirty that night I was engaged in conversation with the deceased in his room, in the company of the two gentlemen,

M. and G. I listened to the three of them telling about a number of recent events that convinced me that in this town, where I only arrived a few days ago, you can't walk around late at night without the risk of running into thieves or murderers. Having no weapon with me at the time, and not being able to get one from the deceased or his friends, I took my leave intending to pass by the room of B. and ask to borrow a pistol I had seen on his table that morning. He loaned it to me, I went on my way, and when I reached my house three men attacked me. It was impossible to run away; my only hope was to shoot at them and take advantage of their confusion to slip inside my house. Everyone who lives there remembers me shouting, and they all came outside with me to the place where I had just seen a man fall. Only then did I realize that this was the unfortunate friend whose room I had just left. Trusting in my innocence, I immediately turned myself in to this jail . . . .

The young man was absolved; but he could never remember this fatal event without deep sorrow.

(*El Semanario*, January 19, 1843)

Elections in Copiapó

They say that in one of the towns in the Argentine province of La Rioja, years ago, they were trying to elect a deputy to the Chamber of Representatives. For this purpose all the voters of the district were summoned to the public plaza, where the political chief awaited them with a company of infantry to keep things as orderly as possible during that solemn act. Having called together all those who were to take part in the election, he had them line up in front of the detachment and opened the session in this manner:

A drum roll.

Company . . . load arms!

Right shoulder, arms!

Prepare, arms!

With the squad assigned to maintain order positioned in this manner, the political chief addressed the voters in these terms:

"Gentlemen."

We're going to proceed with the election of a deputy to the honorable Chamber of Representatives of the province. My choice would be so-and-so. Are there any objections? Answer frankly and in order, starting from the right.

The first voter on the right said:

I-have-no-objection.

The second:

Neither-do-I.

The third:

Neither-do-I.

And all the others said the same thing, until the last one on the left.

The party boss exclaimed with great excitement: *I won! I won! The vote was unanimous! Long live the Argentine Republic! Death to the unitarian savages!*[1]

This procedure of the Rioja leader, in an electoral function, is a bit more simplified than the one we witnessed in Copiapó on the 29th and 30th of the past month. Most of the votes were controlled by the Intendant don Ventura Lavalle.

On the afternoon of the 28th, election supervisors from Chañarcillo, the militia from Tierra Amarilla, Nantoco, and Potrero Grande; militiamen from Ramadilla, and employees from the port, started arriving in groups. All of these, as well as the militiamen from the city, had been clearly warned that if they didn't vote for the government party (which was the name of the Intendant's party), they risked the severest penalties that can befall an insubordinate soldier or a disloyal employee.

On the 29th, on handing each person his registration slip,[2] they put in his hand a carefully folded ticket marked on top with an enormous black seal and a number. *Look*, they said to the voter: *You are number such-and-such; here's your name on the list, so we can check to see if your vote appears in the box. If it's not there, we'll know you supported the other party and that you're an enemy of the government.*

The poor voter was very careful not to say *but* to such a convincing argument. He would march up to the voting table, give them his marked ballot, and be out of his jam.

The authorities have presided over this entire sham, this utter degradation; this riot of corruption has been deemed necessary to achieve a victory: over whom?, over nobody!

Because no other party participated. The supporters of *El Copiapino*, not wanting to fight against the bad faith and excesses that were being prepared and have now been perpetrated, withdrew from the field a week ago. Greater friends of public order than those assigned to preserve it, they chose not to offer fodder to the bilious character of those in power; they chose not to irritate a party that, forgetting its obligations and abusing whatever power it had, would have satiated their spite against the poor wretches who are always elected to be the victims of vengeance simply because they're weak.

The party of the Intendant got what it wanted: "It won everything, except honor." Because there's no honor in serving the government by dishonoring it and by violating and mocking the laws of the Republic; there's no honor in forcing a hundred citizens to prostitute themselves out of fear; there's no honor to be won converting the solemn exercise of popular sovereignty into a farce.

Those who have done this are enemies of their country; they're disloyal to the Government; they're anarchists, not guardians of order.

(*El Copiapino*, April 4, 1846)

Elections in Huasco

It was the Intendant of this province, D. Manuel José Cerda, who tenaciously fomented the war conducted in Vallenar and Freirina between two powerful parties in the election of deputies. That man is responsible for all the crimes the government agents committed in Vallenar and for all the hatred, perhaps irreconcilable, that has been sown between families. And that man goes to confession every week!

D. José Urquieta, governor of Vallenar, was one of the best friends of the candidate of the opposition. But D. José Urquieta hated his neighbor Prado, and Cerda let him know that this Prado was the only one who wanted to defeat him in the election just to embarrass him and show the government and everyone else that Urquieta was a poor man, utterly worthless, a man without prestige. His vanity aroused, Urquieta decided to wage a war of life or death.

Cerda let the civil servants know that if they didn't vote against Vallejo their careers would be finished.

He let others know that if this candidate won the election, they would lose the lawsuits they had pending.

He managed to convince many that *Jotabeche* meant *heretic*, and that his victory would be equivalent to burning down all the temples with all the sacred images inside. However, Intendant Cerda is not a supporter of the administration; everyone knows he betrayed the administration in the elections in Copiapó. He's not a *Monttista*[1] either; we all know the underhanded maneuvers he tried to pull later on, right here, against candidate Gallo,[2] a *monttista* any way you look at him. Exactly what is, then, Indendant Cerda? A madman; a man ruled by blackest bile. If his religious morality is anything like his politics, the Gospel could have no worse enemy. But let's return to the Huasco elections.

Governor Urquieta's strength consisted of (1) some of his relatives, (2) a hundred and sixty registration slips he controlled, (3) the Indians of the Upper Huasco, (4) the marked votes he would distribute to his civil servants, and (5) the general tendency of the multitudes to fear the authorities at election time.

The opposition attacked his relatives with irresistible arrogance; it dispersed the Indians of the Upper Huasco so they couldn't be reorganized by Urquieta in time for the elections; it imitated his marking of ballots, and with an impressively energetic and concerted effort it managed to stifle his abuse of power. The only thing the opposition could not achieve was to arrange for the seized registration slips to be returned to their owners.

Day 25

At nine in the morning, the place the voting table was to occupy was already invaded by the contending forces. At first, only the Conservatives carried clubs in place of canes, but before long the Liberals were also wielding these weapons, which are not prohibited by law even though they're as dangerous as any other.

The voting begins. Forty Liberals deposit their votes in the box without being interrupted, *champions of liberty and the people*. The crowd surrounds the table and the election officials, who complain about all the excitement, muttering the word *disorder* between their teeth.

After this vigorous charge, the Conservatives unleash their attack, pointing to a band of Indians from Upper Huasco, who are being escorted by the governor's vigilantes and agents and being handed their registration slips and ballots just two paces from the table. Here Troy burned. A thousand voices are lifted up against such shameless coercion. The group of Indians is attacked, surrounded, and scattered by the opposition. Their poor braids, ponchos, and hats are tossed in all directions. Everyone is shouting, everyone is hurling insults, everyone is attacking and threatening. The president calls out the guard, and the guard fraternizes with the people. A *pelucón*[3] unsheathes his rapier and loses it; a sword of one of the vigilantes flies twenty yards away, impelled by a blow from a club wielded by a master in the art. A more illustrious battle isn't possible: the spirit of liberty inspired the first group, vanity the second.

The pleas of some members of the opposition managed to calm the fury of both sides, and a complaint was lodged at the table concerning the violence the Conservatives used against the voters from Upper Huasco. The table resolved that the complaint was well-founded, "because the law of elections did not prohibit it."* So the Indians voted amid a frightening chorus of brays, cries from mule-drivers, and neighs that the people directed against them as they voted.

However, in the interval we've just described, there was time to exchange a few votes from the governor for some of ours; since both had the same seal, the voters presented themselves, with little effort, to face the wrath of the commissioner of elections in exchange for mocking him with impunity.

It's impossible to describe the boldness, slyness, and ease the young men of Vallenar displayed in bringing this about. While a few started arguments and lodged heated complaints, others began the conquest of the voters with that persuasive eloquence, that eloquence that is the only thing capable of stealing a few asinine votes from the administration.

But Governor Urquieta had even more eloquent recourses, recourses whose infernal prestige will not pass from the imagination of the people for years to come. The phalanx of Indians, for example, voted under the conviction that if they didn't cast them for Urquieta, the government would take their lands from them. The militiamen, to avoid being called up or going to jail, bought their votes, freeing them from serving in the guard, which was the same as imposing a tax on one group to buy the vote of another.[†]

Finally, after an uninterrupted succession of passionate and stormy scenes, the time came to tally the votes for that day, which was carried out in the presence of the whole town and in an orderly fashion. At this

---

* The conduct of don José María Quevedo, a member of the voting table, was quite impartial on several occasions. The others were corruptly subservient to their party in every resolution they dictated. *Jotabeche.*

† The soldier Silvestre Uveda has been exempted from all service until his next enlistment.—Vallenar, March 25, 1849.—*Urquieta.*

point the arrogance of the Conservatives came crashing to the ground, when they discovered they had won by only fifteen votes, instead of fifty as they had expected. The counterfeiting of the seal had inflicted an incurable wound on them. The Liberals already knew that at twelve o'clock on that same day they had won in Freirina by seventy votes.

Thanks, you slavering poet! You've contributed substantially to the victory of the people. Next time, don't pack the seal in your saddlebags, or leave your horse where those mischievous Liberals can make you look so dumb.

Day 26

The ballot box had been guarded all night by the Liberals. The voting began without incident, except for a few insults exchanged between the two parties. At eleven it was discovered that the Indians who had voted the day before were now voting again using someone else's registration slips, disguising themselves by cutting off their long braids and wearing different clothes. In fact, one of them was caught, but the registrar decided that he could vote, even though there were many witnesses who knew and shouted out the real name of the Indian. The registrar also decided to allow the vote by another twenty year old, who trembled as he confessed that he had never registered.

But among these wretched manifestations of the Urquieta party it's pleasant to recall young Ruperto Peralta who, scorning the threats of the government, shouted as he voted: *I'm not a slave, I'm a Liberal!* It's pleasant to recall the triumphant march the people made around the plaza in honor of the soldier Domínguez, for the clever trick he used to obtain his registration slip and vote against the very one who had seized it.

Since there were many Liberals whose registration slips were being held by the governor, they all went to his house to ask for them, but with smiling effrontery he firmly refused. Then they signed a scathing memorandum complaining about the scandalous retention of their citizen voting privileges: Complaint denied, replied Urquieta. They requested that the election officials order the governor to desist in this devious maneuver, to prevent an imminent riot. The response was that the plaintiffs should take their complaint to the authorities who had originally issued their registration slips, but when they inquired about the location of the bundle of original authorizations, it was discovered that the governor had them along with the registration slips. This trick infuriated them more and more: cries of *To the governor's house* were heard everywhere, and the Liberals had to use much persuasion and patience to control the people, who wanted to go en masse to get the purloined slips. To distract them from this resolution it was proposed that the city council validate the plaintiffs by issuing them legal certificates: when this corporation convened, nothing could be resolved, because the council had no registration book to consult, no book of minutes, no secretary who could sign the authorization, because the latter claimed he had been ordered not to do it.

At last, the final hour of the second day arrived, and Urquieta showed up at the plaza, only to beat a quick retreat to the sound of fireworks and the shouts of the triumphant opposition. It's regrettable that Intendant Cerda, the instigator of the audacious conduct of Mr. Urquieta, wasn't there to witness that and to absorb some of the rockets that exploded against Urquieta's head.

Freirina

There, the Liberal party controlled the battlefield. Despite the efforts that Mr. Campusano, governor of the district, expended to win a few votes, his labor was wasted, to which it should be added that the registration slips weren't seized as they were in Vallenar.

Still, right up until the 23rd of March Campusano was sure of at least forty votes by men who had committed themselves to vote for the worthy García Reyes.[4] Fortunately, don Manuel José Cerda, when he passed through on the steamship for Valparaíso, ordered the governors of Vallenar and Freirina to arrange the vote for don Ramón Rengifo,[5] whereupon the supporters of the government, considering themselves free of their commitment, voted for Vallejo. Thus it happened that Intendant Cerda with his absurd behavior contributed to the victory of the candidate he disliked most.

The conduct of Mr. Campusano in the elections was as noble as that of the noble Blanco Encalada in Valparaíso.[6] His personal influence and the high regard in which Freirina holds his administration could not garner the administration more than ten votes compared to a hundred and five for the opposition. But Campusano, defeated in the campaign, didn't lose a single friend and emerged unsullied and with the glory of not having committed any crime to stifle the will of the people. The minister himself must hold him in higher regard than he does the wretched Urquieta, who lost both the election and his dignity in the plaza of Vallenar.

Day 27

The election was over. All that remained to do was verify the count and officially announce the names of the elected candidates, a result that was already well known since the night of the 26th. The jubilation of the people of Vallenar was as warm as the struggle had been. In Freirina the dancing didn't stop until early morning. Even the employees from the ministry gathered to drown the sad result of their efforts in champagne.

The general verification of the results was to be held in Vallenar: at four in the afternoon the victorious ballot box from Freirina would be arriving there. At twelve, groups of Liberals on horseback started riding out to meet it. On the plains of Perales, which a bold project is today converting into lush, fertile fields, all of these groups joined a multitude of people who were going to this party on foot.

At three in the afternoon a cloud of dust appeared in the distance, and shortly thereafter they sighted the people of Freirina who were escorting the precious chest and waving a banner bearing the noble slogan of UNION AND FREEDOM. The two friendly groups approached each other silently, overcome by the same feeling, their hearts filled with a crushing happiness. As they met they leapt to the ground to embrace one another fraternally, an embrace that exorcised from their generous breasts even the hatred created in the recent struggle. Who could describe such a sublime moment! How does one express the mute tenderness of so many individuals pressed in each other's arms! What idea dominated their thoughts? Country, happiness for the country, the triumph of its freedoms, the rebirth of its glories. Because there is indeed a country and there is glory when an entire people can exclaim: "We're free!," where an entire people have come to believe that their will is superior to the boa constrictor the government has become.

You couldn't tell the Freirinos from the Vallenarinos as they poured into the country home of citizen Aracena, where a snack table had been prepared for the guests. The most common toasts heard were:

"Long live the country! Long live Freirina!"

"To heroic Atacama. May the entire Republic awaken as she has!"

"We swear to reject the candidates of the administration to the end of time!"

"To the victory of Tocornal[7] in Valparaíso and García Reyes in La Ligua."

At five in the afternoon three hundred riders entered Vallenar in files of four. In the vanguard the Chilean flag was waving; at the center of the cavalcade rode the commissioner of elections with the box, the deputy-elect to the right, and the flag of Freirina to the left. The streets were alive with an enthusiastic and excited crowd; the girls waved their handkerchiefs and threw flowers as the box passed by their doors. The hurrahs, rockets, shouts, and general noisiness gave this celebration the appearance of one of those victories that, thirty years ago, the heroes of independence had won.

"Thank God," said a sixty-year-old Liberal, "once again we've seen the country the way it was in the past."

When the box was deposited in the municipal hall, there followed a banquet attended by citizens of all classes. That night the guests were introduced to the young women Liberals of Vallenar, and they danced with them until three in the morning.

The elections in Huasco in 1849 guaranteed forever the brotherhood of its two towns and the triumph of their principles, which no power can ever stifle. Long live the Republic!

(*El Copiapino*, April 4, 7, and 11, 1849)

The Uprising at Chañarcillo

Copiapó, November 2, 1851

The civil war has dug some of its claws into the heart of noble Atacama. Chañarcillo and its town, Juan Godoy, were sacked on the night of the 26th and 27th of last month, by the peasants and vagabonds who rose up to the cries of *Long live Cruz!*[1] *Long live Freedom!*

At three in the morning of the 27th, Intendant Fontanés received this news. Three hours later a hundred men, infantry and cavalry, left here, the infantry riding on the town stagecoaches.

At three in the afternoon this force fell on Chañarcillo and managed to stop the riot, but not to remedy the harm that had already been done.

The entire commerce of that town and the mines of San José and San Francisco suffered horrible pillaging, one of those disasters that cannot be described, because even the imagination cannot comprehend them. Instead of simply stealing what they wanted or needed, the bandits set out to destroy everything.

The government forces, which arrived at three in the afternoon, did what they could to provoke the thousand thieves gathered there to offer some sign of resistance, to voice a single cry of rebellion, so they could proceed against them and teach them a lesson. But it was all in vain: each one of those savages let himself be beaten and tied up like a lamb. Only one offered any resistance, and he fell on the streets of Juan Godoy, where his body still lay on the 30th when our soldiers withdrew.

This mutiny of bandits was inspired by emissaries of the scoundrels from La Serena. The men who presided over all the maneuvers of destruction were disguised and cannot be identified, and they disappeared two hours after having begun the pillaging, when they saw that it was impossible to halt the destruction.

The army managed to recover some of the effects of those who were robbed, but in lamentable condition or in ruins.

The merchants of Chañarcillo are ruined down to the marrow. Don Esteban Rojas loses a hundred thousand pesos. Morales and the others, almost everything they owned.

The bandits of Chañarcillo were also conspiring with others who tried to carry out a similar action in this city at one in the afternoon of the 27th. The plan was to wait until the army left for Chañarcillo, until the authorities were distracted there, to strike. But two hours earlier they were detected and captured in their points of rendezvous.

In short, here we are with the credo in our mouths; here nobody sleeps soundly, because from one moment to the next somebody else might cry out *Long live Cruz!* and the four or five thousand thieves living in this department will fall on us.

(*El Mercurio*, November 6, 1851)

The Last Spanish Caudillo in Araucania

I

The independence of Chile was no longer in question during the epoch I'm going to recall for my readers. Our heroes had beaten and routed the Spaniards from all our soil, soldiers as valiant as they were unfortunate, not so much because of their defeats as because they had invested their honor in the most unworthy of causes.

All the towns to the north of the Maule River were beginning to organize their political administration, swept up in the disorder and excitement produced by the strangeness of their new life, by the inexperience of the new institutions, and by the warlike character and habits they had acquired in fourteen years of campaigns, battles, defeats, and victories. Even Concepción, which during that long period had been laid waste by both armies, burned and sacked by savages and guerrillas, that heroic province that salvaged nothing from the fury of the revolution but the fecundity of its fields and the lushness of its forests, seemed to revive and convalesce, like the soldier whose near-fatal wounds begin to scar over after a long, difficult, and painful cure. Benavides,[1] the most formidable of the butchers who devastated this province during that time, had gone to the gallows in the central plaza of Santiago on the twenty-third of February of 1822.

However, there were still a number of royalist guerrillas on both sides of the Bío Bío River, not unlike those small clouds drifting across the sky immediately after a storm.

One of these bands, led by Colonel Pico,[2] was the largest and most feared. The fearlessness of its chief was made more terrible by the bloody hardness of heart to which he had become habituated during many years of the war to the death that, toward the end, was fought between the champions of Fernando[3] and the independents. Several Araucanian tribes, allies of the colonel, accompanied him on his raids, enticed by the opportunity to pillage and slaughter. Pico's guerrilla band gave no quarter and asked for none: his campsites, battlefields, and the routes of his marches and countermarches were marked by fire and atrocities of every kind. By that time it wasn't a question of trying to defend or reconquer the country. An infernal rage, the thirst for blood and vengeance, the exterminating instinct of the tiger kept the war going and drove the combatants.

Pico was a Spaniard of some forty years, tall, robust, with black complexion, and as savage in manner and habit as the life he led and the profession he followed: his misanthropic stare betrayed the guerrilla in him; two deep scars drastically disfigured the natural lines of his face; his strength would have done honor to any child of Castile, any Araucanian chieftain, and this was the only prestige that maintained any order in the horde under his command. Distrustful by nature, or rather because of the circumstances and men surrounding him, his only friend was a dog that he had named "Rebel," and this animal was his only sentry when he slept, the only escort permitted to walk near the Spaniard.

On the thirty-first of August of 1824, this guerrilla camped in Quilapalo,[4] right beside the mountain and the origin of the torrential Bío Bío.

The rainy season was over, and Pico decided to renew hostilities and risk everything to achieve, if not a surrender, which was too much to expect, then an escape by sea from Chilean territory, where there was nothing left for him except fruitless dangers to overcome. They hadn't put a price on his head, but anyone who brought it back, either by virtue of a victory or an act of treason, would position himself to great advantage with the patriotic leaders and authorities. On this point, Pico knew better than anyone the perilousness of his situation.

The rains of July and August had not allowed the guerrillas to move or receive communications from the few friends Pico had left in the territory occupied by the independents. He had no intelligence about the number or locations of their emplacements, the strength of their garrisons in the towns, or anything else he needed to know to operate with any chance of success. In order to obtain such information, he sent out spies and scouts on both sides of the Bío Bío and determined to await their return in the camp they had made that day.

One hundred princes, all that was left of the brilliant army that under Osorio's command had been victorious at Cancha Rayada[5] and thoroughly defeated at Maipó,[6] wearing the ragged remnants of all the uniforms used by both armies during the war of independence, constituted the flower of Pico's guerrilla band. These occupied, in Quilapalo, the ruins of a shack, apparently the ancient dwelling of some cowhand, judging by the pastures located around it. The Araucanians preferred to camp out in the open and at different spots. The shouts and howls and other noise they made echoed night and day through the forests, as if thousands of wild beasts had invaded them.

Pico took possession of an abandoned hut located about a hundred yards behind the front line and looking out on the Araucanians. Behind the hut was an orchard walled in by a palisade made of the trunks of oak trees. This rundown dwelling had only one entrance, without a door, a circumstance that seemed dangerous to the Spanish colonel in case of a surprise attack. However, since he was accustomed to never showing any fear or nervousness in front of his allies and subjects, he ordered his bed placed in one of the corners of the hut on a wicker frame woven in the blink of an eye by two of his aides. There he received his friends and issued orders to his officers.

Night came, and later, the drum sounded curfew. Pico, after setting up in person several positions in the vanguard and rearguard of the camp and inspecting all the points where he thought he should make an appearance, retired to his lodging, accompanied by no other companion than his dog Rebel. He took the reins off his horse, tied it still saddled to one of the poles supporting the hut, hung a large poncho over the entrance, added wood to the fire; then, grabbing an enormous knife, he climbed underneath the wicker frame and made a hole in the wall large enough for a man to crawl through. Sure of an exit in the direction of the orchard, he took off his spurs, made the sign of the cross, kissed the one on his rosary, and went to bed. Rebel snuggled up at the foot of the wicker frame in a hollowed out space that had once been a hearth-fire and next to the one that was burning pleasantly that night.

Pico preferred these precautions to sentries and guards, which he seemed to think unnecessary. His guerrillas never criticized him for this, simply regarding him as doubly fearless and brave.

II

Are you familiar with the shores of the Bío Bío and its tributaries Laja, Duqueco, and Vergara? You aren't? I'm sorry for you. That's where Paradise is. Because Paradise isn't some fantastic creation; it's nature in its virgin state, nature prior to being conquered and devastated by civilization; nature with its rivers, forests, lakes, mountains, and waterfalls, with its birds and wild beasts, its perfumes and the harmonious sound of its movement and life. If there were any Paradise other than this, the poet would simply be wasting his time trying to imagine it any more enchanting and delightful.

The vast regions that those rivers water and course through have been for three centuries the theater of the war between the Araucanians and their conquerors, or, rather, between the Araucanians and those who have tried to conquer them. Vain endeavor, the only impossible one that brute force, cunning, and courage have encountered on earth! But this war has only managed to destroy men: the natural beauty and grace of the territory remain in their primitive state, in their remarkable lushness. The only thing civilization has succeeded in establishing here, through great travail, is a line of fortresses within which that invincible nature man seeks so vainly to conquer and enslave has enclosed itself as if man had constructed them as its dwelling.

In the period of my story, almost all these fortresses were in ruins, as a consequence of having been captured and lost successively by both antagonists. At the end of the struggle, in 1824, the independents who were camped inside them suffered daily attacks from the savages and guerrillas occupying the plains, forests, and caves surrounding those stone structures.

On the second of September of 1824, Luis Salazar, a guerrilla patriot, and his men occupied the fortress of Nacimiento, one of those deepest inside Arauco territory. Salazar had been born, like all the soldiers who accompanied him, beneath the walls of this fortress, which saves everyone the trouble of wondering whether they were brave or not. Nacimiento has become famous for the contingent of lions hired to sustain the glorious war of our independence.

The sun had just risen. Salazar, standing on the east wall of the fortress, cast curious looks toward the opposite shore of the Bío Bío and the Vergara, which merged at that point. Standing near the commandant, a sentry yawned loudly, thus drawing the attention of his leader, obliging him to ask:

"Have a good night, Coronado?" [7]

"Same as all the others, *mi comandante*. Very cold, lots of watching, not a damn thing to drink or even a Spaniard attacking to warm me up."

"They'll be all over you before long . . . ."

"Or they'll have me all over them, *mi comandante*."

"They've been in Quilapalo since day before yesterday. Siniago,[8] who just passed through, gave me the word . . . ."

"Siniago, *mi comandante*? You mean the deserter who joined the Spaniards two years ago when they stole our horses in San Carlos?"

"That's the one." The sentry made an ugly grimace, shaking his head from side to side. Salazar went on: "From what he says, that bastard Pico is preparing to attack us with more than four-hundred men, counting Indians and Spaniards. We're only thirty-two . . . and there's no hope of reinforcements arriving . . . ."

"It's true: there aren't many of us," said the sentry thoughtfully, scratching the ground gently with the point of his unsheathed sword.

Suddenly, after a short silence, Coronado's breathing became visibly agitated, his head lifted proudly, his eyes shone with furious energy, his face gradually turned dark with blood, and his upper lip, barely covered with adolescent fuzz, began to quiver.

"*Mi comandante*," the young sentry shouted in a frenzy. "That devil has to die."

"Who?"

"That Spanish mother, Pico; I swear by the mother who bore me, the son of a bitch is going to learn that all it takes is one life to finish him off. The devil can have him or he can have me, or both of us, I don't care . . . ."

"Coronado, are you crazy?"

"Yes, *mi comandante*. If I don't kill him, I'll die of rage. I've got this irresistible urge to cut off his head . . . and I'll do it if there's a God in heaven.

"But, where, you young savage?"

"Right where he sleeps, *mi comandante*, in the middle of his damn army. What? Is there some ocean between me and that pig-faced Visigoth to keep me from burying my dagger in his throat?"

"You see those swallows there, fighting over insects? There'd be that many lances tossing you in the air like a pin cushion. It would be better . . . ."

"No, *mi comandante*. If you don't give me four men with good horses, I'll throw myself in the moat and die like a fool because you refused to let me die like a man."

"I know you well, my friend. I know that Lorenzo Coronado is the bravest man ever born inside these walls. But I'm afraid you'll be throwing your life away for nothing. Tell me, boy. What's your plan?"

"To tell the truth, all I can think of is killing the pig. As to how . . . ? Tell me, *mi comandante*. Do you think Siniago can be trusted? The one who went over to the enemy not long ago? I've got this feeling he's Pico's spy, and he's been serving him as aide. So we've got to make sure of him. Look, *mi comandante*. I'm going to tell Siniago I plan to go kill Pico where he lies, wherever I find him, and that to carry out my plan, I need him to advise me on the best way to pull it off, whether I live or die, because I don't care about that. But if I miss and that Spanish witch escapes my dagger, four brand-new bullets are going to zip my friend Siniago straight down to hell. This will give him a reason to be straight with me. Once I've got the directions I need, I'll go with my four men to Quilapalo, which I know like the back of my hand. If anyone's going to die, it won't be the four men you give me, *mi comandante*."

"God help you!" exclaimed Salazar, sighing deeply and squeezing the sentry in his arms. Thus, Salazar took his leave of that interesting victim, the way a priest takes leave of a man condemned to die when the executioner comes for him at the foot of the scaffold.

At sunset, five horsemen galloped over the drawbridge of the fortress; they went single-file down the left side of the Vergara, and after crossing this river in a small boat, Salazar watched them disappear in the Negrete Mountains.

III

It was shortly before midnight on the night of the third of September.[9] Two gunshots away from Pico's camp, four men were crouched behind some thick brambles. From there they could make out the eaves of Pico's shack like a triangular shadow darker than the darkness of the night. The guerrilla band, which had been ordered to march on Santa Bárbara at dawn, slept silently in the camp. Pico was snoring in his bed, sleeping soundly, but Rebel's bark of alarm made him leap to the floor and grab his weapons. He put his hand to his ear; there were no suspicious sounds. But the dog, with his nose pointed toward the orchard, continued growling instinctively.

"Some damn Indian trying to steal my horse," said Pico, and he walked outside the hut wrapped in a large woolen blanket. He soon came back in, shivering with cold.

"I swear on my grandfather's grave," he said looking at the dog, "if you give me another false alarm I'll hang you with that rope from that rafter." He threw some more wood on the fire, dried the dew off his feet, and was about to lie back down, when Rebel started barking with renewed vigor, as if the cause of his alarm was closer than before. Pico gave him a kick that rolled him into the ashes of the fire. The animal, convinced by this that his barking was impertinent, rolled into a ball on the ground and like his master soon fell into a deep sleep.

The coals the guerrilla leader had added to the fire on going to bed were still burning, casting a faint light inside the hut. A man, his head and feet bare, pulled aside the curtain hanging over the entrance, and stepped forward as noiselessly as an ant until he was two yards from Pico's bed. The dog leaps toward him, but is impaled on a long knife through the middle of his body, his growl of attack fading into a muffled death-howl. An instant later, Pico and his attacker are struggling body to body, Pico trying to reach his weapon, the other striking with his; the Spaniard cries out as the dagger pierces his body repeatedly. He manages to drive his knee into the stomach of his attacker and break free of his powerful arms; wounded and crazed, he crawls under the bed looking for the hole he made in the wall three nights earlier. But the hero of Chilean independence renews his attack, grabbing onto him with furious frenzy; together they grapple on the new terrain, together they drag each other through the breach. Fernando's last champion on Araucanian soil[10] utters his final gasp of death as the patriotic dagger sinks into his throat.

By now, the entire guerrilla band was in motion. Alarmed by the strange cries they had heard in the camp, the confusion reached its apogee with a few gunshots fired at that moment from some bushes to the left. They all turned to look in that direction; none of them understood what was happening, but none of them stopped repeating: "Long live Spain! The enemy, the enemy!"

Coronado, holding Pico's bloody head by the hair with his left hand, walked off the battlefield past the terrified guerrillas who, sure they were surrounded by patriots, could think of nothing but mounting their horses and riding for the cover of the forest.

An hour later the five men from Fort Nacimiento had met at the rendezvous point and were galloping their own horses back from their heroic expedition; frightened by the magnitude of their victory, they rode behind Coronado without daring to ask if that was really Pico's head on the croup of his horse.

Coronado and his companions were heroes of the people!

Long live the people!

(*El Copiapino*, September 18, 1845)

Francisco Montero: Memories of the Year 1820

F amous writers of my country and my time frequently undertake the worthy task of relating to us the heroic feats and actions of the leaders of our independence, while they're still alive if they occupy high office, after their death if death ended their misfortunes.

I, a common man, an enlisted man in the ranks of our writers, generally choose my heroes from among the enlisted soldiers of that glorious war. Those who were their great captains can be sure that someone will write down the memory of their virtues, at least an obituary; I prefer to provide this kind of sterile homage to the poor wretches who won the admiration of their peers with rifle or lance, leaving no other monument to their bravery than the legends told around the bivouac fires of the army of the Republic.

Two years ago, I revealed to my readers the forgotten existence of the fearless Lorenzo Coronado:[1] again today, as we dance and drink in public celebration,[2] I propose a toast to the memory of another brave man, another of those lions famous in the battalions of the country.

In the final months of 1820 a savage battle took place, a duel to the death between the conquered and the conquerors of the plains of Maipú. The battlefield of these bloody scenes was the province of Concepción.

Benavides, Zapata,[3] Pico, and other royalists were on the rampage on those plains, giving no quarter to enemies or neutrals.

The patriots Prieto, Arriagada, Boile, Viel, Elizalde, Torres, and García[4] were defending the northern banks of the Ñuble and the Itata to prevent the conquerors of Pangal[5] from laying waste any more territory with their savage onslaughts.

The plains of Talcahuano, which are now covered with the richest and loveliest endowments nature and peace can lavish on a land, were during those months covered with corpses and all the devastation of war. There the bandits under the command of Benavides who occupied Concepción attacked with knives and swords every day at dawn, and a handful of courageous men under the orders of the peerless D. Ramón Freire[6] had set up their defenses in Talcahuano after driving the royalist guerrilla from the territory and decimating his battalions and his inexhaustible bands of savage Araucanians.

Los Perales, the halfway point between the two cities, was the scene of these daily engagements. At times the patriots would drive the enemy at sword point to the heights of Chepe and Gavilán; on other occasions, the latter would drive our men all the way back to the moats and drawbridges of their fortress.

Many months had passed in these exhausting encounters. The hunger and casualties produced by a prolonged and fierce siege were taking their desperate toll in Talcahuano: every steer or nourishment of any sort had to be paid for in blood; the starving horses were of little help to their riders; discouragement was beginning to show on the faces of the men. In every squad curses and complaints were hurled against the government in Santiago that had in this way abandoned our skeletal divisions in the south.

On the other side, Benavides, weary of the assaults and ambushes that always depleted his forces, had reduced the operations of the siege to a wary inactivity, putting all his hopes in the discouragement and anxiety that would afflict those besieged; more than two weeks passed without the patriots having the opportunity to take a prisoner who could give them the news they longed to hear.

It was late afternoon on December 22. General Freire, holed up with Larenas, Díaz, Rivera, and Picarte[7] in a culverin looking out toward Perales from an opening in the fortress, was casting silent glances back and forth between the enemy camp and the approach to the port that led to picturesque Quiriquina.[8] Not a sail in sight bringing reinforcements from Valparaíso . . . no movement from the direction of the royalist enemy!

"This is worse than death," he said, speaking to no one in particular. "By my honor, gentlemen," he added, addressing his comrades, "I've made up my mind I'm not going to die of hunger in this limbo. Tomorrow we eat in Concepción or in hell."

And a fierce courage animated the features of the most dashing and valiant warrior of those times. After a few moments of silence, he exclaimed:

"A prisoner . . . ! How do we get ourselves a prisoner? If we had some idea where the other divisions are camped . . . ! If we only knew what's become of Prieto, Arriagada, and those promised reinforcements! Or maybe those fucking guerrillas have advanced to the Maule . . . ! Damn! I'd give my best horse for a prisoner."

"I'll take the black and gray, *mi general*," came a voice from a few paces back.

"What are you saying, Corporal Montero," barked Freire, "are you taking me up on my offer?"

"By tomorrow, *mi general*, either I'll have won my race with hunger, or I'll be resting with the Catalan Molina, who was cut to pieces by those bastards. Ah, those cowards have it coming for that!"

"Agreed. By tomorrow you'll be a sergeant or a soul in purgatory. I know you; I know you hunt like a jaguar."

"The horse is for me, *mi general;* I'll get me a girl to ride it some other day."

"You can give it to whomever you want. But I need a prisoner who's worth as much as my horse. I need an officer from those thieves."

"That's what you'll get, *mi general.*"

And snapping the back of his right hand against the brim of his hat, corporal Montero spun about on his left foot and marched off with a graceful martial swagger.

The blast of the cannon sounded evening retreat, and two mounted hunters rode out the front gate of the fortress, after singing a rendition of "A Spaniard Worth My Horse" to Lieutenant Bulnes, officer or saint of the day.[9]

Dawn was turning the early sky white. A deep silence had fallen over the plains. It was that sad, solemn hour that all of creation celebrates with exhilaration, and that only the last, fading croaks of the frogs were greeting that morning in the ponds near Los Perales. Two hundred yards from this site, toward Concepción, a straw hut could be seen. The winds and long abandonment had stripped most of the straw roof away and chipped much of the mud from the walls, baring the poles to which it adhered. The door, if there ever was one, had disappeared.

There were two men inside, armed with bare swords and long daggers at their waists. One stood motionless, peering through a hole in the side of the hut that let him view the road from Concepción; the other was finishing a cigarette, holding two saddled horses by the bridles and stroking their manes when they got fidgety.

"Here, finish the cigarette, Pancho," said the one holding the reins to the one watching. "Come over here; let me take the watch for a while."

"Put out that fucking cigarette," answered Montero. "The patrol's almost on top of us."

"And what have we got? Cavalry or infantry?"

"Both. Four . . . five horsemen . . . . Half a squad of riflemen with an officer . . . Ah, we've got ourselves a lieutenant at least! Things couldn't be better."

"Is that what you think? They'll blow us to bits. Really, Pancho, you've got me screwed."

"On your horse, son. As soon as I separate the Spanish devil from the rest, you grab him by the neck or the waist, and fly. I promise you by God's own guts they won't touch a hair on your head. Courage, now. Follow me."

Benavides's patrol was just a few paces from the hut when two demons came charging out at them. Montero's horse forces the detachment to veer to one side; the other presses his horse up against the officer's feet, grabs him by the scruff of the neck, digs in his spurs, and bolts with all the velocity the spurs and terror inspire in the animal. Montero, like a legion of madmen, deals death blows left and right, and only withdraws when he's sure his companion is far enough ahead that he can't be caught and attacked by anyone trying to free the prisoner.

He had to cover the retreat of his companion for a long time, plagued by persistent volleys of shots from the foot-soldiers and sword slashes from the horsemen; blood was running down his face; a bullet had put one of his legs to sleep. But he had knocked two soldiers off their horses, and the other three were staying clear of him, being content to challenge him and feint toward him while keeping a safe distance when their commander spurred ahead of them. Finally, they decided that their best strategy was to declare themselves masters of the terrain and accept what was lost as lost. Then Montero caught up with his falcon, slung his prisoner over the croup of his horse, and a quarter of an hour later General Freire had himself a Spanish captain in exchange for his horse.

It's a fact that on the afternoon of the same day there was a bloody battle between the cavalry of both bands: our hunters emerged victorious. On the following day, the 24th of December, those who had been under siege in Talcahuano marched triumphantly down the Alameda of Concepción: Zapata was defeated and killed near Chillán.

Conclusion

Following this period, there's a lacuna in the life of my hero. It seems that in alliance with Chief Venancio[10] he wandered for many years through Araucanian territory and the Patagonian pampa, winning more and more fame for his bravery. When he came to the end of his life, he was as brilliant as he had been throughout his career.

One day years ago, a colonel presented himself to the security guard of the Suipacha battalion, which was headquartered in Buenos Aires, announcing that he was carrying a sheet of paper for the commander of that body, and he was taken before him.

Fifty years of age, a tall man with a desiccated, bony body, white, bristly mustaches, oldfashioned uniform, rusty epaulets, and a sword of enormous size, this individual inspired more respect than ridicule.

After exchanging the standard greetings, the commander read the sheet of paper that had been handed to him, walked out of the room, then came in again after several minutes.

A squad of riflemen stood at ease at the door.

"You are Colonel don Francisco Montero?" the commander asked the old soldier we have described.

"At your orders, and Chile's."

"Thank you. Are you aware of the contents of the paper they've had you bring to me?"

"They told me it was an order for you to give me lodging."

"You're mistaken, Colonel, and I'm sorry. Be so kind as to read it."

"I don't know how to read, *comandante*."

"Then, listen." And he read the following: *Long live the Argentine Confederation! General Headquarters in Buenos Aires, etc., etc. The commander of the Suipacha battalion will have the bearer of this paper, Colonel Francisco Montero, shot immediately; so it is ordered. God and Liberty!*

The commander stopped without reading the signature, then added: "Prepare yourself, Colonel. The squad will await your orders in five minutes."

Montero was pale when that reading was concluded. A loud sigh was expelled from that broad chest, and a huge tear slid down his cheek. The lion saw that he was irremediably surrounded by dogs.

Meanwhile, noticing that his prisoner was beginning to tense his body like a tiger about to attack, the commander ordered him imperiously to surrender his sword.

"First, tell me," replied Montero. "Are you determined to carry out this order to murder me?"

"Well, what do you think, colonel. Do you think I want to end up tomorrow in the spot you're in now?"

"In that case, defend yourself. Francisco Montero's sword will belong to whoever finishes him off."

And unsheathing it, he fell like lightning on that commander and all those who tried to come to his aid. Montero, amidst a confusion of cries of alarm and moans from dying men, his chest pierced by a bullet, fell to the ground with his arms around his Tizona.

(*El Copiapino*, September 18, 1847)

Editor's Notes

I COPIAPÓ AND THE MINING ZONE

Copiapó (page 3)

1. The official name of Argentina at that period.

2. Probably a song connected with the popular Spanish drama *El Trovador*, first produced 1836, by Antonio García Gutiérrez (1813–84), on which Verdi's *Il Trovatore* was based.

3. More commonly known as the *zamacueca* or simply *cueca*, a handkerchief dance of Peruvian origin that became the national dance of Chile. Known in Peru as the *marinera* and in Argentina as the *zamba*.

If They Could See You Now! (page 8)

1. Diego de Almagro (?1475–1538)led the first, unsuccessful expedition of Spanish conquistadors into Chile (1536).

2. Subdelegates *(subdelegados)* governed the main subdivisions within each Chilean province; provinces themselves were each governed by an Intendant *(Intendente)*. The titles of these officials, first used under Louis XIV in France, were introduced by the Spanish Bourbon monarchs into Spanish America in the late colonial era. Independent Chile retained the colonial terms—in the case of Intendant, up to the present day.

The Mines of Chañarcillo (page 12)

1. Under Spanish colonial mining law, an unworked mine or claim, if "denounced" after a set period, was forfeit to the denouncer, the purpose being to stimulate continuous mining.

2. A foundry of the period at Copiapó.

The Discoverers of the Chañarcillo Mines (page 14)

1. See note on p. 173.
2. Argentine Liberal opponents of the dictator Juan Manuel de Rosas were known as *unitarios*. The "federal agents" would have been Rosas' spies and informants, much feared by Argentine exiles in Chile.

The Theater, Steamships, and the Chañarcillo Hospice (page 19)

1. See note on p. 173.
2. In October 1845, during the period of political agitation preceding the re-election of President Bulnes, some of the opposition Liberals founded a Democrat Society, to counteract the pro-government Society of Order.

Candlestick Mine (page 23)

1. The Huasco valley.

The Map to the Lode of the Three Mountain Passes (page 27)

1. Juan Manuel de Rosas (1793–1877), Governor of Buenos Aires and Argentine "federalist" dictator (1829–32, 1835–52), from whose regime many of the Argentines in Chile had fled.
2. Fr. José Félix Aldao (1785–1845), priest and general. He and his brothers Francisco (1787–1829) and José (1788–1830) were veterans of the wars of independence who established themselves as guerrilla leaders in the Cuyo region of Argentina. José Félix allied himself with the La Rioja caudillo Facundo Quiroga and with Rosas, and in 1842 became governor of Mendoza, where he decreed (31 May 1842) that all Liberals were officially demented.

The Cangalleros (page 32)

1. *Cangalla*, the theft and smuggling of ore, practiced by *cangalleros*, mineworkers themselves or semi-organized gangs, was universal in the mining zone, and very difficult to control. A mineworker caught in the act could usually expect a flogging.
2. Jotabeche never did.

Vallenar and Copiapó (page 36)

1. The main town in the Huasco valley, very roughly halfway between Copiapó and La Serena, and founded in 1789 as San Ambrosio de Vallenar by the Spanish colonial governor Ambrosio O'Higgins. Vallenar is a hispanicized form

of Ballinary, the place in County Sligo, Ireland, where O'Higgins claimed to have been born.

2. The distance by road today is about 150 kilometers.

The Port of Copiapó (page 42)

1. The *Chile* and the *Peru* were two steamships that had begun service in late 1840 between Chile and Peru, operated by the new Pacific Steam Navigation Company (PSNC), a British line whose passenger vessels were a familiar sight on the Chilean coast until the 1960s.

2. The rocky promontory of Quintero was a well-known shipping hazard further south.

3. Captain George Peacock, the PSNC's first senior officer.

4. The Peruvian president Agustón Gamarra had invaded Bolivia the previous year, only to be defeated by General José Ballivián (1805–52), president of Bolivia (1841–47), who then threatened Peru with invasion. This international conflict was still simmering at the time Jotabeche was writing this essay, but was ended by a Chilean-brokered peace treaty a few weeks later.

5. The overabundance of poets clearly paid off: twentieth-century Chile would have more good poets than any other South American country.

II PICTURES OF SOCIETY

Carnival (page 51)

1. See note on p. 173.
2. The opening words of the Argentine national anthem.
3. That is, of Ash Wednesday, the first day of Lent.

Corpus Christi (page 56)

1. Fr. Francisco de Paula Taforó (1816–89), a priest of well-known Liberal connections who was conducting mission work in the north at the time. He was later the center of a major episode, when the government nominated him to the papacy as archbishop of Santiago (1878). Pope Leo XIII rejected the nomination, and relations between Chile and the Holy See were broken off for several years.

Lent (page 60)

1. Hughes-Felicité-Robert de Lamennais (1782–1854), radical-liberal French-Catholic writer whose *Paroles d'un croyant* (1834) aroused indignation among European governments and won condemnation from Rome. In April 1850 the radical newspaper *El Amigo del Pueblo* started to serialize Lamennais's book (in

Mariano José de Larra's translation), but the uproar in Santiago was so great that only the first extract was printed.

2. The (rather limited) student milieu in Santiago was experiencing a moment of radical enthusiasm, partly under the spell of the youthful Francisco Bilbao (1823–65), who only a few weeks later published his article "Sociabilidad chilena" in the magazine *El Crepúsculo*. Under the press law of the day, the article was condemned as "blasphemous" and "immoral" (though not "subversive"), and Bilbao found it prudent to go into exile.

3. Verses by José María Núñez and engraved on the entrance to the general cemetery in Santiago.

4. José Rivera Indarte (1814–44), Argentine Liberal writer, who had published a pamphlet *Es acción santa matar a Rosas* (It is a Holy Act to Kill Rosas).

5. A dig at Domingo Faustino Sarmiento, who had proposed a radical reform of Spanish orthography. This proposal was what occasioned Vallejo's description of Sarmiento as a "literary anti-Christ." Andrés Bello also had some ambitious ideas of orthographic reform, from which Sarmiento may have derived some of his own. Some minor changes (using the "i" in place of "y," for instance) went into effect in Chile and were widely used there until around 1910.

Copiapó: Today's Tertulias (page 65)

1. A popular medication (probably a placebo) of the time.

2. See note on p. 174.

3. Manuel Oribe (1792–1857), Uruguayan general and president (1835–38) and "federalist" ally of Juan Manuel de Rosas, who supported him in his long-running siege of Montevideo (1843–51).

4. General Nazario Benavidez (1805–58), "federalist" caudillo of the Argentine province of San Juan.

5. See note on p. 174.

Afternoon Walks (Second Article) (page 75)

1. General Andrés Santa Cruz (1792–1865), Bolivian general and creator (1836) of the short-lived Peru-Bolivian Confederation, destroyed by Chile at the battle of Yungay (January 1839), his Waterloo.

2. Allusion to Argentine dictator Juan Manuel de Rosas (commonly known as the "Illustrious Restorer of the Laws," or simply "The Restorer") and his struggle with the French, whose warships blockaded Buenos Aires from 1838 to 1840.

3. *Mayorazgo* technically a strict Spanish form of entail that bound estates to a particular family for generations. Very few *mayorazgos* had been set up in colonial Chile and their holders (also usually referred to as *mayorazgos*) were regarded as vaguely noble, but also, by progressive spirits, as retrograde and idle. The continued existence of *mayorazgos* had been a major political issue in the 1820s; they were finally abolished in the 1850s.

Letter from Jotabeche to a Friend in Santiago (page 85)

1. The italicized phrases in this section are another dig at Domingo Faustino Sarmiento, who had used them in recently published articles.

2. The Argentine national holiday.

3. The article, by Vicente Fidel López (1815–1903), appeared in the May 1842 number of the short-lived *Revista de Valparaíso*. Anyone reading it today would be inclined to agree with Jotabeche that it is, to say the least, mildly confusing.

4. Robert Lovelace, character in Samuel Richardson's novel *Clarissa* (1748), whose name became a symbol for notorious seducers, a usage still known in the early twentieth century.

Letter from Jotabeche (page 89)

1. Standard nickname ("bigwigs") for Chilean Conservatives, first used in the 1820s.

2. Standard nickname ("greenhorn") for Chilean Liberals, first used in the 1820s.

3. General Angel Vicente Peñaloza (1799–1863), known as "El Chacho," Argentine "federalist" caudillo, who later met his own brutal death at the close of the last of his many campaigns.

An Illness (page 93)

1. See note 2 above.

2. Guillermo (William) Blest, immigrant British or Irish physician, the best-known doctor in Santiago at the period, and father of novelist Alberto Blest Gana.

3. Allusion to St. Veronica, who, according to Catholic tradition, wiped the face of Christ on the way to his crucifixion.

A Word about Fools (page 97)

1. The legendary first emperor of the Incas—hence Peruvians, rhetorically, are the sons of Manco Capac.

2. It is not clear who Jotabeche has in mind here. Obvious candidates would be the liberator-dictator Bernardo O'Higgins or his successor in office, Ramón Freire, both of whom had to go into exile, or Diego Portales, who was murdered. Jotabeche does not seem to have shared the Chilean Conservatives' reverence for Portales, although the real cult of him only developed in the later 1850s.

3. An allusion to the opulent wedding (or as it turned out, nonwedding) of the "rich man Camacho" in Part II, chapters 20–21 of *Don Quixote*.

The Provincial in Santiago (page 101)

1. Teresa Rossi, Italian soprano who visited Chile with opera companies in the 1840s.

2. A game vaguely similar to hockey, part of Chile's Araucanian heritage.

3. A poor district, no longer known as such, to the south of downtown Santiago, roughly in the area of the present-day Avenida Matta. Taking its name from a Franciscan religious house, it later became a district in which *conventillos* (tenements) proliferated.

4. The main avenue in Santiago.

5. The Church of La Compañía, destroyed by fire in 1841 and then rebuilt, and destroyed again by fire in 1863 (when 2,000 worshippers were killed) and not rebuilt. The Congress building later occupied the site.

6. The neoclassical Moneda Palace, built as the royal mint at the end of the colonial era, and used from 1846 onward as the presidential palace.

7. Chile's leading educational institution, both a secondary school and a place in which university courses were taught until the University of Chile acquired its own building in the 1860s.

8. Nowadays called, as in colonial times, the Plaza de Armas.

The Renegade Provincial (page 109)

1. Possibly José Manuel Novoa, well-known lawyer of the time.

2. Almost certainly Juan de Dios Vial del Río, lawyer and politician.

Gossips (page 113)

1. The Argentine province just across the mountains.

The Liberal (page 117)

1. Allusion to the 1828 Constitution, which Chilean Liberals revered as a talisman for several decades after its replacement by the Conservative constitution of 1833. St. Bernard (of Clairvaux) and Peter the Hermit (*L'Ermite*) preached in favor of the first and second Crusades (Peter for the first, Bernard for the second).

2. Mariano Egaña (1793–1846), prominent Conservative politician and ideologue (and major influence on the 1833 Constitution) whose death on 24 June (he had collapsed and died in the street) had caused a minor sensation in Santiago.

3. First (1817) of the two battles that secured Chilean independence.

4. During the political agitation surrounding the reelection of President Bulnes in 1846, Conservatives (and some prominent Liberals) had formed a Society of Order to support the government.

5. Chile's first national government was installed on 18 September 1810, and 18 September is still the national holiday.

III JOURNEYS AND EPISODES

Items of Interest (page 125)

1. Battles and skirmishes of the wars of independence.

2. Quotation from a poem by Andrés Bello.

3. The battle of Rancagua (1814) marked the downfall of the first Chilean national state, and the city streets named for the heroes who fell in the battle are still there. The street named for the state (formerly for the king) gives Jotabeche an opportunity for some humor, since the Chilean state, unlike the heroes, revived and went through further "martyrdoms," that is, the political upheavals of the 1820s and 1830s.

4. See the note on p. 176.

5. Another name for Concepción, whose inhabitants are still referred to as *penquistas.*

6. Allusion to Gabriel Alejandro Real de Azúa (1803–79), an Argentine who settled in Copiapó (and later Valparaiso) and who made a fortune in mining. He made several trips to Europe, where he died. His *Poesías diversas* and *Fábulas* (the two books Jotabeche refers to) were published in Paris in 1839, and his *Máximas y pensamientos diversos* in 1856.

7. The mining camp of Juan Godoy at Chañarcillo.

Letter (Visit to the Maipo Canyon) (page 129)

1. Manuel Talavera, close friend of Jotabeche.

2. The Maipó (or San Carlos) Canal runs for thirty miles and links the Maipó and Mapocho rivers. The biggest engineering scheme of late colonial times, it was designed to irrigate the land to the south of Santiago, and was completed in 1820, just after independence. Maipó normally has an accent nowadays; we follow Jotabeche's usage in the text.

A Little Journey by Sea (page 133)

1. Articles on legal cases printed in the newspaper *El Mercurio,* often sent in by litigants.

2. Well-known trader in Copiapó and Valparaíso, a partner in the house of David Ross & Co., established at Copiapó in 1835.

3. Dance better known nowadays as the *refalosa.*

4. Allusion to Domingo Faustino Sarmiento, one of whose pseudonyms at the period was "Zamora de Adalid."

5. The most populous and "popular" district of Valparaíso, contrasting with the business streets (with, even in the 1840s, their faint air of London), and the location (perhaps Jotabeche is implying this here) of the port's main bordellos.

Excerpts from My Diary (page 138)

1. The original name of Copiapó, long out of use by Jotabeche's time. His use here is presumably jocular.

2. Not an Englishman, in fact, but an American, Samuel Averell, a mason and builder well known in La Serena at the period.

3. The new La Serena cathedral was finished the following year.

4. One of the obstacles on the Valparaíso-Santiago road; nowadays a tunnel runs through it.

More Excerpts from My Diary (page 143)

1. See note on p. 173.

2. See note on p. 177.

3. Santiago's first daily newspaper, which ran from 1842 to 1853.

Elections in Copiapó (page 151)

1. See note on p. 173.

2. Registration slips (popularly known as *calificaciones*) were issued to citizens enrolling as voters several months before the elections. They were handed in at the voting tables at election time prior to the vote being cast. No identification was demanded. It was open to both government and opposition to accumulate as many of these certificates as possible and to use them fraudulently. The government nearly always had the upper hand, using methods illustrated by this essay.

Elections in Huasco (page 153)

1. Supporter of Manuel Montt, future president of Chile (1851–61).

2. Miguel Gallo, son of the millionaire miner of the same name, and brother of Pedro León Gallo and Angel Custodio Gallo, future leaders of the Chilean Radical party.

3. See note on p. 177.

4. Vallejo's friend Antonio García Reyes, who was standing for election elsewhere. It was permissible for candidates to stand for more than one district.

5. Ramón Rengifo (1795–1861), businessman, politician, and poet, was also standing for election elsewhere.

6. Admiral Manuel Blanco Encalada (1790–1876), hero of the wars of independence, was currently Intendant of Valparaíso, and had instructed the militiamen of the port to vote as they pleased—not part of his duties as understood by the government. He was subsequently vilified by the government press.

7. Vallejo's friend Manuel Antonio Tocornal.

The Uprising at Chañarcillo (page 159)

1. General José María de la Cruz, leader of the anti-government forces in the civil war of 1851, defeated at the bloody battle of Loncomilla in December that year.

The Last Spanish Caudillo *in Araucania* (page 160)

The story told by Jotabeche in this essay was a real historical incident, but some of the details he gives were inaccurate. Diego Barros Arana, Chile's greatest historian, and an admirer of Vallejo, describes this narration as "half history, half novel."

1. Vicente Benavides (1777–1822), a very active and cruel guerrilla chief on the Spanish (royalist) side during the wars of independence and the scourge of the southern provinces until his capture.

2. Juan Manuel Pico, a former Spanish trader who had offered his services to the royalist guerrillas in the south and was named Colonel by the Viceroy of Peru. He had been Benavides' second-in-command.

3. King Ferdinand VII of Spain.

4. Colonel Pico's encampment was in fact close to the modern town of Mulchén, about fifteen miles from Quilapalo.

5. Patriot defeat in March 1818.

6. The decisive patriot victory in April 1818, securing Chile's independence.

7. Luis Coronado, Captain Salazar's nephew, who was accompanied on the hunt for Pico by another of his nephews, Angel Salazar.

8. The real name was Verdugo. There were two of them acting as informants: Pedro and Manuel.

9. The date is now accepted as 28–29 October.

10. Though Pico has always had the credit, he was not quite the last. Another Spanish officer, Miguel Senosiaín, led a guerrilla band until January 1827, when he finally surrendered. Back in Spain, he rose to the rank of general.

Francisco Montero: Memories of the Year 1820 (page 167)

Little is known about the real-life Francisco (also called as Juan de Dios) Montero. He was certainly a soldier in the patriot army during the wars of independence, and won a reputation for bravery. In May 1817, at the battle of Carampangue, he saved the life of Colonel Ramón Freire (see note 6). He later became a follower of Venancio Coñoepán, a celebrated Araucanian leader friendly to the Chilean government, and he married an Araucanian woman: his descendents still live in the Chol Chol area (IX Region, Chile). He accompanied Coñoepán across the mountains to Argentina, where the chief fell in battle against Pampa Araucanians near the modern city of Bahía Blanca. Montero's dramatic end as recounted by Jotabeche cannot be authenticated historically, though it is not beyond the bounds of possibility that he was taken to Buenos Aires as a prisoner and shot there.

1. In fact Luis Coronado.

2. The article was published on 18 September, the Chilean national holiday.

3. José María Zapata, the first of the royalist guerrilla chiefs to take the field (1817) as the main wars of independence in Chile were concluding. He was eventually defeated and killed (as noted in this narration) in December 1820.

4. Joaquín Prieto, Pedro Ramón Arriagada, José María Boile, Benjamín Viel, Francisco Elizalde, Domingo Torres, Manuel García: Chilean army officers. Viel was French born and had fought at Waterloo. The most prominent figure mentioned, Prieto (responsible for the death of the guerrilla chief Zapata in December 1820), was later a general and president of the republic (1831–41).

5. Royalist guerrilla victory won by Colonel Pico in January 1820, one of three serious reverses that month for the patriot government.

6. General Ramón Freire, later Bernardo O'Higgins's successor as leader of Chile (1823–25, 1827).

7. Enrique Larenas, Francisco Díaz, Juan de Dios Rivera, Ramón Picarte: Chilean army officers.

8. Quiriquina Island in Talcahuano Bay.

9. Manuel Bulnes, later a general and president of Chile at the time Jotabeche wrote this essay.

10. See general comments before note 1.

Glossary

cangalla	The theft and smuggling of ores from the mines, hence *cangallero,* someone who practices *cangalla.*
chañar	Type of bush found in the Chilean north, from which the Chañarcillo mining district derived its name, as does the modern port of Chañaral.
chicha	Partially fermented grape or apple juice, still popular in Chile.
chueca	A stick-and-ball game originating in pre-Hispanic Chile; the stick vaguely resembles a hockey stick.
dadín	Plant of the *Asteraceae* family (which includes asters, daisies, etc.).
empanada	Turnover or pasty of variable size, filled with meat, onions, cheese, etc.
gringo	Foreigner (primarily non-Hispanic European).
horchata	*orgeat:* a cool, syrupy drink normally made from barley or almonds.
huaso	Chilean peasant (often an *inquilino,* sometimes a ranchhand) owning a horse.
inquilino	Tenant-peasant on a Chilean hacienda (specialized Chilean use of a common Spanish word).

lúcumo	Chilean fruit tree of the *Sapotaceae* family whose fruit is the *lúcuma*, about half the size of an apple, and nowadays a common flavor in Chilean ice creams.
malilla	Card game.
mate	Paraguayan tea (*yerba mate*) popular in Chile since colonial times.
moza	Nickname for the traditional final dance of the evening.
pejerrey	Small fish abundantly found in Chilean waters (and elsewhere).
Pelucón	Nickname for Chilean Conservative.
peso	Chilean currency unit (worth approximately ninety U.S. cents in the 1840s).
Pipiolo	Nickname for Chilean Liberal.
quimagogo	Popular medication of the period (probably a placebo).
real	Traditional Spanish currency unit: one-eighth of a peso (the *peso de a ocho reales*, the "peso of eight reales" is the origin of the expression "pieces of eight").
sajuriana	Traditional couple dance, with a good deal of foot tapping, common in Chile and Peru at the period.
tarasca	Serpent figure common in traditional Corpus Christi processions.
tertulia	Social gathering for conversation, music, dancing, etc. (see Jotabeche's essay "Copiapó: Today's *Tertulias*").

Bibliography

Editions and Anthologies of Jotabeche

Colección de los artículos de Jotabeche (J. Joaquín Vallejo) publicados en El Mercurio *de Valparaíso, en* El Semanario *de Santiago, y en* El Copiapino, *desde abril de 1841 hasta setiembre de 1847* (Santiago, 1847), preface by Antonio García Reyes.

Colección de los artículos de Jotabeche. Don José Joaquín Vallejo. Artículos literarios, políticos y de costumbres publicados en varios periódicos de Chile (La Serena, 1859), reprint of 1847 edition, and the reprinted obituary by Diego Barros Arana in *El Correo Literario* (Santiago, 1858).

Colección de los artículos de don Joaquín Vallejo, publicados en varios periódicos bajo el seudónimo de Jotabeche (Valparaíso, 1878), introduction by Abraham König.

Jotabeche. Artículos y estudios de costumbres chilenas, escritos por don José Joaquín Vallejo (Santiago, 1885). Biblioteca Chilena, ed. Luis Montt and J. Abelardo Núñez.

Obras de don José Joaquín Vallejo (Santiago, 1911), ed., with introductory essay by Alberto Edwards. Biblioteca de Escritores de Chile.

El provinciano en Santiago y otros artículos de costumbres (Santiago, 1966), ed. Pedro Lastra.

José Joaquín Vallejo. Antología (Santiago, 1970), ed., with introductory essay by Raúl Silva Castro.

José Joaquín Vallejo. Artículos de costumbres (Santiago, 2001).

Biography and Criticism

Amunátegui, Miguel Luis, *Ensayos biográficos*, Vol. III (Santiago, 1894).

Amunátegui, Miguel Luis and Gregorio, *Don José Joaquín Vallejo* (Santiago, 1866).

Arteaga Alemparte, Domingo, *Vida y escritos de don José Joaquín Vallejo* (Santiago, 1866).

Durán Cerda, Julio, ed., *El movimiento literario de 1842*, 2 vols. (Santiago, 1967).

Pinilla, Norberto, *Panorama y significación del movimiento literario. José Joaquín Vallejo. Sobre el romanticismo* (Santiago, 1942).

Pinilla, Norberto, *La generación chilena de 1842* (Santiago, 1943).

Rojas, Manuel and Canizzo, Mary, *Los costumbristas chilenos* (Santiago, 1957).

Salvat Monguillot, Manuel, "Exégesis de la 'Carta de Jotabeche a un amigo en Santiago,'" *Boletín de la Academia Chilena de la Historia*, No. 92 (Santiago, 1981).

Silva Castro, Raúl, *José Joaquín Vallejo, 1811–1858* (Santiago, 1969).

Torres Caicedo, José María, *Ensayos biográficos y de crítica literaria sobre los principales poetas y literatos hispano-americanos*, Primera serie, tomo II (Paris, 1863), pp. 357–84.

Vicuña Mackenna, Benjamín, "La niñez de Jotabeche," *El Mercurio*, Valparaíso, 28 September 1880.

9 780195 128673

Printed in the United States
By Bookmasters